THE WATER DREAMERS

Michael Cathcart was born in Melbourne in 1956. He has worked as a schoolteacher, university lecturer, theatre director, radio presenter and a television host. Michael's first book, *Defending the National Tuckshop*, was published in 1988. Since then he has published an abridgement of Manning Clark's epic *A History of Australia* and an anthology of Australian speeches.

THE WATER DREAMERS

THE REMARKABLE HISTORY OF OUR DRY CONTINENT

MICHAEL CATHCART

Text Publishing Melbourne Australia

The paper in this book is manufactured only from wood grown in sustainable regrowth forests.

The Text Publishing Company
Swann House
22 William St
Melbourne Victoria 3000
Australia
www.textpublishing.com.au

First published by The Text Publishing Company, 2009

Every effort has been made to trace the original source material contained in this book. Where the attempt has been unsuccessful, the publisher would be pleased to rectify any omission.

Cover design by WH Chong
Page design by Susan Miller
Maps by Tony Fankhauser
Index by Russell Brooks
Typeset by J&M Typesetters
Printed and bound in Australia by Griffin Press

National Library of Australia
Cataloguing-in-Publication data:

Cathcart, Michael, 1956-

The water dreamers : the remarkable history of our dry continent / Michael Cathcart.

ISBN: 9781921520648 (pbk.)

Water-supply—Australia—History. Water-supply—Social aspects—Australia. Water-supply—Social aspects—Australia—History. Water-supply—Environmental aspects—Australia. Water-supply—Environmental aspects—Australia—History. Australia—History.

363.610994

For my mother,
Muriel Cathcart

CONTENTS

INTRODUCTION
How Water and Silence Made Australia   *1*

1   The Cadigal Stream   *8*

2   The Valley of the Tank Stream   *19*

3   Mr Busby's Bore   *39*

4   The Silent Continent   *48*

5   Sounds of Water   *66*

6   Ruins of Hope   *76*

7   The Myth of the Inland Sea   *82*

8   River of Dreams   *99*

9   Silence Victorious   *124*

10   Mapping the Silence   *148*

11   Necronationalism   *154*

12   The Great Artesian Basin   *166*

13   Dick Hardwicke to the Rescue   *179*

14   Change of Heart   *198*

15   Australia Unlimited   *219*

16   New Beginnings   *246*

NOTES   *261*

ACKNOWLEDGMENTS   *299*

ILLUSTRATIONS   *300*

BIBLIOGRAPHY   *301*

INDEX   *320*

INTRODUCTION
HOW WATER AND SILENCE MADE AUSTRALIA

History is geography set in motion.

JOHANN GOTTFRIED HERDER

Late in the night, as we lay burning with thirst and dreaming of
water, a species of duck flew over our heads which, from its peculiar
note, I knew I had previously heard on the Darling.

MAJOR THOMAS MITCHELL

This is a book about dreaming of water on the most arid
continent on earth.

In 1944, the economic historian A. G. L. Shaw observed that
the history of Australia could be written as the struggle to
conquer two obstacles—great distances and a lack of water.
Geoffrey Blainey's classic *The Tyranny of Distance* (1966) took on
the first part of this challenge. His sweeping study of how
distance shaped our colonial history articulated a preoccupation
in Australia after World War II. The aeroplane, railways, radio,
cheap cars and improved roads were at once challenging and
reinforcing Australians' sense that great distances separated
them from each other and from the rest of the world. Since
then, the world has grown smaller. Australians' anxieties about
isolation have diminished. During that same period, the challenges posed by the continent's lack of water have become even
more acute.[1]

Water is the fundamental limit on how Australians live. It determines where we establish our cities, how we think about country, how we farm it, build on it, defend it and dream about it. Of all the inhabited continents, Australia has the lowest average annual rainfall (almost half the rainfalls of Europe and North America), and the lowest level of river discharge (around one-sixth that of Europe and of Asia). There is a broad consensus that, as Australia's population climbs towards 22 million, our capacity to grow any larger depends on how we manage water and how we cope with the extreme variability of our rainfall from one year to the next. Though the country is dry, Australia has more water per person than any other continent. By that measure, we are not running short of water. Yet many rivers and catchments are in crisis. Our problem is not an excess of people, but a lack of understanding. We are still getting it wrong.[2]

In an age when many Australians are starting to acknowledge the scale of the challenge, one might be tempted to write another study of environmental damage. But if we are to learn from our successes and our failures, we must first come to grips with the diverse ways in which Australians have struggled to understand the country. We have to articulate the values, myths, aspirations and anxieties that have shaped our cultural geographies.

There are many studies of particular rivers, catchments and corporations, and a few local histories that deal with water. Joe Powell's many works on historical geography and water policy have been indispensable to the writing of this book. My challenge has been to synthesise the real world approach of the physical geographers (which, for the most part, we might call environmental determinism) with the ways our experience and interpretation of the world are shaped by our cultures. In this, I have been inspired by Roslynn Haynes' *Seeking the Centre* (1998) and by many other historical works about culture and country, notably those by the historians Tom Griffiths and Tim Bonyhady. These writers resonate with Australian environmentalists such as George Seddon, William J. Lines and Tim Flannery, and with such US historians as Donald Worster and Marc Reisner, whose respective books *Rivers of Empire* (1985) and *Cadillac Desert* (1986) remain touchstones of environmental history. These writers (despite their substantial disagreements) are each telling a story of destructive exploitation—a story, in historian Geoffrey Bolton's phrase, of 'spoils and spoilers'.[3]

The English historian Simon Schama has summarised the argument of his magisterial book *Landscape and Memory* (1995) in one sentence. 'Landscapes are culture before they are nature; constructs of the imagination projected on to wood and water and rock.' He elaborates this axiom by pointing out that 'once a certain idea of landscape, a myth, a vision, establishes itself in an actual place, it has a peculiar way of muddling categories, of making metaphors more real than their referents; of becoming, in fact, part of the scenery'.[4] This dictum could stand as the manifesto for several of the powerful works about landscape and empire written since the 1980s, notably Paul Carter's luminous and vexing 'spatial history' *The Road to Botany Bay* (1988), Stephen Greenblatt's *Marvelous Possessions* (1991) and Mary Louise Pratt's influential *Imperial Eyes* (1992). To say that we 'project' cultural landscapes on to the world rescues us from a naive belief that our categories, including the idea of nature itself, are facts rather than interpretations. But I want to draw a caution. The notion of 'projection' can also imply that the world is merely a blank field, waiting to be imprinted with our land-scapes of desire: that there is only language. The reality is that the world answers back. Project whatever you like. If you fail to find water, you will die.

This is also a book about silence.

Quite early in my research, I was struck by the ways

colonists often represented the settlement of Australia as a process of bringing civilised sound and redeeming song to a timeless, silent land. Though I had set out to write a history of water, I soon found what the explorers found—that the water runs out. And that beyond the water, out there in the dry country, there is a silence that refuses to be colonised. Titles such as *Imperial Eyes*, Simon Ryan's *The Cartographic Eye* (1996) and Bernard Smith's *European Vision and the South Pacific* (1985) indicate how, over the past three decades, academic literature has paid a good deal of attention to the 'imperial gaze', to the ways in which empires *saw* the various lands and peoples they colonised. Essentially, these studies are critiques of the imperial traveller who dramatises himself as 'master of all that I *survey*'. I want to draw attention to the ways in which colonial geographies not only *saw* but *heard* the lands and peoples of Australia.

In fact, there is a growing number of writers who are *listening* to the past. In *The Sound in Between* (1992), Paul Carter has listened to the sounds, babbles and conversations in which Europeans and Aborigines made contact with each other. Similarly, the American historian of the senses Mark M. Smith has captured the cacophony of American experience in a range of books and articles with such titles as 'Of Bells, Booms, Sounds, and Silences: Listening to the Civil War South'. He shares interests with Shane White and Graham White, whose book *Sounds of Slavery* (2005) explores how African slaves, in their thirst for meaning and solace, unleashed a deluge of music, sermons and speech on to the American south. More broadly, the American sound artist Douglas Kahn, the author of *Noise, Water, Meat: A History of Sound in the Arts* (1999), has pioneered the study of what he calls 'auditory culture', especially in the arts.[5]

Some writers on the topic have become campaigners for 'aural history', as if vision exercises a kind of tyranny over our understanding. I am more inclined simply to attend to sound—and to silence—as another way of getting at how the colonists experienced and interpreted their world, because they themselves write about it so often. As Mark Smith writes, 'If hearing were demonstrably important to people in the past, and if they left evidence to that effect, then the topic demands and deserves our attention'.[6]

In 1922, the English novelist D. H. Lawrence and his German wife Frieda spent three months in Australia. During this brief stay, Lawrence became both fascinated and appalled by what he called the 'weird silent timelessness of the bush'—a force that he wrote about as if it emanated from the land itself, reducing settler Australians to a state of mute resignation. Lawrence was experiencing afresh an anxiety, a feeling of alienation, that was fundamental to colonial Australia. Once the colonists failed to find mighty rivers in the interior, many were overcome with a sense that silence (with its connotations of stasis, lethargy, primitivism and death) was the ruling principle at the arid heart of their continent.[7]

In 1949, the power of this image was noted by the University of Melbourne's Professor G. L. Wood, an expert on population and resources in Australia. Writing in the popular magazine *Walkabout*, Wood argued that, for the purposes of development, Australia fell roughly into three zones, divided by what we know today as the 250-, 500- and 750-millimetre isohyets, or lines of average annual rainfall. The land beyond the 250-millimetre isohyet was desert, and therefore 'useless'. The zone that fascinated him received an average rainfall between 500 and 750 millimetres. This was the hard, dry country of pioneering sweat and struggle, 'the pastoral belt of Henry Lawson, of Banjo Paterson, and of many of the Australian poets and writers'.[8]

Wood pointed out that it was here that the 'climate halts permanent settlement': this was the hinterland to which 'the aboriginal nomad has been pushed back by the forces of occupation'. Wood rounded off his point by quoting a tenacious pioneer of the Northern Territory named Jessie Litchfield. In the desert, she wrote, she had found:

> arid rock on either hand
> Veiled with drifting red-brown sand.
> And nothing the aching silence stirred,
> No insect's chirr, nor song of bird,
> Just desolate, silent loneliness.

That stanza—standing alone—could be interpreted in several ways. It could be read as a challenge ('Let's roll up our sleeves and bring some life to this place.'); as a stark fact about the climate ('It's dry out there. Get used to it.'); or as a hymn of resignation—a surrender to melancholia. And these were exactly the choices colonists constructed for themselves at the end of the nineteenth century.

This story is played out in Aboriginal country. It is a story in which the white myths of the land as vacant are contradicted by the vivid presence of Aborigines—not only in the country itself, but in many of the accounts written by the colonists. I have not attempted to write in detail about the Aboriginal meanings or significances of water. That would be a different book. But this book arises from the understanding that the contact between white settlers and the Aboriginal owners triggered a battle for resources. In a country where water was scarce—and where it was central to the cultures of the Aboriginal peoples—the battle for land was also a battle for water.

To construct this account, I have looked at the journals of those primal myth makers the explorers, and writings by settlers, as well as novels, poems and newspaper articles about settlement, and books, political speeches, and magazine articles about pioneering, development and hydro-engineering. I have tried to understand how explorers, settlers and writers made sense of the process of settlement itself. It is an investigation that returns again and again to one overwhelming fact. In Australia, the success or failure of settlement has been largely determined by rainfall.

I explore three ideas that have been at the heart of what might be called geographical nationalism in Australia: the desert, the centre and the inland sea. Like most people educated in Australia during the twentieth century, I learnt at school that the early colonists 'believed in an inland sea', and that most explorers went in search of it. In the initial phase of my research, I attempted to track down references to this inland sea from the early colonial period. As part of this quest, I spent a couple of months in three English archives: the Royal Geographical Society, the vast library of the Institution of Civil Engineers, both in London, and Rhodes House in Oxford (where key Australian manuscript material was catalogued as 'Non-Africania'). It was at Rhodes House that I faced a daunting truth. There was almost no material on the notion of the inland sea in early Australia. The reality was hard to fathom. There was nothing to find. Something was wrong with the received account of Australian history. Whenever the myth of the inland sea entered our national cosmology, it was not during the era of exploration. As we will see, it appeared much later.

Early versions of sections of this book have appeared in *RePublica* (1995), the *Australian's Review of Books* (March 1997), Adam Shoemaker (ed.), *Sea Change* (1998), Tim Bonyhady and Tom Griffiths (eds), *Words for Country* (2002) and the Indian journal *Lemuria* (2006).

1

THE CADIGAL STREAM

But when I came to man's estate,
With hey, ho, the wind and the rain,
'Gainst knaves and thieves men shut their gate,
For the rain it raineth every day.

WILLIAM SHAKESPEARE, *TWELFTH NIGHT*

Wet-country people

The First Fleeters were wet-country people. Water coursed through their industries, their farms, their buildings, their class relations, their faiths and superstitions, their songs and their games. As the convicts and their keepers set sail from England, water was soaking into the places they left behind—into Hertford, Stafford, Deptford, Chelmsford, Poole, Kingston upon Hull, Southwark and Monmouth.[1]

These were watering places—towns or districts whose geographies, whose very names, were fashioned by water. This was water for which English men and women had a score of words: they spoke of rivulets and millstreams, millponds, ponds and pondages, of lakes, canals, cascades and falls, of cataracts, reservoirs, bogs and brooks, of fens and marshes, of moats and rills and rivers. These were waters where children played, where anglers fished, where industries pumped their sludge and farmhands watered stock.

Water pumped and gurgled through the arteries of industrial Britain: water ferrying commerce along the rivers and canals and seething in the great steam engines that thumped and clanked night and day. Above the crowded cities, tireless chimneys billowed with smoke and soot, choking the slums and encrusting the courts of the mighty with oily grime. Without let, the factories, tanneries, abattoirs and towns were creating the wonders of the industrial revolution, and spewing their filth into the waterways of England.

On a wide and rolling ocean—far from the clank and clamour of the factories—eleven tiny ships were opening a pathway to the far side of the world. The wooden vessels were crammed with convicts—along with soldiers, clerks, weapons, official documents and ledgers, goats, sheep, corn, barrels of salted meat, barrels of water, nails, hammers, hoes, shovels, axes and the tonnes of other equipment and provisions needed to build a prison camp on a coast mapped by Captain James Cook eighteen years before.

Among the creatures confined in the heaving belly of the ship *Alexander* was a London cutpurse named Robbie Abel. Aged just fifteen, Robbie was sentenced to seven years' transportation, for stealing five shillings. We may imagine him at night, lying filthy and near-naked, in the stench of the male convicts' quarters. Pressed around him, criminals are sleeping, farting, snoring or eyeing off the wild young boy. Robbie lies awake, listening to the creaking of the ship, while far behind him the plainsong of the poisoned Thames continues without pause, its music grown dark with the power and misery of industrial Britain.[2]

He was headed, along with the rest of them, for the driest continent on earth.

As this *terra incognita* hove into view, Captain Arthur Phillip scanned the alien shore. His instructions from Whitehall were clear. He was to establish his settlement at Botany Bay, a location chosen on the basis of Cook's survey as 'possessing a commodious harbour and other advantages which no part of the coast hitherto discovered affords'. He was explicitly instructed to waste no time searching for a more congenial site.[3]

On 18 January 1788, Phillip sailed into Botany Bay. From the quarterdeck of the *Supply*, he could see forty naked black men, or 'Indians', gathered on the southern beach, shouting and making what Lieutenant Watkin Tench described as 'uncouth signs and gestures'.[4] On the opposite beach, however, there was a party of just twelve such Indians. Phillip decided to take his chances with this smaller group, and set out towards them with a group of officers in a boat.

The crewmen rowed the boat parallel to the beach for some distance, 'the Indians keeping pace with her on the sand'. Each group was watching the other. The Aborigines jogged along the shoreline holding their long, flexible spears, while the British officers sat alert in their red and blue uniforms with their muskets ready. Then, reports Tench, one of the officers 'made signs of a want of water, which it was judged would indicate his wish of landing'. The Aborigines 'directly comprehended what he wanted' and pointed to a watering spot where the strangers should come ashore.[5]

For Arthur Phillip, a great deal hung on the next few minutes. Perhaps even men's lives. The forty-nine-year-old naval officer climbed out of the boat and stepped on to the sand to meet the owners of the land. According to his own account, when he 'approached with signs of friendship, alone and unarmed, they readily returned his confidence by laying down their weapons'.[6] The other officers clambered out of the boat and joined the men on the beach—the one group strangely dressed, the other strangely naked. The intruders saw their mime-show through to its conclusion by drinking at the

Aborigines' watering place and found the water to be 'very good'.[7] It was one of Botany Bay's tiny creeks, a run of cool water gurgling over rocks, shaded by green ferns, melaleucas and tea-tree.

We can picture the officers squatting among the reeds on the edge of the Aboriginal wetlands, scooping up the water with their hands or drinking out of their hats, while the Aborigines looked on warily from thirty metres away. When the drinking was done, the Aborigines advanced closer as Phillip and the officers clowned about and offered them presents. The surgeon, George Worgan, was in no doubt that these men were still fearful of these intruders. But the water ritual was a kind of communion between the two groups. A day later, another meeting was filled with laughter, comedy and dancing.[8]

This initial transaction concealed deep differences of meaning. The Aborigines were engaged in a social exchange they knew well: they had welcomed strangers with water. But when Governor Phillip stepped ashore, *his* purpose, as Lieutenant Tench saw it, was 'to take possession of his new territory and bring about an intercourse between its old and new masters'.[9]

As the foundation legend of white Australia famously records, Phillip judged that Botany Bay was too shallow and too dangerously exposed to provide an all-weather harbour. On shore, the prospect was even worse. He found the ground was either too sandy for cultivation or too swampy for building. Today we would celebrate this water-country as wetlands. But Phillip and his officers reviled it as marshes, subscribing to an idea as old as Hippocrates, that these were unhealthy places, emanating miasmic gases. His fellow officer David Collins agreed: the place 'was deficient in that grand essential—*fresh water*'.[10] It was sickness country. It would not do.

The next day, Phillip left the ships anchored in Botany Bay and took a team to investigate an opening that Cook had reported a few kilometres up the coast. And so it was that a group of officers and oarsmen in three British boats passed between the bluffs that guard the entrance to the fishing grounds of the Eora people. There Phillip had 'the satisfaction', he wrote, 'of finding the finest harbour in the world'.

Sydney's enigma

Visitors to modern Sydney are so dazzled by the glories of this same harbour that few notice an astonishing absence. This shining, prosperous city has no river flowing through its centre.

But Circular Quay, the city's busy ferry terminal, masks the underlying geography. The Quay and the noisy city block behind it actually sit astride the V-shaped estuary of a creek. If you leave Circular Quay and join the crowds walking up the gentle slope of Pitt Street, you can trace a depression in the land that shows where this Aboriginal watercourse seeps through a tunnel buried beneath the roadway. The first intersection you reach is busy Bridge Street, so named because, in the first year of settlement, the convicts built a log bridge here, close to the spot where the creek opened into the estuary.

One block further inland, the contours of the city indicate that the underground creek has drifted to the right of the street. By the time you reach the bustle of Martin Place, the creek is running directly beneath the stately General Post Office building, now occupied by boutiques, restaurants and the brass-and-polished-timber of an exclusive hotel. In a musty basement room, ignored by the noisy crowds, there is a small historical display that explains that this creek is the Tank Stream. There, at the bottom of an excavation in the basement, is the curved brick roof of the drain through which it now flows.

Once, an Eora family could walk the entire 600 metres of this waterway in a few minutes. Their stroll would end at the source—a reedy pond, alive with calling birds, splashing fish and the rustle of paperbark trees. This favourite camp site is now a roaring city block, immediately south of Sydney's futuristic Centrepoint Tower.[11]

In 2000, this lost watercourse was signposted with a series of elegant glass and steel markers set into the footpath, created by the sculptor Lynne Roberts-Goodwin. The Tank Stream is not forgotten. Its humiliation has been reworked as a poignant heritage tale—an act of desecration that has become part of the city's mythology. This entombed stream is the chief reason that Sydney exists.

As Phillip explored the Eora's coastline, his eye lighted on a cove called Warran or Cadi, in the territory of a clan called the Cadigal.[12] Two features of the place caught Phillip's attention. The little bay provided a good anchorage. And it was the estuary of a stream. As he explained to Lord Sydney:

> I fixed on the one that had the best spring of water, and in which the ships can anchor so close to the shore that at a very small expense quays may be made at which the largest ships may unload. This cove, which I honoured with the name of Sydney, is about a quarter of a mile across at the entrance, and half a mile in length.[13]

By 26 January, all the ships of Phillip's convoy had reassembled in Sydney Cove. The weather was 'uncommonly fine'.[14]

The geography of silence

It was at this place—on the banks of the Cadigal stream—that the newcomers first heard the great silence of Australia. It is the central image in an account that has become a foundation text for white settlement. David Collins, the judge advocate (chief judge) of the new prison settlement, described how a work party went ashore to clear a site for the camp.

> The spot chosen for this purpose was at the head of the Cove
> near the run of fresh water, which stole silently along through
> a very thick wood, the stillness of which had then, for the first
> time since the creation, been interrupted by the rude sound of
> the labourer's axe and the downfall of its ancient
> inhabitants.[15]

By 'ancient inhabitants' Collins meant, not the Aborigines, but
the trees. The axe, he continued, brought these ancient trees
crashing down, breaking the 'stillness and tranquillity which
from that day were to give place to the voice of labour, the
confusion of camps and towns, and "the busy hum of its new
possessors"'.

The humming reference is Collins' reverential allusion to
John Milton's poem 'L'Allégro', a celebration of an idealised
medieval past, where 'Towered Cities please us then,/And the
busy hum of men'. Collins was daring to hope that he and his
company were liberating the sounds of a new civilisation.[16]

When Collins refers to a 'wood', it is tempting for the
modern ear to hear him as a newcomer who has not yet learned
to use the language of 'the bush'. But, as Simon Schama points
out, the wood, the greenwood and the forest carry deep and
shifting symbolic meanings, across time and between cultures.[17]
Collins was using an image that would soon become commonplace in the colony. He was imagining the wood as the primal
condition of the landscape, as a kind of aboriginal forest, that
was dark, dormant and outside time.

This imaginary geography has a long lineage in the west.
Both Virgil and Dante locate a gloomy primordial forest at the
entrance to the underworld. In such fairy stories as *Hansel and
Gretel, Red Riding Hood* and *Snow White*, the dark woods are a
menacing zone that precedes history. The colonial Canadian

poet George Martin wrote of 'the primal grandeur of the solemn woods' that 'no white man's axe…had marred'. As the French philosopher Gaston Bachelard puts it, the forests have a 'before-us' essence: they 'reign in the past'. In Collins' mind, then, the woods on Sydney Cove were the dominant feature of a great timeless and silent continent—a land waiting to be possessed.[18]

In the same vein, Phillip wrote to Lord Sydney six months later, 'The climate is a very fine one, and the country will, I make no doubt, when the woods are cleared away, be as healthy as any in the world'.[19] Phillip was returning to his old theme. His metaphor was not silence, but *health*. For him, the woods, like the swamps, were somehow airless and unwholesome. By clearing them away, the civilisers would ventilate the bracing—and, implicitly, British—potential of the land itself.

For the Europeans, this journey into the woods was an encounter with nature, but not a nature husbanded by farmers, landowners and woodsmen as they knew at home. Here, in the 'untamed wilds', they found a kind of raw and nameless ur-nature, which was sometimes beautiful, sometimes menacing, often somnolent—and almost always alien. It preceded the 'art'—the building, farming, road-making, gardening and naming—through which civilisation had orchestrated the natural world in Britain. And, often, it was silent.[20]

This sensation was amplified in a popular *History of New South Wales* published in 1802, which explained that, 'The convicts landed that morning near a stream of fresh water, at the head of a cove. On this first inhabited spot, from that time, tranquillity ceased and the foundation of a new country usurped the seat of silence.'[21]

In fact, this passage is plagiarised from David Collins. (The phrase 'a stream of fresh water, at the head of a cove' simply flips Collins' wording.) The book was sold as the work of a debonair pickpocket named George Barrington. But literary scholars now acknowledge that it was written by an unknown hand in England, briskly reworking other accounts of the distant Sydney settlement. This provenance is revealing. The ghost writer has chosen to underline the significance of Collins' image. The silence, he recognises, is a symptom of vacancy. It confronts the settlers with their destiny to possess and civilise this land-in-waiting. The logic was later spelled out by the convict novelist James Tucker. It was part of the global mission of the British race, he wrote, to 'rescue the most untamed soils from the barbarism of nature and bid the busy sounds of industry and art awaken the silent echoes of every primeval forest in which they are placed'.[22]

Aboriginal water

On the Aboriginal side of the frontier, this felling of the trees had a different meaning. To the Eora, the traditional owners of Sydney Cove, the clearing of their trees was the destruction of the most dominant features of their ancestral lands—a devastating and unprecedented act of trespass. It was the first cause of friction between the two peoples. As the gentle Lieutenant William Bradley noted, when the axemen began their work, the Aborigines' pleasure evaporated and they 'wanted them to be gone'.[23]

Phillip, like the shepherd kings who followed him, was looking for arable land supplied with water. This was bound to lead to conflict with the Aboriginal peoples, whose cultures—whose lives—depended on rivers and waterholes. In hundreds of distinct countries spread across the entire continent, the various Aboriginal peoples valued their own water resources down to the last drop. As the explorer and bushman Edward Eyre was later to observe, 'they know the very rock where a little water is most likely to be collected, the very hole where it is the longest retained'. In the western deserts, the people dug and maintained wells to store precious rainwater as it ran off great slabs of flat rock. Other groups had perfected methods of harvesting groundwater, of storing water in hollow trees, carrying it in the skins of animals, and extracting it from plants. In time, the explorers would learn to rely on Aborigines to show the way to their traditional watering places—a kindness which, in the early contact between the two cultures, the Aborigines often seemed happy to perform.[24]

The explorer Major Thomas Mitchell was quick to adopt indigenous knowledge, noting how his Aboriginal guides would scoop a bowl in the sand at the edge of a hot, muddy pool. When muddy liquid had seeped into the hole, the Aborigines threw in bunches of long grass, through which they sucked cool, clean water. 'I was very glad to follow the example', wrote Mitchell, reporting with delight that 'the sweet fragrance of the grass' afforded 'an agreeable addition to the luxury of drinking'.[25]

Mitchell's bitter rival the explorer Charles Sturt observed that Aborigines who lived on the Murray were sensitive to the subtlest rises and falls of the river. They knew exactly when the river would transform 'all the dried up lagoons' into ponds, teeming with birds and fish.[26] And where fish swam, the Aborigines built fish traps. Among the wetlands of Toolondo in western Victoria, the Jaadwa excavated a wondrous eel trap nearly four kilometres long.[27] At Brewarrina, on the Darling River, the Ngemba people built Ngunnhu, the largest network of stone fish traps in Australia, a looping maze of solid stone walls that extended downriver for five hundred metres. Like most water-holes, Ngunnhu is a place bathed in spiritual power: it was fashioned by the great dreamtime ancestor Baiame, who first spoke its many names and taught the people how they should use it. (You can still see his giant footprint on the bed of the Darling River.)[28]

As the Aboriginal historian Marcia Langton explains, the various lands and waters were a 'living drama of history'. Waters flowed with sacred meanings and memories, and with the social obligations by which each individual defined him or herself as a person of that place. Langton tells how the elders of one Cape York community sometimes 'baptise' newcomers with local water. By participating in this ritual, strangers make themselves known to the land, and signal to the ancestors that they will treat the land with respect. [29]

Before their lands were invaded, Aborigines, like all human populations, lived in the greatest numbers where rainfall was highest. The rainfall dictated that the east coast, the south-west corner and the north-west were more densely settled than the rest of the continent. This was not a cultural choice. It was a biological necessity. In a land where water was scarce, there was literally none to spare. Estimates of the population in 1788 range from 300,000 to one million. The number climbed during wet periods, when the survival rate of young children and old people increased, and declined when the rains did not come. The hundreds of Aboriginal territories that made up the continent were full. Conflict with the white invaders was inevitable. [30]

2

THE VALLEY OF THE TANK STREAM

The trouble with water—and there is trouble with water—is that they're not making any more of it.

MARQ DE VILLIERS, *WATER*

Strangers

On the day after the first British convoy dropped anchor in Sydney Cove, the surgeon John White and some others took a boat on to the harbour and began fishing. A few local Eora men joined the party. They 'behaved very friendly', even helping the intruders to drag their net ashore. 'For this kind office,' wrote Mr White, 'they were liberally rewarded with fish, which seemed to please them and give general satisfaction.'[1]

A few days later, a meticulous and reflective naval officer named Captain John Hunter took a party of men in a six-oared boat to explore some neighbouring nooks of the harbour. On a beach where Sydneysiders now jog in the early morning or sunbake as they listen to their iPods, Hunter and his comrades spent an entertaining summer's day with local Eora men. They learned each other's songs. They danced the hornpipe. They danced Aboriginal dances. Black men and Europeans laughed together as they competed on the beach in games of strength and skill, throwing spears, not in conflict, but in shared enjoyment. When the fifty-one-year-old Hunter returned to his tent that night, he was exhilarated. His neighbours were 'a very lively and inquisitive race', he wrote. They were cheerful, athletic and uncannily accurate in their use of the spear. Like Phillip, he anticipated that the colonisation of the Aboriginal territories could be achieved in a spirit of cooperation and goodwill. [2]

During these days of mutual wonder, the Eora men moved freely about the camp that was taking shape on the banks of the Cadigal stream. But there were signs of caution. Surgeon White was convinced that they knew and dreaded the power of the white man's guns. The Eora women stayed away almost entirely: only one, a very old woman, entered the camp. The Aboriginal men took presents from the officers. They watched the newcomers labour to fell more trees and build shelters in a place which, for the Eora, was already perfectly habitable. They saw the convicts lay out gardens and build yards for their sheep, cows, pigs and chickens. They saw too how drunk and randy white men raged through the settlement, carousing and rutting in the women's camp. Also watching was Lieutenant Ralph Clark, pining for the young wife he had left behind in England. He was sickened by this wanton 'Seen of Whordome'. To him, the natives were a civil and noble people, while the mass of convicts were drunken, carnal brutes. [3]

Then suddenly the Eora stopped coming. The officers were bewildered by the change of mood. There had been no quarrel. Perhaps the wretched convicts, who were free to wander the surrounding country, had injured or abused the local people. Perhaps the strangers' manic felling of trees had simply become intolerable. But David Collins suspected that relations had soured because the French explorer the Comte de la Pérouse, now anchored a few kilometres away in Botany Bay, had become involved in a confrontation with the local people and had 'been compelled' to shoot at them. Whatever the case, the Eora stayed away, even though, as Collins wrote, 'we were occupied in works that indicated an intention of remaining in their country'.[4]

The axis of the British settlement was the Cadigal stream. It flowed through a sandstone gully that sliced through the middle of the camp. In this new geography, the stream upheld the distinctions of the Georgian class system. On the eastern side of the stream, the men assembled the governor's prefabricated house and hoisted a British flag on a white flagpole out the front, right on the harbour's edge. The officers erected their tents in the prime position—along the banks of the stream itself, while the regular soldiers and the convicts mostly had their tents on the other side of the stream, on the western side of the cove. The parade ground lay between the male and female convicts' camps.[5]

Close by stood the Hanging Tree. On 27 February, the company assembled under its branches for the first time to see the rebellious, flash-talking Thomas Barrett executed for stealing food from the government store. Ralph Clark watched him die: 'the Ladder was pul from under him and he Lanched into the other world without a gron'.[6]

As Barrett's corpse hung silent from the tree, everything on Sydney Cove was dripping wet. The hot air smelt of rain, damp earth and eucalyptus. It was a season of wild, summer storms. A fortnight earlier, wild lightning had struck the camp, splitting a tree in two and killing several livestock. The day after the hanging, another storm sent dark clouds and thunder rampaging across the harbour, while wild rain drenched the strangers and pelted their possessions. Ralph Clark sheltered in his tent as it snapped and thumped around him. 'My God, what a Terrible day this has been of Rain,' he wrote. 'I never Saw that I Recollect it Rain harder...all the time it rained [as] if heaven and earth was coming together.'[7]

These storms revealed that the stream was not the only place from which the settlers could draw water. The porous sandstone beneath Sydney acts as a solid sponge. Throughout that steamy February and March, the rocks of Sydney oozed with cool waters that trickled down the gullies and into the sea. The settlers were soon following a practice, centuries old in Britain: they were sinking wells, from which they lifted scoops of clean, pure water. A survey map drawn by William Bradley shows that, just five weeks after the British arrived, there were two such wells alongside the hospital garden on the western side of the cove. Phillip reported that the men had also dug an 'excellent' well beside his own house.[8]

When it came to water, Phillip had reason to be optimistic. Despite its reputation for sunshine, the home of Bondi Beach is actually a very rainy place. Sydney's average annual rainfall (1223 mm) is *double* the average of London (a mere 593 mm). And it almost doubles Paris (642 mm). Yet Sydney *is* a sunny city. The reason is that Sydney receives its rainfall in much larger doses than the other two cities: on average, it experiences just 138 rainy days each year compared with drizzly London's 154 days.[9]

Equally pleasing to Phillip was the subtropical lushness and variety of the vegetation. This warm, humid country supported a cornucopia of plants. Over 140 species of eucalypt raised their branches to the hot blue sky. Luxurious ferns grew thickly beneath the gum trees, while grasses and vines festooned the rocky cliffs bordering the harbour. The forest blazed with strange antipodean flowers—the flaming waratahs, red and yellow banksias, and the weird, blood-red gymea lilies, perched like savage crowns atop their five-metre stalks. Phillip was reassured, too, to find edible plants that reminded him of vegetables from home: 'wild celery, spinages, samphose [the succulent salt marsh plant, samphire], a small wild fig, and several berries, which have proved very wholesome'.[10]

Not all the newcomers shared Phillip's optimism. Daniel Southwell, a lowly mate from the *Sirius*, wrote miserably that, 'We meet with no thing that is deserving of the name of fruit, and its quad's [quadrupeds] are scarcely above vermin.' He went on, 'There are no rivers of water, and we are indebted to the frequent rains that supply the little runs that furnish us with this article.' Phillip's deputy was Major Robert Ross, a cantankerous veteran of campaigns in Canada and America. He dismissed this 'vile country' as being 'so very barren and forbidding that it may with truth be said here nature is reversed'. These two disgruntled men had a point. Sydney's copious rains and diverse plants did not signal rich soils or plentiful water. Quite the opposite. The plants of the Sydney region are adapted to grow in poor soil, and to survive on low levels of moisture.[11]

The reason for this paradox is Sydney's ubiquitous sandstone. Over millions of years, it has broken down to produce a thin layer of poor, highly porous soil. The few nutrients tend to leach into the sea. The sandstone base itself is so permeable that rainwater is drawn into the rock and then drains away. This was no place for English-style farming. Sydney Cove, for all its rain, was country designed to dry out.

So it was that Phillip and the other officers were soon scouring the harbour for fertile soils and a more reliable water supply. They were dismayed to discover that all the trickles that flowed into Port Jackson 'proceed from swamps' where 'perpetual damps prevail, and the air itself appears to stagnate'. As Tench put it, the men found 'not a single rivulet' worthy of the name, and 'were under a necessity of supplying themselves with water from standing pools'. Being an optimist, Phillip foresaw that, in time, man-made channels would drain these malignant marshes, swelling the streams and making the country 'habitable and salubrious'. This, he said, was 'the great improvement which may be made by the industry of a civilised people in this country'.[12] The water dreaming of white Australia had begun.

Theft

Meanwhile, the relationship between the convicts and the Aborigines was growing uneasy. The Eora stole from the intruders. And the intruders stole from the Eora. On Garden Island (now used as a naval base), three men were preparing a vegetable garden, when a group of thirty Aborigines made off with some tools. As the thieves fled, one of the gardeners fired a gun, stinging an Eora man in the leg with small-shot. The wounded man dropped a spade, and scrambled to safety.[13]

April came. The weather cooled and the rains eased. With winter approaching, the exiles started building sturdier shelters from local timber. The best tree for planks was one which 'resembles the fir tree'. But the intruders cut down so many that they soon had to lug timber from other parts of the harbour, and were vexed to discover that they could not tow these logs across the harbour because they became waterlogged and sank.[14]

As the building continued, two convict lads named Bill Okey (aged about eighteen) and Sam Davis (about twenty-one) walked to a nearby mangrove swamp to collect rushes for thatched roofing. The place is now known as Rushcutters Bay, a leafy corner of inner Sydney, where gracious houses preside over a green park and sleek yachts sway expensively on their moorings. In that solitary cove, Eora warriors attacked the two young men. As Sam Davis fled into the mangroves, the Aborigines drove three spears into Bill Okey's guts and then broke open his head with a club. When a search party found his corpse the next day, Okey's brains were oozing from his shattered skull and birds had eaten his eyes. The searchers found Davis's body a short time later, wedged in a tangle of mangroves. When Surgeon White examined the corpses, he concluded that Davis had died in the night of cold and terror. A month later, the Eora slew another convict and wounded his companion. In all, convicts killed three Aborigines that first year. The Aborigines killed seven convicts and one soldier.[15]

In years to come, such killings by Aborigines would trigger murderous reprisals. But in these first weeks of the settlement, the British officers held the Eora in high regard. Watkin Tench had no doubt that the attacks by Aborigines had been provoked by 'outrages committed upon them by unprincipled individuals among us'—in short, by the convicts themselves. When it emerged that the dead rushcutters had stolen an Eora canoe, David Collins—mindful of his role as the colony's chief legal officer—sided with the killers. Okey and Davis had acted as common thieves. The Eora, he said, had every right to execute them for their 'act of violence and injustice'. Phillip reinforced that opinion by ordering would-be trophy hunters not to steal 'spears, fizgigs [harpoons], gum, or other articles' from the Aborigines. He was determined to treat the Aborigines 'with the greatest humility and attention', hoping that they would learn the art of farming from the newcomers and thereby 'render their situation more comfortable'.[16]

The stealing and the violence continued, but so too did the wary exchanges of goodwill. A couple of days after the attack on Okey and Davis, Phillip and a group of officers were walking along the nearby coast in search of the men responsible for the deaths. The Englishmen stumbled on three hundred Aborigines—men, women and children—gathered on a beach, a little to the north of Botany Bay. The Aboriginal men were hostile and warned the intruders away. But Phillip offered them fish-hooks, beads and a looking-glass. In response, wrote Surgeon

White, 'they in a few minutes mixed with us, and conducted us to a very fine stream of water, out of which some of them drank, to shew that it was good'. The Aborigines shared their water with the intruders—and no more was said of the attack.[17]

Shortly afterwards, Phillip set out again in search of water and arable land. Accompanied by a party of ten soldiers and officers, he sailed to the western end of the harbour. They found what they had dreamed of—a confidently flowing river teeming with fish and birds. The local Burramattagal people, whose huts, fish traps, canoes and middens were all around, took their name from the river, the Burramatta, or Parramatta—Eel River. Phillip renamed the country 'Rose Hill', not after the English flower, but in honour of George Rose, a Whitehall powerbroker and leading campaigner against slavery.[18]

The following November, Phillip sent a detachment of convicts, soldiers and overseers back to establish a farm on a pleasant slope of rich volcanic soil lapped by the waters of this fine river. On the edges of a natural amphitheatre, now signposted as a heritage site, they constructed stone buildings including a small fortification in case of Aboriginal resistance. But, for the time being, the members of this new outpost were mostly on good terms with the people of the Burramatta. Neither the unwilling convicts who dug the rich alluvial soil under the whispering gum trees, nor the bored soldiers who kept guard, had any knowledge of agriculture, and the convoy had brought no plough. So progress was tardy. But a local lake provided water for the farm even when the river was depleted. There was hope.

In 1789 and 1790, the summers were hotter than any the exiles had ever known. Supplies ran low. The crops failed. In Sydney, convicts and soldiers alike grew miserable and dejected. By now, the soldiers' uniforms were in tatters. The convicts were wearing rags. And the distinctions of rank, which had been so carefully laid out in the catchment of the creek, were blurred by boredom, hunger and discontent.

The suffering among the Eora and their neighbours was even worse. In 1789, smallpox suddenly descended upon the Aborigines. It killed hundreds—perhaps thousands—of people in the Sydney region. The historian Judy Campbell argues that the epidemiological evidence shows that the disease was introduced into northern Australia by Indonesian fishermen and was already spreading death across the continent when the whites arrived. Whether that is so—or whether smallpox was introduced independently by the convicts—the epidemic was a catastrophe. The officers could not contain their horror and dismay as they reported that human corpses were rotting in every cove and inlet of the harbour. It was, wrote Tench, 'an extraordinary calamity'. Such were the grief and social breakdown which this foreign plague inflicted on the Aborigines of Port Jackson that the few wretched survivors seemed determined to avoid the settlers altogether. It was a year of misery on both sides of the frontier.[19]

When the ever-thoughtful Watkin Tench led a party of two officers, two marines and a convict on a short expedition, inland from Parramatta, in search of new sources of water, he was overwhelmed by a melancholy sensation that the country was unpeopled.

> Before us lay the trackless immeasurable desert, in awful silence...We continued to march all day through a country untrodden before by an European foot. Save that a melancholy crow now and then flew croaking over head, or a kangaroo was seen to bound at a distance, the picture of solitude was complete and undisturbed.[20]

Tench was not using the word 'desert' in its now familiar sense: this country was well-vegetated and fertile. In the young colony, the word 'desert' simply meant a place that seemed empty and unused. Tench's efforts were rewarded by the discovery of the Nepean River, which remains a vital source of water for Sydney to this day.

The struggle for the Tank Stream

Back in the settlement, Phillip had already resolved to protect the Cadigal stream from the heat of the sun, and from rubbish and faeces, by proclaiming a fifteen-metre green belt along either bank, where settlers were forbidden to cut down trees, keep animals or erect buildings.[21] As the creek withered to a trickle, Phillip ordered the stonemasons to carve three rectangular holes—each the size of a modern backyard swimming pool—into the sandstone abutting the stream. One was excavated on the eastern bank. The other two were on the opposite side at today's Bond Street. (Part of the track that led to this source of 'spring water' is today's Spring Street.[22]) The colonists called these cisterns 'the tanks'—an Anglo-Indian term derived from the Gujarati word *tankh*, meaning reservoir.[23] And so, the Cadigal watering place became the 'Tank Stream', a name that spoke, not of England, but of the empire. It was Australia's first government-funded hydro-engineering project.

The torments of heat, hunger and thirst, which unleashed such misery on the settlement in 1790, were no respecters of rank. In a much-celebrated act of egalitarianism, Phillip placed everyone—soldier, officer, convict and governor alike—on equal rations. But British justice was merciless with hungry lawbreakers. In June, young Robbie Abel—the boy we met cradled below the decks of the *Alexander* on the voyage out—stole some sugar. As punishment, the flogger lashed him 200 times; each stroke cutting flesh away from his spine, reducing his back to a bloody pulp. When justice was spent, Robbie was stretchered semiconscious to the hospital, where Surgeon White bandaged the boy's ruined body.[24]

At the same time, Phillip relieved the pressure on Sydney Cove by consigning several hundred convicts and soldiers, under the odious Major Ross, to an outpost Phillip had already established on the remote and windswept Norfolk Island. Despite his attempts to protect the Tank Stream, the settlers continued to foul the creek. By now, the sandy beaches around the cove were rank with rubbish and filth.[25]

Though the next year remained dry, the broad Parramatta River continued to flow at the far end of the harbour, and the sixteen-hectare farm on its banks at Rose Hill began producing food—despite the grudging labour of the convicts. But elsewhere around Port Jackson, the lagoons and wetlands were drying out and the Tank Stream itself had withered. Phillip struggled to make sense of it all, reporting to his masters in Whitehall that 'I do not think it probable that so dry a season often occurs'.[26] In fact, he had no idea. How could he? He had governed the valley of the Tank Stream for just three years.

It would take a century for the settlers to understand what was happening. Unlike England, where the climate patterns are fairly regular, in most parts of Australia the climate varies greatly from year to year. In Europe, the average rainfall figure is an indication of what is most *likely* in any given year. In Australia, the average figures tell you nothing about what is likely. This year may be wet. Or it may be dry. The only certainty is variability.

An exhausted Phillip departed for England in December 1792, entrusting the administration to the senior military officers of the New South Wales Corps with their commanding officer Major Francis Grose acting as governor. Grose was an amiable fellow, embedded in the culture of the officers' mess. To him, the settlement was a military encampment and he had no truck with Phillip's feudal dreams of an agrarian utopia. To the officers, the convicts were an inferior breed of humanity, whose destiny it was to be exploited as a source of cheap, vexatious labour. The officers used their newfound power to take control of trade in and out of Sydney. They abolished a prohibition on trading rum established by Phillip and controlled the supply, which they used as currency, earning their regiment a place in history as the 'Rum Corps'. As their wealth and influence grew, Grose abandoned Phillip's green-belt regulations, allowing his comrades to build more substantial houses and keep animals alongside the Tank Stream.[27] Land being the right of officers and gentlemen, Grose signed over prime riverside country at Parramatta to such fellow officers as William Cummings and the tough man of Sydney, John Macarthur. At the same time, Grose appointed Macarthur to the post of government administrator of Parramatta, allowing him to lay the foundations on which he would build the Australian wool industry and his own power and fortune.[28]

Grose and his successor, a fellow officer named William Paterson, wielded supreme power for less than three years. But the damage to the Tank Stream was done. Paterson was relieved in 1795 by the second official governor, the wily and grizzled Captain John Hunter, who attempted to reverse the abuses by erecting protective fences along either bank. But the pattern was now set for acrimony between successive governors and the officers of the Rum Corps. Residents who had built houses near the stream (many of whom were officers) ripped off the palings to take shortcuts to the water. Some fattened pigs at the rear of their houses and, when it rained, a slurry of pig shit slithered into Sydney's drinking water. The result was so noxious that on 22 October 1795 Hunter decreed that people who broke the fences or kept pigs near the stream would be removed and have their houses demolished. But that last sanction was unthinkable—and the situation got worse. By May 1797 the water was so foul that Hunter believed it had caused the 'disorders of which several have lately died'. The following summer there was an outbreak of dysentery. Hunter issued further orders against fouling the stream or vandalising the fences, but they made no difference.[29]

The famine of the early years was now in retreat. Not only was the government farm at Rose Hill producing food, but it was being overtaken by newer farms owned and run by the officers themselves, using convict labour. Any hope of a reconciliation between the British interlopers and the local Aboriginal groups (known collectively as the Darug) now seemed vain. As the settlers' land-grab spread from one watering place to the next, a deadly resistance was led by a Darug wise man or sorcerer named Pemulwuy, whose first victim had been Governor Phillip's game hunter, John McIntyre. In 1800, the new governor, Philip Gidley King, ordered that Pemulwuy be killed on sight. When soldiers finally gunned the Darug fighter down in the streets of Parramatta two years later, King declared him 'a brave and independent character', and sent his head, pickled in a barrel, to Sir Joseph Banks in England. It is now lost.[30]

Back in Sydney Cove in 1803, King was engaged in a dour struggle with the free-wheeling Rum Corps, gaining some respite when he sent their arrogant champion, John Macarthur, to face court martial in London. In an attempt to defend the creek, King built fences around the tanks themselves and reinforced the regulations. Any person throwing filth into the stream, cleaning fish or washing in the water, or erecting pigsties close by was liable to be fined five pounds and—once again—to have his house demolished.[31] That same year, King outlawed indiscriminate tree-felling along the banks of all rivers and streams in an attempt to reduce the erosion and the blockages that were becoming all too evident. These might have been avoided, observed the very sensible Governor King, 'if the trees and other native plants had been suffered to remain'.[32]

Meanwhile, David Collins established a new colony (today's Hobart) on the Derwent River in Van Diemen's Land. Determined to avoid the disaster he had witnessed in Sydney, Collins was quick to post regulations protecting the 'rivulet' that provided the settlement's water. His General Orders of 21 February 1804 cautioned the people 'against polluting the stream by any means whatsoever' and forbade anyone 'going into, or destroying the underwood adjacent to the water, under pain of being severely punished'.[33]

In Sydney itself, there were a few prosecutions. One James Anderson was fined fifty shillings in the magistrate's court in 1808 for rinsing hides in one of the tanks. In his defence, he pleaded that 'it had never occurred to him that he was doing harm since, being a knight of the order of St Crispin, he had accustomed himself to the taste of water in which he had steeped his leather'. Mr Anderson was no knight. St Crispin is the patron saint of shoemakers. Mr Anderson was a cobbler who had soaked his skins in the town's drinking water. And, as his smart-arse defence indicates all too plainly, he frankly did not care. That same month, the government issued the regulations yet again, containing all the familiar prohibitions against washing, cleaning fish and allowing pigs and cattle to foul the stream.[34]

Two decades of colonisation had now passed. The British had established new centres of settlement inland on the Parramatta, northwards on the fine farming country along the majestic Hawkesbury River and at Hobart. They had learned that droughts—and their attendant bushfires—were not the only trial to which the climate might subject them. There were also floods. The Hawkesbury—a wide river that even today glistens with serene assurance—soon proved that it was capable of transforming into a wild killer, bursting its banks in a deluge that submerged farms, and drowned both stock and people.[35] In Britain there were floods too. But, over the centuries, the British had built levee banks and weirs and learned to harmonise their agriculture with the cycles of river water gurgling over the meadows. In Australia, the floods were more unruly—and no technology would ever quite get the better of them.

Sydney was now a noisy port where officers of the Rum Corps had adopted a code of swagger and ambition that made them contemptuous of the fetters placed on them by government. It was an impatience that erupted in 1808, when the officers were confronted by a new and determined governor. He was Captain William Bligh—the same Captain Bligh whose violent manner had driven so many of his officers to mutiny aboard HMS *Bounty* in the waters off Tonga in 1789.

The corps had no economic incentive to protect free, clean drinking water. Indeed, as the Rev. Samuel Marsden observed, the controllers of the rum economy had a vicious interest in maintaining their convict workforce in a state of alcoholic dependency.[36] The Rum Corps' neglect of the Tank Stream was obvious: the protective fences were falling into disrepair and would soon completely disappear.[37] At the same time, housing was about to become an exceedingly inflammatory issue. For the most part, Sydney's householders did not possess freehold title to the land on which they had built. If a resident's lease expired or was forfeited by his misconduct, the governor was entitled to remove the house itself since it stood on crown land. So affronted was Bligh by the disorder of Sydney that he did what no previous governor had dared. He began demolishing such houses in an attempt to clear the ground for more congenial urban planning. To the householders of Sydney, among whom the officers were the most powerful group, this was an assault on private property and an affront to their fundamental rights as Englishmen. The commander of the corps, Major George Johnston, saw to his alarm that Bligh's 'gross frauds and shameful robberies' were driving the officers towards mutiny. When an armed deputation marched on Government House in the notorious Rum Rebellion, Johnston was at its head, reluctantly declaring himself acting lieutenant governor.[38]

Though Bligh was left seething under house arrest, his Tank Stream regulations remained in force. Indeed, the magistrates reissued the now-standard regulations forbidding people to foul the area around the tanks. There was one change to the previous rules: there was no longer any threat to demolish offenders' homes.[39]

The military authorities in Britain had always expected its officers to become frontier capitalists: after all, the first qualification demanded of one of His Majesty's officers was that he be a gentleman of property. But in Sydney, the conflict between the officers' private interests and their military duty had unleashed scandal and rebellion. From the distance of Whitehall, the British government re-established its authority by recalling the Rum Corps in 1809 and appointing the visionary Lieutenant-Colonel Lachlan Macquarie as the next governor of New South Wales.

Macquarie

Macquarie achieved what Bligh had failed to do: he cleaned up the town. He standardised the names of streets and localities, and established a plan for development. Macquarie was appalled by the squalor of the Tank Stream. Noxious waste from tanners, slaughtermen and brewers oozed into the stream. And it seemed that every household in the valley was adding to the problem. Macquarie observed that it was common practice to throw 'Ashes, Filth, and Dirt of every description [sewage] in the Street, on the Footpaths, and into the Drains...to the great prejudice of the Tanks and streams to which those Nuisances are carried down by the Rains'. In his first year, Macquarie issued a lengthy schedule of prohibitions and ordered that stone diversion walls be built along the banks, and that slaughter-houses, tanneries and privies which fouled the stream be pulled down.[40] But once again, short-term considerations triumphed. Nothing really changed. In any case, it was too late. What Macquarie could not know was that this filth was leaching into the groundwater, which in turn flowed out of fissures in the sandstone and into the stream. The germ theory of disease lay seventy years in the future. But it was common knowledge that the Tank Stream made you ill. As the angry *Sydney Gazette* put it, people who drank there were either 'choaked (sic) with soap-suds, or poisoned with infectious filth'.[41]

Increasingly, residents had come to depend on the wells—though these tended to dry out in the summer. For people with money, the best option was to buy water carted at some expense from swamps and lagoons near the town.

In 1814, the convicts of Sydney were joined by Joseph Lycett, a forty-year-old artist who had been transported for forgery. Throughout the 1820s, Lycett painted dozens of watercolours of Sydney and the surrounding countryside. At the same time an officer named Major James Taylor painted three panoramas of Sydney in a similar illustrative style. Their works depict a thriving harbour town filled with bright new houses surrounded by neat gardens and orderly fences. Soldiers, men of affairs and noble Aborigines stand around engaged in conversation as if they are characters in an allegorical play. In the fields, men are driving carts and tending cattle while other Aborigines sit beside their huts or hunt for food in a sort of ethnographic display. On the harbour, English ships ride purposefully on the waves, while tiny windmills, looking as if they belong in Holland, sit atop the hills catching the breezes in their outstretched arms.[42]

What these cheery, idealised views of the settlement cannot convey is the stench. On a hot summer's day, this busy Sydney, especially the area around the Rocks, reeked of swill, rotting rubbish and shit. It was chronic in the summer of 1826, when, once again, the fat subtropical rains failed to arrive. The pastures around Sydney died off and the vegetable gardens wilted under the ferocious sun. The heat reduced the Tank Stream to a rancid gutter, crawling between two rows of houses, butchers' yards and tanneries, and disgorging a toxic plume into the blue waters of Port Jackson.[43]

The following summer, a young military officer named Charles Sturt arrived in Sydney aboard a convict transport. As formal and ambitious as a hero in a Jane Austen novel, Captain Sturt was intent upon serving his God and making his name and his fortune in New South Wales. He was charmed by the prosperous township that his countrymen were building on the slopes of Sydney Cove, seeing at once that this was an outpost of British civility. 'I had not pictured to myself, nor conceived from anything I had ever read or heard in England,' he wrote, 'that so extensive a town could have been reared in that remote region, in so brief a period.' But as he soon realised, he had arrived in a colony that, for all its mercantile clatter, was gagging with thirst.[44] Not only could he smell it. He could read about it in the newspaper.

That year, a grand jury—a committee of citizens set up to advise the court on the state of Sydney's public facilities—conducted an official inspection of the Tank Stream. (In the absence of a parliament, the court functioned as the major political forum, in which the governor's powers were subjected to review, individual rights were tested and civic values were affirmed.) As the committee men made their way along the sad little waterway, they were overpowered by 'the stench proceeding from the slaughterhouse of Mr David Kelly' and strongly recommended that all such abattoirs be removed to nearby Darling Harbour. They also complained that the Tanks had become a favourite gathering place for the town's thieves and hoodlums, particularly on Saturdays, when rowdy convicts and their associates splashed about naked in a froth of soap suds as they laundered their clothes.[45]

A host of people could see the problem—but they lacked the civic will to solve it. After all, life in industrial England was no different: the urban rivers were vile, and common people often drank beer or spirits because most city water was so nauseating. That same year, *The Times* reported that the Thames itself was undrinkable. The river was reduced to a foul brew of raw sewage combined with 'the refuse of hospitals, slaughterhouses, colour, lead and soapworks and manufactories'.[46]

By now many of Sydney's wells were drying up. The rest were poisonous. An official survey, carried out by a new government engineer named John Busby, found that, 'In all of them the water, from being more or less impregnated with mineral substances, is unfit for many domestic purposes, and is very generally considered prejudicial to health.'[47]

This was good news for the water carters. Their purses were chuckling with the sixpences they charged for every bucket of water they hauled from the nearby Lachlan Swamps. It was good money: sixpence was the price of a pound of pork, or a full day's wage for a convict. In Sydney, as in England, clean water was becoming the privilege of the rich.[48]

Since private interest had so comprehensively fouled the waterways and abandoned poor folk to their squalor, it was only logical, in both England and Australia, that reformers should argue that clean water and public health were the rightful responsibilities of government. One champion of water reform in Sydney was the outspoken, nationalist *Australian* newspaper, edited by Robert Wardell. Its co-founder was W. C. Wentworth, who was fast establishing his reputation as the most pugnacious advocate for the rights of former convicts and their families, the so-called emancipists. The *Australian* was in high rhetorical mode as it addressed the immorality and disorder of the convict quarter, the Rocks. The debaucheries arose, it said, not from innate human failings, but because the people were living where slops and shit congealed in the muddy roads and alleys.[49] These were people who could 'not afford to pay sixpence for a bucket-ful' of clean water. The time had come for the government to put that right.

> Let the Authorities cast their eyes upon the Rocks; up there, who [that] have spent their childhood in the very midst of them, will not *sing* pæons in praise of them, if they are disposed to admit, that to the scarcity of water may be attributed three-fourths of the filth in which the inhabitants live, and with which they are surrounded...
>
> It is downright ill-nature—it is absolute inattention—it betrays almost a wanton indifference to our interests—to the health and welfare and prosperity of the Colony, not to proceed forthwith to afford the town of Sydney a supply of water...
>
> We have a right, on behalf of our fellow-colonists, to demand the best services of the Government in removing one of the heaviest calamities which a people can have to submit to...THE WANT OF PURE WATER![50]

As it happens, the paper believed that the answer to Sydney's water problems was artesian water—and it urged the government to drill. We will return to this miraculous innovation. For the moment, the great hope for redeeming both Sydney's water supply and its underclass lay in a swamp.

3

MR BUSBY'S BORE

Earth felt the wound; and Nature from her seat,
Sighing through all her works, gave signs of woe
That all was lost.

MILTON, *PARADISE LOST*

Lachlan Swamps

John Busby was born in Northumberland and worked as a mineral surveyor before arriving in Sydney in 1824 as the colony's chief engineer. Appointed by the government to report on Sydney's failing water supply, Busby recognised that the Lachlan Swamps, so favoured by the water carters, were an ideal source.[1]

The swamps were a system of ponds and marshes three kilometres long, with a catchment eight times larger than the valley of the Tank Stream. The main pond was just three kilometres south of Sydney Cove, in the area now occupied by the undulating lawns of Centennial Park. The swamp itself was part of a much larger chain of lagoons, marshes, heathlands and sand dunes that extended south, all the way to Botany Bay. Ironically, these wetlands were the far side of the same 'unhealthy' swamps that had so dismayed Arthur Phillip four decades earlier.

If we could walk through Centennial Park as it was in

Aboriginal times, it would strike most of us as a place of lush, subtropical beauty. Here, birds landed in the branches of the paperbark trees and then swooped down to the reeds and rushes that grew in the lagoons. The water was swirling with eels and splashing with fish. At night, the air on the marshes was filled with the thrumming of frogs and the whine of insects, while in the warm, orange light of morning, kangaroos and wallabies grazed on the grassy flats. Beneath them, water gurgled through the earth, some of it seeping into ponds, some trickling into the springs and creeks.[2]

But when the portly Mr Busby muddied his boots here in 1825, he saw this not as an Aboriginal waterhole, nor as the environmentalist's pristine wilderness, nor as one of Phillip's miasmic swamps. He saw it as a reservoir. Fifteen years earlier, Governor Macquarie had gazetted the area for the grazing of stock, calling it the 'Sydney Common'. So while Busby may have spotted kangaroos among the trees, he would also have met the settlers' goats, pigs, horses and cattle, drinking at the ponds, ripping out the grasses and trampling the wetlands. Along the ridges, the settlers had widened the Aboriginal paths that linked the waterholes, creating cart tracks connecting Sydney to Botany Bay. They felled so many trees that one settler complained the region was fast 'being denuded of its scanty covering of timbers'. At the top end of the swamp, a paper mill and a flour mill were both in operation, while market gardeners were beginning to grow vegetables in the 'uncommonly fertile' soil.[3]

In his official report, Busby described the swamps as a 'great sand sponge' carrying water at a depth from thirteen to thirty metres. He noted that the water was clear and 'free from every taste and smell'. He proposed to pump this water into a holding reservoir on the highest point of what is now Centennial Park and then allow it to flow down into Hyde Park through pipes, cast of solid English iron.[4]

In distant Whitehall, Earl Bathurst—a shrewd and efficient administrator with views so moderate that they alarmed no one—looked over the proposal. The request from Sydney for pipes and pumps entailed considerable expense—and Busby's plans were compiled in haste. Bathurst appreciated that water was an 'essential article of life', but, until he saw more detailed plans, he would not approve the expenditure.[5]

Meanwhile Busby changed his mind. Forget the pipes. In just three years, he would drive a tunnel underground from the swamps, downhill to a capacious reservoir in Hyde Park. True, at £20,000 it was nearly double the price of the pipe, but, since the tunnel would operate without a pump, it would cost almost nothing to run. In essence, he proposed to dig a mine shaft.[6]

The government approved expenditure on the shaft, but not on the reservoir, and in September 1827 Busby's convict workers began breaking open the earth near the south-eastern corner of Hyde Park. The *Sydney Gazette* expressed a 'deep debt of gratitude' to the latest governor, the imperious Lieutenant-General Ralph Darling, for this promise of 'wholesome water'. At the same time it welcomed the fact that, thanks to the government, new 'wells of considerable magnitude are being sunk in every principal street'.[7] Things were looking up.

But work on the tunnel was troubled. According to Busby's own records, he tried to encourage his convict labourers by paying them on completion of set tasks—after which they could knock off for the day. But he complained that the men remained 'vicious and lazy', constantly finding ways to sneak out of the tunnel so they could sleep, earn extra money elsewhere, or get drunk. Absconders were dragged before the magistrate. Some were whipped. Others were tormented by days of mindless labour walking on the heavy treadwheel, a punishment that the convicts called 'the endless staircase'. A few were thrown into Sydney's stinking prison. But these ordeals made no difference.

As the historian John Hirst bleakly observes: 'Busby sent the men to the floggers without anger or hope of reform; the men certainly did not reform, but neither did they rebel or run away.'[8]

So Busby's Bore was hewn out of fatalism and misery. The work-crews blasted and hacked four-fifths of the tunnel through Sydney's sandstone. And where they struck unstable ground, they stacked blocks of stone into ramshackle walls which they covered with a rough ceiling of stone slabs.

At any given time, there were around one hundred convicts toiling on the project. But nothing happened quickly in that tunnel. Unskilled and brutalised, the men advanced at the heart-stoppingly slow rate of one metre a day.[9] (Just one centimetre per man per day.) By 1832, the Colonial Office was growing impatient at the delay and the escalating cost. But in Sydney, there was an unforeseen bonus. Because the convicts were tunnelling through porous sandstone, groundwater (referred to as 'seepage springs') began to collect in the tunnel. By 1830—a full seven years before the tunnel reached the Lachlan Swamps—around 150,000 litres of free drinking water were flowing down to Hyde Park every day. In 1833, workers installed a pipe to carry some of this water further downhill to Circular Quay where it was sold for the supply of ships.

As the project stretched into its seventh year, yet another governor was in residence—Governor Richard Bourke. He became furious, reporting to London that the rosy-cheeked Mr Busby—now in his sixties and pocketing a gentlemanly salary—simply refused to go below ground with the convicts. Some versions of the story claim that the overseers, Busby's own sons, also refused to sully themselves in this way. As one journalist put it in 1903, Busby was relying on 'reports supplied by the less-disagreeable members of his working staff'.[10] This exaggerated display of class superiority signalled Busby's social alliances. Sydney may have been a society where subversive 'Australians' were trumpeting their ideas about Jack being as good as his master, but Busby had aligned himself with the British 'Exclusives', those officers and large landowners who enforced social distinctions with a fastidiousness that was the hallmark of their kind throughout the empire. Witness the action of Lieutenant-Colonel Harry Despard, who in September 1832 positively refused to allow the soldiers of his regiment to demean themselves by joining 'the local Australians' in a cricket match. The nationalist paper, the *Currency Lad*, declared that, 'We regret this exceedingly, for we did hope that a more liberal era had dawned.'[11] Mr Busby, we may be sure, took the colonel's part.

The convicts did not complete their miserable work until 1837, and only after Governor Bourke had curtailed Busby's control of the project and docked his pay.[12]

Assessments

In 1988, a survey by engineering geologists M. J. Dale and Peter Burgess judged that the tunnel was 'a major feat of construction for a colony only thirty-nine years old'.[13] In fact, engineers had been building tunnels exactly like this since Biblical times. The ancient *qanats* of Iran are a series of sloping tunnels that carry underground water to deep collecting wells or to small reservoirs on the sides of hills. Unlike Busby's excavation, which became unstable in thirty years, some of these have been in operation for 3000 years. Equally old are the *foggaras*, tunnels hacked out of the limestone beneath the Sahara. Some still carry water from oases into the desert as far as five kilometres— slightly further than Mr Busby's Bore.[14]

It would be fairer to say that Sydney's water tunnel was the best that could be done with poor materials, a sullen workforce and inept management. Busby's Bore was crudely built. A Sydney water engineer reported in 1855 that 'a rougher piece of tunnel-ling can scarcely be imagined'. As the tunnel neared the Lachlan Swamps, the floor level began to rise and fall like a roller-coaster. In its dimensions, the tunnel ranged from narrow passages, through which a man could scarcely crawl, to chambers 2.5 metres high. It also wandered into six blind alleys, the largest being 160 metres long.[15] Given the record of convict shenanigans on this job, you can only wonder whether the labourers were using these subterranean spaces for some illicit purpose. In any case, the project had stretched out for ten years. All this to carry water just three and a half kilometres.

The tunnel delivered around 1.5 million litres per day to Sydney—slightly less than the capacity of one Olympic swimming pool. This modest supply was sufficient for the needs of that minority of the 20,000-strong population who could afford to pay, for the water was not used to alleviate illness and public squalor—it was treated as a commercial commodity. The bore was little more than a way of replacing the water carters with a more convenient, and far more profligate, means of delivering water to the well-to-do. Since Busby had not installed sluice gates inside the tunnel and there was no reservoir at Hyde Park, there was no way of stopping the flow or storing unused water. Every night 'hundreds of tons of surplus water' drained down from the swamps and gushed, unused, through the streets of Sydney—a situation that was not rectified until holding dams were constructed the following decade.[16]

In 1842, responsibility for Sydney's water passed from the imperial government to the new Sydney Corporation—the fore-runner of the city council. Dominated by unelected gentlemen, it had no interest in providing safe water to Sydney's poor. In any case, the corporation was legally prevented from borrowing money to finance public works. As a result, it laid water mains only to areas where it could count on a quick return. By 1844, pipes were connected to just seventy-five houses and businesses—mainly flour millers, brewers, tanners and manufacturers of soap—who had the means to afford the luxury. Those were the official customers. The corporation eventually discovered that it was being short-changed by several business owners who had secretly tapped into the mains and were stealing the water.[17]

There were technical problems too. The pipes had already started to rust. Eels from the swamps took up residence in the mains where they died and putrefied—making the water stink. By the late 1840s, the tunnel's impact on the Lachlan Swamps was plain. They were drying up. In the 1860s one eyewitness described the former wetlands as 'a tract of barren sandhills'.[18]

And what of the Tank Stream? It was now a squalid relic. The swamp that fed the stream was drained in 1850 to create land for building. In 1860, the section of the stream from Hunter Street almost to Bridge Street was buried in a brick pipe and left to disgorge into the ocean as a sewer.

For the poor, Busby's wretched bore changed nothing. In 1851, the *Herald* was still campaigning for better water, better drainage and proper sewers, reporting that the inhabitants of Parramatta Street around Ultimo and Glebe 'cook in dirt—they eat in dirt—and they sleep in it, they are born, bred and they die in dirt; from the cradle to the grave, they pass through life in filth—society tolerates it, and they look upon it as their inheritance—it was so in the old country'.

This was now the eve of the New South Wales goldrush. The transportation of convicts had come to an end, and a new class of free-born colonials and immigrants was setting the tone of the working classes of Sydney. As the colony boomed, the *Herald* warned the authorities that they neglected the social discrimination of the water system at their peril: Chartism and revolution were fed by the filth and misery of the common people.[19]

Industry was expanding and Sydney's manufacturers were clamouring for more dependable supplies. In 1853, the governor dismissed the corporation, and responsibility for public works passed to a panel of three commissioners, who were no more popular. An official inquiry into the problem recommended that the more distant wetlands on the shores of Botany Bay were the ideal source of cool clean water.[20]

And so it was that a ramshackle scheme was built in the so-called Botany Swamps by the city engineer, and commenced its thirty years of operation in 1859. These were the very swamps that Phillip had scorned in 1788 because they contained no healthy water. Meanwhile, a makeshift sewerage system was completed in 1859, but it was 1889 before a functioning system was constructed, incorporating the infamous Bondi Ocean Outfall.[21]

In the Botany Swamps, the familiar pattern of environmental ruination was played out a third time. In 1869 John Smith, the Professor of Physics at Sydney University, chaired a government commission into Sydney's latest water crisis. Smith found that the Botany wetlands, including the Lachlan Swamps, had substantially dried out. He identified several reasons: the clearing of the thick scrub, the compacting of the soil by cattle, and the city engineer's practice of cutting drains through the swamps to increase the harvest of water during droughts. All these had caused much of the surface to harden. As a result, heavy rains ran off to the sea 'instead of being, as formerly, absorbed by the spongy ground, and keeping up a full stream for weeks after'.[22]

Though Charles Moore, the prickly Irish mayor, and Edward Bell, the city water engineer, were drowning in scandal, they were defiant in their evidence to the commission. The mayor insisted that Sydney could be supplied for another thirty years by pumping still more water out of the swamps. In truth, the wetlands had already been destroyed. Professor Smith recommended a dam on the Nepean River, thereby inaugurating the system of reservoirs on the Nepean and Hawkesbury Rivers that are now the heart of Sydney's water supply.[23]

By mid-century, the pattern of Sydney's water use was characterised more by mistakes than by lessons learned. Sydneysiders had exploited and destroyed three vital sources of water—the Tank Stream, the Lachlan Swamps and the Botany Swamps—as if there was always more water, further out. It was to be a common story in Australia over the next two centuries—the harvesting of resources that could not be renewed. It is also a sign that the coastal dwellers had not yet learned the implications of the very limitation they had rued from the beginning—that this continent was dry. The colonists had the values, aesthetics and aspirations of a culture that was steeped in water. If they were to become Australian, they had to learn how to prosper in an entirely new climate. To do that, they had first to make sense out of silence.

4

THE SILENT CONTINENT

Water is H$_2$O, hydrogen two parts, oxygen one, but there is also a
third thing that makes water and nobody knows what that is.

D. H. LAWRENCE, *PANSIES*

On the politics of maps

When I was in Grade 6, the teacher pinned a chart to the wall of
our classroom. It consisted of several maps of Australia, each
labelled with a year. On the earliest map, Australia was a black
silhouette, except for a tiny white spot labelled 'Sydney'. On
each of the maps that followed, the white area expanded, indicating that yet another sweeping corridor had been opened by
an explorer. In the final map, Australia glowed white with
knowledge, and the story of exploration was complete.

Such a chart also appeared in the *Australian Encyclopaedia*
(1958), and similar diagrams were a feature of history textbooks
in post-war Australia. Today, it is unthinkable that an educa-
tional publisher would be blind to the racial subtext of these
maps—a black Australia overrun by a white Australia. What,
then, did those black and white regions indicate? They map an
ethos that I call 'the geography of silence'.

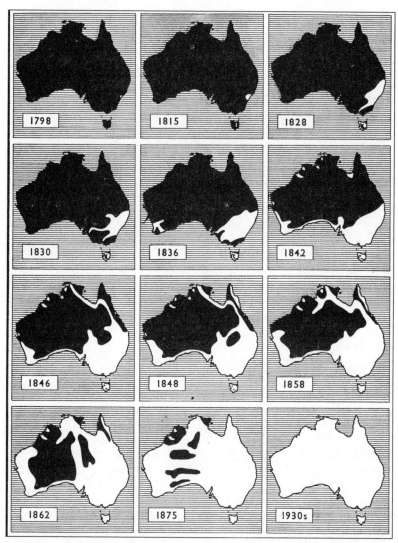

'Opening up the continent'

Writing in 1930, the British geographer Hugh Mill celebrated geography as an imperial science, declaring that, 'Geographical instincts worked in each of the conquering races, Roman, Teutonic and Scandinavian.' He suggested that the origins of British geography lay in the writings of Julius Caesar, 'who came and saw and conquered two thousand years ago'.[1]

Viewed in this light, geography is an inventory of conquest—a way in which an invader assesses new territory in order to control it.

Most post-colonial scholars would agree. Since the 1970s, such academics have been preoccupied with analysing imperialist geographies in order to uncover alternative 'geographical imaginaries' and to interrogate the ways in which geographical knowledge acts as a form of power.[2] But imperial geographies were not solely expressions of destiny, control or belonging. In Australia, a good deal of colonial writing about the country was also attempting to make sense of anxiety and failure. In expressing this paradox, the metaphor of silence has played a key role.

Of blanks and silence

If colonial Africa was the 'dark continent' in the British imagination, then colonial Australia was the 'silent continent'. As the historical geographer Patrick Brantlinger points out, the British myths of the dark continent were filled with complexities and contradictions, but they came down to this. The British and other Europeans invented the dark continent as a place that demanded to be colonised—to be brought out of darkness, as the Victorian explorer Sir Samuel Baker put it, and 'enlightened by English colonisation'. The moral, religious and scientific arguments all agreed. It was Britain's destiny to bring darkest Africa into the light.[3]

The image of Australia as a silent continent has been an enduring one. As recently as 1980, the eminent British geographer and educationalist T. W. Freeman wrote that in 1830 (when London's Royal Geographical Society was formed) Australia was 'virtually *terra incognita*'. Less than five per cent of the continent 'had been explored'.

The other 95 per cent of the continent has been aptly described as 'a blank', a vast and silent wilderness, immeasurably old, bereft of all appearances of either water or life...one of the last empty spaces in the maps of the world, simply waiting to be filled in.[4]

This passage contains all the key elements of Australia's geography of silence. The continent is big, dry, vacant and, of course, silent. It is ancient or 'timeless': so old and inert that history has been bleached from it. And we are to understand that this silent land-without-a-history is waiting to be rescued... in this case, by explorers from the Royal Geographical Society. Freeman is not ventriloquising this attitude for critical effect. On the contrary, it is an interpretation he endorses: Australia, he says, is '*aptly* described as blank'. Of course, he knows that colonial Australia was the home of Aborigines and supported distinctive plants and animals: he says so later in the article. But it is this dialectic, this ability to represent Australia as if it existed simultaneously in two realities—one with Aborigines and one without—that explains the potency of the image. It enabled the colonial imagination both to acknowledge the existence of the Aborigines and simultaneously to deny their relevance to any account of the new reality that the process of colonisation was about to unveil. Freeman is simply re-affirming sentiments that were commonplace in colonial Australia. As the Tasmanian explorer James Calder wrote in the 1840s, 'The country we describe is as yet without a history, without traditions, and indeed without association. Its past is a veritable blank.'[5]

One of the many writers who have challenged that way of thinking is Australia's leading conservative historian Geoffrey Blainey. His opposition to the principle of native title established by the High Court's 1992 *Mabo* decision is well known. Yet his book *The Triumph of the Nomads* (1975) was built on a fact that many white Australians found hard to grasp—that Australia had an Aboriginal *past*, not merely an Aboriginal no-time that preceded history. Despite this insight, the geography of silence occurs, albeit momentarily, in Blainey's own work. In *A Land Half Won* (1980), he tells the story of two famous overlanders, Joseph Hawdon and Charles Bonney. In 1838, the pair set out with a small party of stockmen to drive several hundred sheep and cattle from the Goulburn River in New South Wales to Adelaide. They opened up—as the saying went—a new stock route through the back country, passing through Aboriginal territory previously untravelled by whites. Drawing on Hawdon's own journal, Blainey vividly retells the story of the journey—of their encounters with Aborigines, their struggles to find water, and Hawdon's own restless interest in almost everything. Just as their thirst was becoming desperate, the party stumbled upon an Aboriginal lake whose name was Nookamka, but which Hawdon renamed 'Lake Bonney' in honour of his partner. As Blainey tells it, Hawdon 'was pleased that no European had seen the sights he now saw'. Blainey goes on: 'On the shores of still water, the silence of the land filled him with astonishment. Sometimes he fired his gun and listened to the bounding echo.'[6]

This scene is pure invention. Here is Hawdon's original account. I have marked all his references to sound with italics:

> March 12th…I discovered a fine lake of fresh water, about thirty miles in circumference, and on its margin we encamped. Kangaroos appeared to be rather numerous here. The Blacks were encamped further along the Lake, and from the *noise* they made, we knew they must have noticed our arrival. It was a beautiful moonlight night, and I strolled out along the edge of the lake to shoot some ducks which were seen on the water in thousands. On discharging our guns, *the echo of the report rolled along the water magnificently; one would have supposed that a hundred shots had been fired at the same moment.* As the reports

died away the lake became perfectly alive with the myriads of
live fowl in motion on its surface *screaming and cackling with
alarm at the novel sound.*

Gradually the *flapping of their wings* and *the splashes as they
alighted in the water* ceased, and they again settled upon the
Lake in solemn stillness. *The wild, sweet musical note of the
swans was heard over our heads,* as they returned to rest upon
the bosom of the Lake, after feeding during the day amongst
the reeds on the river. As we lay enjoying this delightful scene,
we could now and then catch *the distant noise of a tribe of Natives
as they were disputing, with much emotion about this extraordinary
inroad upon their territory.*[7]

Nowhere in his journal does Hawdon comment on 'the
silence of the land', much less say that he was 'astonished' by it.
When Hawdon fired his gun, he did not listen to the echo
bounding through the silence. The men's gunshots (Hawdon
was not alone at this moment, though he does briefly imply that
he was) set off a great 'screaming and cackling' of startled birds.
The Aborigines, far from being silent, were talking loudly at
their camp across the water, in an argument provoked by the
intrusion of the strangers. Indeed Hawdon actually imagined
that the Aborigines were asserting their ownership of the
country. So this was no silent place. That evening, Hawdon's
experience of the country and its people was principally shaped
by sound—and Aboriginal ownership was part of the
conversation.

This intrusion of the geography of silence into Blainey's
prose is so momentary that you could miss it. Indeed, for the
most part, he evokes a frontier bustling with Aborigines. But
this instant allows Hawdon to become the kind of man Blainey
most admires—the lone risk-taker who strikes out into uncharted
territory, and opens up a new commercial activity. Indeed,

Blainey is fully conscious of the ideology he invokes, writing, 'It was almost as if the sound of the gun reminded him that his technology made him the master of a hostile land.'[8]

In introducing this image to the story, Blainey draws on one of the shared—almost unconscious—myths of white Australia. It was a myth nurtured by those many explorers and colonial writers who, unlike Hawdon, *did* dramatise the shattering of the Australian silence in this kind of scene. The explorer Major Thomas Mitchell, for example, described an expedition up the Glenelg River just two years earlier, on which 'We pulled on through the silent waters, awakening the slumbering echoes with many a shot at the numerous swans or ducks'. Similarly, Watkin Tench led a party through 'awful silence' until they found the Nepean River, covered in ducks. The men fired their weapons, and Tench remarked, 'Nothing is more certain than that the sound of a gun had never before been heard within miles of this spot.' His point was simple. The land had just changed forever. [9]

Before *terra nullius* was a legal concept in Australia, it was a state of mind.[10] We've already seen it in David Collins' description of the settlers clearing Sydney Cove. The continent is covered in a dark and silent forest. The settlers announce their arrival by cutting down trees. As the trees crash into the ancient forest, they shatter the silence. They announce that history has begun. The place now has a story. Time has arrived in the timeless land. In this moment, when silence is transformed into the 'hum of industry', the Aborigines are nowhere to be seen or heard. Yet, Collins was extremely sympathetic to the Aborigines. He wrote about them often, and—as we've seen—even sided with them when they murdered convicts. But they have no place in his epic tale of a new flag raised and a new civilisation planted on the banks of a stream where the primeval forest had been cleared away.

This pervasive ideology was neatly expressed half a century later by Major Mitchell, who developed a deep respect and empathy for the Aborigines. Yet he entered unfamiliar territory, proud in the assurance that he was 'commencing the first chapter of its history. All was still new and nameless, but by this beginning, we were to open a way for the many other beginnings of civilised man, and thus extend his dominion over some of the last holds of barbarism.'[11]

This differentiation between European history with its forward momentum and a perpetual Aboriginal no-time did have a cultural basis. Thanks to the industrial revolution, the British lived in a world where minutes and even seconds disciplined both their work and leisure. If they were to conquer the continent, then, as the historian Graeme Davison has pointed out, they had to invest it with time.[12] Aboriginal hunter-gatherers, by contrast, regulated their lives according to a cycle of complex seasons defined by the life cycles of animals and plants. In some ways, Aborigines lived in a time-world that was perpetual—one might just as well be going back as heading forward to gather honey-ants or to fish in a river. Furthermore, as the archaeologist Harry Lourandos explains, a tribal Aborigine might describe an event that occurred a thousand of years ago as if it occurred yesterday.[13] It is tempting to see Aboriginal time as grounded in 'nature' and to regard European time as a mechanical invention. But the precision of linear time is itself born out of a scientific engagement with 'the natural world', specifically from the mariners' demands for a clock that was accurate to the second, so they could fix their longitude at sea. Like indigenous time, western time is grounded in the need to know and understand an individual's relationship to place. It tells people where they are. But the colonists were focused on the future. For them, it was as if the Aborigines were somehow absent. They were living in a different tense.

This notion endured well into the twentieth century, even among writers who were sympathetic to the Aborigines. In 1963, the popular bush novelist George Farwell imagined a scene in colonial Sydney with 'aborigines all around this great harbour, moving silently through the scrub, stalking kangaroos with boomerang and spear. These dark, stone-age nomads belonged to the land in a way Europeans had not yet learned.' He tells us that the young Charles Sturt 'envied them their freedom. The way they roamed so widely through the silent and mysterious bush.'[14] This is a dignified description born of respect. Yet, quite unwittingly, it serves the logic of *terra nullius* by placing the Aborigines into a parallel and doomed dimension. They become a people without a history—creatures of timelessness and silence.

They are here, but not here. Here, but not heard.

Silence in retreat

In one generation, the penal colony at Port Jackson had grown into a busy harbour town; the Miltonian hum which had been initiated by the crash of falling trees on Sydney Cove was now a civilising racket. As W. C. Wentworth explained, the hills inland of Sydney were still smothered by 'one vast forest'. But even here, the colonists were beginning to stake out the future. On the summits, Wentworth saw clearings made by the axes of his fellow settlers. These 'cultivated openings', he wrote, 'tend considerably to diminish those melancholy sensations' that the 'gloomy monotony' of the forest would otherwise inspire.

In his sprawling epic poem *Australasia* (1823), Wentworth orchestrated Sydney as a clamouring harbour, where the 'noisy workmen' and the 'creaking crane' unloaded fruits and other cargoes from across the world. Out on the harbour, he writes,

'As the merry boatmen row along,/The woods are quicken'd with their lusty song.'[15]

Wentworth himself had played a role in putting the silence to flight—and his poem is partly an exercise in self-promotion. To the west of the settlement, silence had raised its ramparts. For a quarter of a century, Sydney's colonists were confined to the fertile coastal strip, able only to imagine what fabled lands might lie beyond the canyons and gorges of the Blue Mountains. Though the settler population of Sydney was just 13,000, the local ecology was already reeling. The grasslands were scarred by overgrazing, erosion and parasites. In 1813, a serious drought exposed the extent of the damage. The pastures withered. Sheep and cattle grew gaunt and died. So it was that a thirst for water and a hunger for new pastures drove three of Sydney's sheep men to seek a path across the Blue Mountains. Wentworth's companions were an ambitious young lieutenant named William Lawson and the wealthy landowner Gregory Blaxland, who led the expedition. They took four servants, including an experienced kangaroo-hunter named James Burns as their guide, Blaxland believing that Aborigines were not useful in this role outside their own territory.[16]

Wentworth told how, high in the Blue Mountains, he and his companions challenged the gloomy 'Austral giant' who presided over this vacant world—a world where silence alternated with the wild, meaningless roar of water.

> How mute, how desolate thy stunted woods,
> How dread thy chasms where many an eagle broods,
> How dark thy caves, how lone thy torrents' roar,
> As down thy cliffs precipitous they pour,
> Broke on our hearts, when first with vent'rous tread
> We dared to rouse thee from thy mountain bed!

After an arduous, month-long expedition the men stood on a cliff-top looking inland across the wide, undulating 'grazing lands' and 'cheering smokes' of the interior.

In fact they did not set foot on the lands beyond. Moreover, there is evidence that they were not even the first white men to cross the range. And, of course, the local Aborigines knew their way about that country perfectly.[17] But Wentworth was a great publicist. He wrote himself and his companions into history as pioneers who brought the land to life. This 'boundless champaign burst upon our sight,' he declared, with an almost American sense of destiny, 'op'ning like Canaan on rapt Israel's view'. The giant, 'the mournful genius of the plain', had fled, 'and fixed his drowsy throne/In untrod wilds to muse and brood alone'.

Blaxland also wrote about the journey as a confrontation with the geography of silence, recalling how, one night on their homeward journey, they 'heard a confused noise arising from the eastern settlements below, which, after having been so long accustomed to the death-like stillness of the interior, had a very striking effect'.[18]

There was room in this silence for Aborigines, and Blaxland said so. He told of the Aboriginal pathways they followed and of the smoke from Aboriginal fires they saw above the trees. He describes how he and his companions stood on a cliff and watched a group of Aborigines moving about their camp in the gully far below. In the shadowy forests, Blaxland also noted the sounds of animals. They heard an emu 'calling continually in the night' and were unsettled by a 'most tremendous howling of native dogs'. Even allowing for the drought, the men must also have heard birdsong: those deep, luxuriant gullies resonate with the sounds of around 300 species, including gang gangs, screeching white cockatoos, warbling magpies, laughing kookaburras, wagtails (which sing at night), golden whistlers and tinkling bellbirds.[19]

So how do we account for the silence? The point is that the silence expresses the moral condition of the land—the lethargy and stasis of a primordial forest. The silence is a dimension that exists before time. The 'howling' of the wild dogs, the 'screeching' of the native birds, even the conversation of the Aborigines themselves, do not disperse the silence. They inhabit it.

How glorious it was, then, when the silences and the occasional howling of the land were redeemed and enlivened by the orderly sounds of civilisation. It was in this spirit that Sydney's new Presbyterian minister, the lively John Dunmore Lang, told his congregation that, thanks to them, Sydney had been 'reclaimed from the lowest stage of barbarism':

> It is delightful, in those vallies where the wild beasts of the forests roamed so lately, to hear the bleating of sheep and the lowing of oxen. It is delightful, on that spot where the rude savage had so lately a boundless solitude upon him, to behold a rising city, and to hear the speech of civilised men.[20]

The youthful Charles Sturt was equally delighted by the sounds of civilisation, assuring intending migrants from Britain that Sydney Cove was a place where 'a flourishing town stands over the ruins of the forest'. Here, 'the lowing of herds has succeeded the wild whoop of the savage; and the stillness of that once desert shore is now broken by the sound of the bugle and the busy hum of commerce'.[21]

As the American historian Mark M. Smith points out, a similar ideology of hearing was acted out in the United States. The Baltimore journalist Hezekiah Niles exalted over the progress of American colonisation by declaring that: 'Everywhere the sound of the axe is heard opening the forest to the sun...The busy hum of ten thousand wheels fills our seaports, and the sound of the spindle and the loom succeeds the yell of the savage or the screech of the night owl in the late wilderness of the interior.' In Australia and the USA, colonists had their ears pricked. They were optimistic that the 'busy hum'—that's the recurring and orderly phrase—would continue to advance, deeper and deeper inland.

As Mark Smith observes, the sound of an axe ringing against a tree was heard by American settlers as an 'aural victory over howling wilderness'.[22] In Canada and Australia, too, the axe scored the frontier. Australian explorers inscribed their advance into the Aboriginal country by blazing trees with their initials, often accompanied by the date or a Roman numeral showing the number of their camp. These marks became signposts for other travellers to follow and expansions of the king's domain.

Following a practice already established in Africa and America, settlers and explorers would use hatchets as gifts to conciliate Aborigines. Mitchell reported that he distributed them 'liberally', often in exchange for the right to draw water from local rivers and waterholes. The custom became so common that by 1831 Mitchell found that almost all the natives in contact with Sydney owned a tomahawk, and that their use had spread beyond the frontier.[23]

The symbolism of the axe as the instrument of possession—and of dispossession—was so potent that, on 12 August 1828, the foundation of Perth was marked by a ceremony in which the settlers gathered on the banks of the Swan River to watch Mrs Helen Dance, the wife of a naval officer, chop down a small gum tree. In 1844, the English painter George French Angas visited the Aboriginal bushland around Mount Barker in South Australia just as it too was falling to the settlers. Angas reported that, occasionally, in some 'deep glen of the forest' he would come upon a gypsy-like encampment where a group of men was busy at work, surrounded by fallen timber and sawn planks. And all the while, he wrote, 'the sharp sound of the axe rings, echoing through the solitude, proclaiming the dawn of civilisation and industry'.[24] Just as it had done that first day in Sydney Cove.

So exhilarating was the sound of timber crashing through the forest that Governor King found it necessary, as early as 1803, to legislate against the reckless and indiscriminate felling of trees. But wood-cutting was not only an essential economic activity, it was also a manly way of letting off steam. In the 1850s, the cocky young diggers on the Victorian goldfields often ended their working day in displays of virility by chopping down gum trees, which, as one English visitor to the goldfields observed with regret, 'you hear continually falling with a crash'. There was some point to this orgy of axemanship: the goldfields were ravenous for timber. But more primal motivations were also at work. The sound and spectacle of a great tree crashing to the ground were exhilarating. And when the miners weren't chopping down trees, wrote the Englishman, they were setting off a 'thunder of guns, pistols, and revolvers…I verily believe for the sake of the noise'.[25]

The axe was just the first of the tools of civilisation whose sounds proclaimed that the era of silence—and of the untamed 'howling wilderness'—was ended. As one South Australian colonist, a Mr Bennett, expressed it:

> the original quiet solitude is disturbed by the merry ring of the black-smith's anvil and the carpenter's hammer; the uniformity of the far-stretching plains is relieved by the scattered cottages of the settlers; and the ever-green but dreary forests, which then echoed only to the howl of the wild-dog, the screech of the parroquet, or the yell of the savage, now resounded with the bark of the shepherd's dog, the bleating of sheep, and the lowing of cattle.[26]

The howling wilderness

Writing in 1662, the poet Michael Wigglesworth famously dramatised the interior of North America, before the arrival of the Puritans, as:

> A waste and howling wilderness,
> Where none inhabited
> But hellish fiends, and brutish men
> That devils worshiped.

These four, simple lines from a poem called 'God's Controversy in New England' are packed with imperial ideals. Christian readers, well-versed in their Bible, would recognise the reference. In the book of Deuteronomy (32: 9–14), Moses sings a hymn telling how God led Jacob and his people out of 'a waste and howling wilderness' and into a land of milk and honey. The expression became a stock phrase in colonial American literature. Whenever Americans refer to the wild lands of North America as 'a howling wilderness', they evoke, almost subliminally, a landscape which, in its primal condition, was godless and cursed, but which speaks to them of their 'manifest destiny' as the new chosen people of God who will sanctify this wildness with civilising grace.

Unusually for North America, the paradox of *terra nullius* is here too. The land is represented as a place 'Where none inhabited', except for those 'hellish fiends, and brutish men', who seem scarcely human at all—more like evil land-spirits to be exorcised by virtuous whites.

Where Australian colonists often heard the land as silent, American writers often evoked the *cacophony* of the uncolonised United States—as if a mighty tumult was crying out to be tamed by the harmony or syntax of civilisation. The triumph of civilised sound is acted out in a classic biography of Daniel Boone, which opens with the legendary 'Indian fighter' declaring:

Thus we behold Kentucky, lately an howling wilderness, the habitation of savages and wild beasts...Here, where the [Indian] hand of violence shed the blood of the innocent; where the horrid yells of savages, and the groans of the distressed, sounded in our ears, we now hear the praises and adorations of our Creator; where wretched wigwams stood, the miserable abode of savages, we behold the foundations of cities laid, that, in all probability, will equal the glory of the greatest upon earth.[27]

Like Australian myth makers, US nationalists also had it in their repertoire to write about North America as if it were vacant. In their best-selling history *America: The Story of a Free People* (1942), the liberal historians Allan Nevins and Henry Steele Commager have plenty to say about 'Indians'. But in their heroic preface, they represent the great continent of America as wild and unoccupied. 'The story of America is the story of the impact of an old culture upon a wilderness environment,' they write. The first settlers 'were not primitive but civilised men, and they transplanted here a culture centuries old'.[28] On this account, it was the bracing, pristine environment that transformed old-world values into a uniquely American vision of freedom, ambition and hope.

In the nineteenth-century American classic *Walden* (1854), Henry Thoreau revelled in what he called 'the tonic of wildness', using the terms 'wildness' and 'wilderness' interchangeably to express the inexhaustible energy that binds men to the natural world.[29] Today, this is the dominant tradition in the US and Canada, where people tend to hear the word 'wild' in the word 'wilderness'.

It evokes towering mountains, roaring rivers and herds of wild beasts. The wilderness promises a 'power and majesty' experience of nature: a brisk, life-affirming antidote to what the environmental writer Wallace Stegner decried in the 1960s as 'the noise, the exhausts, the stinks of human and automotive waste' of American urban life.[30] This bracing tradition has links back to the eighteenth-century notion of 'the sublime'. The sublime, wrote the English philosopher Edmund Burke, 'comes upon us in the gloomy forest, and in the howling wilderness, in the form of the lion, the tiger, the panther, or rhinoceros'.[31] In the howling wilderness, faced with raw power and imminence of death, a man knew that he was fully alive.

By contrast, colonial Australians generally imagined the 'wilderness' not as wild, but as a bleak and lifeless emptiness. Thus the explorer Ernest Giles reported that central Western Australia was a 'howling wilderness', so devoid of water that 'it seems intended by the great creator that civilised beings should never re-enter here'. To the explorer John Oxley, the Murrumbidgee Valley was 'a howling wilderness', a 'barren desolation' to which 'civilised man' would never return. To the adventurer David Carnegie, the endless sand ridges of the Great Sandy Desert were a 'vast, howling wilderness', a place of 'ghastly desolation and endless dreariness'. Each of these travellers reached for the phrase 'howling wilderness' without hearing the relentless noise that thunders through the Biblical image. In the writings of these explorers, the word 'howling' conveys, not noise, but torment—as though the dreadful silence has provoked a howling in the soul. The writer Henry Lawson heard what was really going on. In 1892, he gazed in defeat over the dusty plains on the border of Queensland and New South Wales. The country was 'a blasted, barren wilderness that doesn't even howl,' he wrote. 'If it howled it would be a relief.'[32]

But these laments lay in the future. Early colonial Australia was confident that a noisy, bustling zone of civilisation was destined to conquer this silent continent. When the settlement of Melbourne was founded in 1835, nearly half a century after

Sydney, the geography of silence continued to reverberate with new world optimism. In the early Melbourne novel *The Recollections of Geoffry Hamlyn* (1858), young Hamlyn imagines the place before the British arrived: it was a kind of limbo where 'the Yarra rolled its clear waters to the sea through the unbroken solitude of a primeval forest, as yet unseen by the eye of a white man'. Exactly like the Tank Stream. In Melbourne—just as in Sydney—we hear new arrivals rejoicing in the sounds of civilisation. In 1843, for example, the squatter John Cotton reflected that, just a few years earlier, this place 'lay in silent primitive nature, as it were fresh from the hands of its Almighty Creator, the abode of the wild native untaught man'. Now he was 'most agreeably surprised' to discover that this silent world was transformed into 'a large rectangularly built city with all the activity, hum and bustle of its 2500 inhabitants'.[33] The silent continent was realising its destiny.

5

SOUNDS OF WATER

The isle is full of noises;
Sounds and sweet airs, that give delight.
WILLIAM SHAKESPEARE, *THE TEMPEST*

The Yarra Falls

In 2006, the old Sandridge Bridge in central Melbourne was recommissioned as a pedestrian walk and decorated with stylish outdoor art. The squat iron bridge, pock-marked with steam-age rivets, spans the Yarra River at an oblique angle. It was, until recently, the rusting relic of the Sandridge railway line that once connected central Melbourne to the port. The bridge marks the location of the water feature that determined the very site of Melbourne itself—the now-vanished Yarra Falls.

Let's visualise the morning that British history records as Tuesday, 1 February 1803. We are in the territories of the Kulin nation—in the wetlands on the south side of the river—in the very place where, fifty years from now, workmen will build the railway line. It is the hottest time of year. Most of the ponds and lagoons have dried out. Another lagoon has shrunk to a salty puddle. While swans and ducks fuss about in the reeds in search of food and pelicans doze in the sun, women of the local Bunurong tribe are chatting and laughing as they gather edible plants in the wetlands. To the local people, this is *bulluk*—swamp country.[1] This place, the intersecting homelands of the Bunurong and the Woiworung peoples, is shaped by water and rich in food: fish and eels, edible plants, birds, kangaroos and possums. And it is at the watering places—at the billabongs, falls and the confluences of rivers—that the local clans most often gather for the talking and music of ceremonial occasions.[2] As the sun strides across the high blue sky and the day grows hotter, people of the two tribes are resting in their shady huts on opposite banks of the river. They watch as their children play and laugh in the gurgling water. Other children climb a tree that overhangs the river and dive into the water with a great splash.[3]

On Wednesday 2 February, the weather continues hot, and that night the humidity boils over—as it so often does there at this time of year—into a spectacular electrical storm. Lightning slashes through the darkness, briefly illuminating the aboriginal coast, and thunder rumbles across the ocean. Then the blackness feeds the land with fat, cool rain. As the water sheets down, let's say that a group of Bunurong men are talking on their beach beyond the wetlands. They are watching strange lights flickering on the far side of the darkness. Out there, a small two-masted schooner named *Cumberland* is riding at anchor as black waves slap against its hull. A few sailors lie bare-chested on the bobbing deck, as the rain tumbles out of the night and soaks their weary bodies. Or, if you wish, they are below decks sheltering from the rain. The point is they are there.

The local people call this part of the river Birrarung. The bay into which it flows is the centre of their lives, created, like everything else, by Bunjil, the wedge-tailed eagle.[4] To the English intruders, the bay is a strategic harbour that has recently caught the attention of that snooping French explorer Nicolas Baudin. So for the past fortnight, the survey party on the *Cumberland*, led by the efficient surveyor general of New South Wales Mr Charles Grimes, has been charting the bay, beach by beach. They are carrying out a detailed investigation of Port Phillip. Their reconnaissance will take them another four weeks. The heat, the storm, the birds, the native hut, the boat, the exhaustion and the presence of the natives—all these details they note in their official journal.[5]

The journal records that the summer heat was still intense the following dawn. The survey party lowered a boat in the waters of the bay, and rowed through the mouth of the Birrarung and headed upstream into the Kulin homelands. One of the officials in the boat was James Fleming, a rough-handed convict gardener whose work on the farms at Parramatta had won him the favour of Governor King. With a keen eye for plants, country and water, Fleming was an ideal member of the survey team, and it was his role to document the country. But there was tension in the boat: Mr Grimes refused to share his charts with the industrious young ex-convict. Quite so. A man may employ a convict as his shepherd. Or travel in a boat where convicts pull the oars. But no gentleman—duly qualified in his profession— willingly shares his office with a convicted thief.[6]

A day later, ten kilometres from the mouth of the Birrarung, Jim Fleming reported that the ill-matched duo had found 'excellent water, where we saw a little hill'. In fact, the party had reached a small waterfall beyond which was a reef—a sort of rock shelf—which formed gentle rapids extending over at least one hundred metres. At low tide, the drop in the falls was about one metre. At high tide, the rocky shelf was almost submerged and the drop at the falls was just a few centimetres. For the local clans, the bank alongside this rocky reach was a camp site, a meeting spot and a convenient place to cross the water from the hilly northern bank to the marshy floodplains on the south. Most important, the falls divided the river into two sections—fresh water above, and salt water below. Next morning, the crew returned to the falls and filled the ship's barrels with clean drinking water. Meanwhile, Grimes and Fleming documented the river as the 'Freshwater River'. It was not so much a name as a signpost for later Europeans to follow.[7]

They spent a week surveying the river and then sailed back into Port Phillip to continue their work. While Mr Grimes worked on his fine map, laying out the potential of the region for settlement, Jim Fleming methodically described the hills, the plant life and the quality of the soil. Wherever he went, he looked for lagoons, dry creeks, small rivers and waterholes and estimated the height of floods in the rainy season. Their meetings with local people were few—and apparently accidental. At the end of February 1803, the survey was complete. Fleming concluded that there was too little fresh water and that soil was too poor to support a settlement just about anywhere on the bay. But if there was to be a colony here, then 'The most eligible place for a settlement that I have seen is on the Freshwater River'—at the Aboriginal falls.[8]

It was a sound judgment—but one which came too late for David Collins. He was already on the high seas, transporting three hundred convicts, troops and officials in two ships from England where he had returned five years earlier. He had orders to settle in Port Phillip.

Silence descends on the Kulin nation

So it was that in October that same year, Collins dropped anchor in the shelter of a cove just inside the entrance to the bay. Here the convicts began to build a settlement. At first, Collins' deputy Lieutenant James Tuckey was optimistic that their venture would succeed. One evening, the adventurous young Irish officer left the convicts to their squabbles and strolled into the wooded hills of what is now the prosperous seaside town of Sorrento. 'Here,' he wrote, 'Contemplation, with her musing sister Melancholy, might find an undisturbed retreat.' It was almost as if the silence was welcoming him to the wilds. As the sun set over Port Phillip Bay, lines came to him from Milton's poem *Il Penseroso*. Surely this was a place, he mused,

> Where the rude ax with heaved stroke
> Was never heard the nymphs to daunt,
> Or fright them from their hallow'd haunts.

The place was tranquil. But it was also indolent—and faintly melancholy. As for the Aborigines, they were scarcely present.

> The last hymn of the feathered choiristers [sic] to the setting sun, and the soft murmurs of the breeze, faintly broke the death-like silence that reigned around; while the lightly trodden path of the solitary savage, or the dead ashes of his fire, alone pointed out the existence of human beings.[9]

But it took more than a primal silence to guarantee success. Ominously, Jim Fleming and Mr Grimes had marked their map with a warning. This location was 'Swampy—very bad ground'. Collins slowly realised that poor soil and a lack of water spelled ruin. Four months later, he and Lieutenant Tuckey moved their charges across Bass Strait to the island of Van Diemen's Land (Tasmania). There, on banks of the Derwent River, they established the settlement that grew into the city of Hobart.

Batman

John Batman was a product of that venture. In 1821, he left his birthplace of New South Wales and joined the settlers who were running sheep in the lush hills and valleys of Van Diemen's Land. Shortly after he arrived, the settlers and the Aborigines plunged into a decade of bloody warfare as they fought each other for possession of the rivers and grasslands of the island. It was a conflict fanned by Hobart's *Colonial Times* in 1826 when it penned its most notorious editorial. The settlers would endure the violence of the Aborigines no longer. 'We make no pompous display of Philanthropy,' it warned. 'The Government must remove the natives—if not, they will be hunted down like wild beasts and destroyed!'[10]

Just three years earlier, Presbyterian minister John Dunmore Lang sailed into Hobart on his way to Port Jackson, where he was destined to build a church and a school, and become a champion of immigration. As his ship approached the coast of Van Diemen's Land, the young Scotsman listened to the forest, which dominated that 'voiceless shore', and heard nothing:

> But all is still as death! Nor voice of man
> Is heard, nor the forest warbler's tuneful song.
> It seems as if this beauteous world began
> To be but yesterday, and th'earth still young
> And unpossessed...[11]

These were lines written in youthful innocence. But, in retrospect, they were unwittingly cruel. As stories told by present-day Aborigines and research by several historians (most recently James Boyce) show, the sheep men were responding to the Aborigines' campaign of resistance with deadly brutality. The young John Batman was known to be a conciliator between settlers and Aborigines: he called them 'that much injured and most unfortunate race'. Yet so pervasive was the fighting that, in September 1829, Batman himself led a squad of 'Sydney native blacks' in an attack on a camp of some sixty Aboriginal men, women and children. As the families fled, Batman writes, 'I ordered the men to fire upon them.' By his own reckoning, his party killed at least twelve people. He took two bleeding men, one woman and a terrified child as prisoner. But the following morning, the two men were unable to walk. So, writes Batman, 'I was obliged to shoot them.'[12]

By 1835, there was just a handful of Tasmanian Aborigines left, most of them pining to death on the sad confines of Flinders Island, while a few misused women survived among the lawless whalers and sealers who worked the seas around islands in Bass Strait.[13]

Now it was the sheep themselves that were the colonists' problem. They kept multiplying. New Aboriginal grasslands had to be found. In May 1835, Batman made a covert voyage in the ship *Rebecca* across Bass Strait to Port Phillip. He went, he wrote, with the intention 'of secretly ascertaining the general character and capabilities of Port Phillip, as a grazing and agricultural district'.

On the coast near the place we call Geelong, Batman (aided by a couple of his 'Sydney natives') had several encounters with local Wathaurong people that culminated with a corroboree and an exchange of gifts. Batman received baskets and spears; the locals got blankets, glass beads, looking-glasses, sweet sugar apples and handkerchiefs. In Batman's mind, the Wathaurong landscape was melting away—and sheep runs were taking form. 'I never could have imagined it possible that so fine a country existed on the face of the globe—gentle hills, plains, and downs, on which 5000 sheep might have been allowed to feed with little trouble to the shepherd.'[14]

But the Wathaurong kept their most precious asset to themselves: they did not escort this stranger to the lush banks of the Barwon River. And so Batman reboarded his ship unsatisfied. The land was as fine as any he could imagine, but he left believing that the place suffered from 'a great deficiency of water'.

As he sailed further up the bay surveying the Aboriginal coastline, he next encountered the great Werribee grass plains, a land 'entirely congenial to the ripening of my intentions'. On a walk up the Werribee River, he discovered what he was looking for—excellent fresh water. He reported that his party passed at least a dozen stone fish traps that the Aborigines had built across the creek. Each trap consisted of three or four stone walls spanning the river, each wall having gateways of sticks and bushes to allow fish to pass from one enclosure to the next.[15] As he admired their ingenuity, Batman must have known what his arrival meant. Unless he succeeded in his plan to negotiate a treaty with the Aborigines, there would be a battle for the waterholes in the district of Port Phillip. As one observer would report just five years later, 'the creeks, watercourses and rivers' of this region were 'the first to be occupied'. By then, the settlers and Aborigines each regarded the other as 'intruders'.[16]

Finally, Batman's voyage brought him to the head of the bay where a substantial river flowed into the sea. It was the Kulin people's Birrarung—Grimes' Freshwater Creek. Batman's colleague, the surveyor John Hedler Wedge, reported that he stood at the falls with some Kulin men and, by using signs and noises, asked them what they called this place. When the men replied 'Yarro-Yarro', Wedge took this to be the name of the river. But Wedge later conceded that he had misunderstood. It was in fact the name of the falls. (The historian Paul Carter has called this story into question, doubting whether this *was* the Aboriginal name for the falls and suggesting that Wedge told this story simply to reinforce his claim to be the first colonial name-giver.) The misunderstanding—if that's what it was—was never undone: the river lost its name and entered white geography as 'the Yarra'.[17]

The falls formed a barrier. A ship sailing upstream could proceed no further. Just below the falls there was a deep basin, where ships dropped anchor and unloaded at the noisy dock, providing the adjoining market with every kind of produce and manufacture. And it was here, at the entrance to the city, that the government built its fine Customs House, now home to Melbourne's Immigration Museum. Meanwhile, the water from above the falls became the first water supply of Melbourne.

In 1839, a youth named Edward Curr was one of the hundreds of Vandemonian sheep men who travelled into Melbourne by a second route. He disembarked at a jetty that had been built on the bay nearby, and made his way to the settlement along a road that followed a sand ridge through the wetlands, where 'signs of civilisation' were 'completely absent'. All around him were the lagoons, where seagulls swooped for fish and raucous white cockatoos perched in the tea-tree. Despite this profusion of birds, what struck the ambitious young man most was, he recalled, 'the stillness of the bush'.[18]

Arriving at the same time, the pioneer William Westgarth had a similar sensation. The Yarra wetlands, he later recalled, were:

> an immense wilderness, where the kangaroo skipped about in undisputed happiness and emerged in troops upon the flats, from the dense woods. The branches of the trees were filled with black and white cockatoos, and innumerable parroquets, whose gaudy plumage sparkled in the sunlight, while their incessant chattering imparted life to a scene, otherwise hushed, in the presence of man, and the total absence hitherto, of his noisy but enlivening commerce.[19]

Why 'otherwise hushed'? Westgarth was not implying that these wetlands were ripe for colonisation. This was the tranquillity of nature going about its business on a summer's day—a silence to be savoured. Just four years after the settlement of Melbourne was laid out, Westgarth was welcoming this fertile wilderness as a sanctuary from the 'noisy but enlivening commerce' of the town.

He was expressing the contentment of a man strolling near the banks of a river. But in the distant, dry inland, where the hum of industry had not yet been heard, the silence of the scrub was more ominous.

6

RUINS OF HOPE

In Europe such a discovery would have meant that he had come on the remains of a past civilisation…But this was Australia, the land without a history, the one country in the world without a past.

ERLE COX, *OUT OF THE SILENCE*

Gentlemen's parks

As John Oxley, the government surveyor, rode with his men across the plains of inland New South Wales in 1818, he was alone in his despair. A man could die out here. Or lose his mind. And who would notice? Not the scorched earth. Nor the limp, silent trees. Not the emus running nowhere. Nor the Aborigines, whom he saw going about their business in the distant heat. But even in these deserts of despair, Oxley encountered oases of hope. He found parks.

Three times on this expedition, Oxley rode out of the silence and into grasslands, which he recognised as superbly 'adapted for grazing', and his spirits soared. On the banks of a river near present-day Tamworth, he could even visualise an English gent riding to the hounds across 'the finest open country, or rather park, imaginable'. And when this 'fastidious sportsman' tired of hunting kangaroos, wrote

Oxley, he might hunt emus with equal success.[1]

In fact, as several commentators have observed, it was common for colonists encountering such country to rejoice in how closely it resembled 'a gentleman's park'. Ideally—but not always—these parklands occurred alongside rivers. Thus the pioneer sheep breeder Elizabeth Macarthur enthused that the Aboriginal grasslands of the Hawkesbury River were 'like an English park, and the trees give to it the appearance of a wilderness or shrubbery, commonly attached to the habitations of people of fortune'. In 1803, Lieutenant John Bowen declared that the land around Hobart was 'more like a nobleman's park in England than an uncultivated country'. To Governor James Stirling, the newfound grasslands on Western Australia's Swan River were like a park where a farmer could graze his stock with no preparation whatever. Unlike the alien limbo of the 'dark and gloomy woods', the open grasslands, set about with a few well-spaced trees, were reassuringly English—'just like a nobleman's park nicely wooded', declared Adelaide's Governor George Gawler in 1838.[2]

These parks were pastures lying idle. They were, as John Batman put it, 'delightful to the eyes of the sheep farmer'. It was as if the scions of an ancient line had returned to claim their patrimony. As the English artist and travel writer George French Angas explained when he toured the Adelaide Hills, one could easily imagine that this 'one immense park' was 'skilfully arranged by the hand of man, rather than a natural paradise prepared for his reception'.[3]

George Angas should have trusted appearances, for it was indeed 'the hand of man' that was responsible, if not for the creation of these grasslands, then certainly for their upkeep. In 1969, the archaeologist Rhys Jones challenged white Australia's ideas of the 'natural landscape' when he argued that the great grasslands of Australia were created by Aborigines using a process he called 'fire-stick farming'. The truth appears to be more nuanced. Scientists who have analysed the age of pollens stored in the earth now argue that at least some of these grass-lands were established, long before the Aborigines arrived, by lightning fires and by the grazing of giant marsupials.[4] The role of Aborigines in maintaining this open country, however, was exactly as Jones described it. They burnt off the long dry grass and saplings, encouraging sweet new grass to shoot. This fresh grass attracted kangaroos and wallabies, which Aborigines hunted for food. As early as the 1790s, John Hunter appreciated that the Aborigines used fire for clearing. In 1848, Major Mitchell explained in detail how 'Fire, grass, kangaroos, and human inhabitants' were 'all dependent on each other for exis-tence'. And, as many settlers soon realised, once the Aborigines were driven out of a region and the burning stopped, the grass-lands were either destroyed by stock or rapidly became overgrown.[5]

So the great Aboriginal grasslands did not *resemble* parks. They *were* parks. For the Aborigines who owned and nurtured them, they had the same purpose as any nobleman's park in Merrie England—to allow stock to graze and game to be hunted.

Hunger for history
The gentleman's park was just one of the images used by colo-nists attempting to define a place for themselves in country that was alien. Daniel Southwell was twenty-four when he arrived in Sydney Cove as a junior officer in 1788—a good lad who kept a journal and wrote regularly to his mother. During that first May, Southwell spent a happy day sailing on the sparkling blue waters of Port Jackson. As his boat winged past the various 'small islands that are dispers'd here and there', he was delighted to see

that he was surrounded by 'charm'd seats, superb buildings' and 'the grand ruins of stately edifices'—as if Sydney was the site of an ancient civilisation. But it was all a trick of the mind. Those mighty castles, museums and temples were all just rocks and stones and trees. 'Tis greatly to be wish'd,' he sighed, that 'these appearances were not so delusive as in reality they are.'[6]

Southwell was not the last to experience such architectural longings. Edward Eyre imagined the cliffs of the Great Australian Bight as 'massy battlements of masonry'. In central Australia, the explorer John McDouall Stuart saw a line of hills as 'old castles in ruins'. Sturt, too, saw a rocky outcrop that 'strikingly resembled an isolated castle'. Mitchell described a gorge where:

> there stood a sort of watch-tower, as if to guard the entrance, so like a work of art, that even here, where men and kangaroos are equally wild and artless, I was obliged to look very attentively, to be quite convinced that the tower was a work of nature only.[7]

When the explorer Ernest Giles and his party camped in the desert near the towering, red bluffs of Kata Tjuta, the sacred rocks displayed themselves to the astonished Europeans as a city of 'rounded minarets, giant cupolas, and monstrous domes'. To Giles, it seemed that he was in the presence of cosmic history. Those domes had stood there, he wrote, 'as huge memorials of the ancient times of earth, for ages, countless eons of ages, since its creation first had birth'.

A few days later, Giles climbed a hill in Pitjantjatjara country and looked down to a wide plain, thick with native grasses, 'level as a billiard table and green as an emerald'. This time, he could not help thinking what a glorious spot this would make for 'a display of cavalry manoeuvres'. Cocking an imperial ear, he could even hear, he wrote, the 'shouting of the slayers' and the 'screeching of the slain'. (The lines come from Macaulay's drawing-room favourite, *Lays of Ancient Rome*.) Giles was so stirred that he renamed this Aboriginal park the *Champs de Mars*—the Fields of War.[8]

These explorers were agents of an empire whose books were filled with stories of King Arthur and Sir Lancelot, of Horatio defending the bridge, and Thomas à Becket murdered in the cathedral. They knew stories of the Virgin Queen and Sir Francis Drake, and a score of other heroic tales. This was history-as-romance, set in a world of castles, walled cities and ivy-clad ruins. The plots and pageants of this romance were not mere entertainment. They reminded the explorers that, like their heroes of the past, they were on a quest to colonise and civilise the future. At the same time, as the cultural historian Simon Ryan observes, their imperial daydreams erased Aboriginal presence by re-imagining the land as vacant.[9]

We should not overstate the potency of this fantasy, however. These mind games were rare. Furthermore, the explorers did not project these battlements on to the land by some conscious act of will. On the contrary, they wrote as if they were surprised, startled and delighted whenever such visions appeared. These battlements were an architecture of solace—an illusion of familiarity in a strange and often hostile land—which is why both Southwell and Mitchell expressed such disappointment when their castles vanished into air.

Paul Carter's *The Road to Botany Bay* (1987) changed the way Australian historians thought about exploration. Carter highlighted the means by which the explorers' descriptions and maps reinvented the country they described—naming it, as if for the first time. Since the book was published, it has been commonplace for scholars to write as if the explorers laid out the landscape that the later colonists inhabited—almost as if the explorers were white Australia's dreamtime ancestors who fashioned the new terrain. But the explorers did not cleanse the land, nor render it pristine in the moment they crossed it. They did not transform it into an imperial domain, simply by wishing it so. In fact, the explorers' journals express anxiety, tedium and alienation more often than they proclaim a triumphal geography. Furthermore, some explorers questioned the very imperial endeavour on which they were embarked. Thomas Mitchell and Edward Eyre in particular were sickened by the decimation of the Aborigines. In his 'Manners and Customs of the Aborigines' (1845), Eyre reported that 'the better, and right thinking part of the community' were anxious 'to promote the interests and welfare of the natives'. But, 'these poor wanderers of the woods are looked upon as intruders in their own country, or as vermin that infest the land, and whose blood may be shed with as little compunction as that of the wild animals they are compared to.' In England, in 1837, a select committee of the House of Commons expressed outrage at the killing of Aborigines, the 'wretchedness' inflicted upon them, and the neglect of their 'territorial rights'.[10]

The truth is that the explorers' journeys opened up corridors of hiatus and uncertainty across the Aboriginal territories. For all the explorers' early optimism, the land too often betrayed them. More often than not, it mocked their dreams that somewhere beyond the frontier new grasslands and mighty bodies of water were waiting to be discovered.

According to the history books, the most luminous of these exploration fantasies was the myth of an inland sea.

7

THE MYTH OF THE INLAND SEA

Though inland far we be
Our souls have sight of that immortal sea
Which brought us hither.

WILLIAM WORDSWORTH, 'INTIMATIONS OF IMMORTALITY'

The quest

Near the core of the Australian imagination lies the lost inland
sea. Schoolteachers and history books have told us that the
explorers went in search of it. It has become a symbol of white
Australia's disappointed hopes. And now, in times of disaster, it
taunts us: whenever there is a flood in inland Australia, some
journalist will reach into the bag of clichés and tell us that the
outback is now 'an inland sea'. As West Australian hydrogeolo-
gist Philip Commander observes, the continuing enthusiasm for
watering the desert is shaped, not by science, but by the fact that
there is a 'deep-seated quest for the "inland sea" in the Australian psyche'.[1]

Indeed, Australians are inclined to suppose that this imagi-
nary inland sea is awash with meanings of a distinctively
Australian kind. But this is not the case. In the 1590s, Sir Walter
Raleigh went in search of the fabled city of El Dorado that was

said to lie on the shores of a great inland sea named Lake
Parima, in South America. Writing in 1850, the US historian
Bayard Taylor endowed Utah with a sacred geography when he
described how the Mormons settled 'beside an inland sea', a
new-world counterpart to the sacred Sea of Galilee. Around the
same time, we are told that America's Sacramento River flooded,
creating 'a vast inland sea'. A century earlier, map makers represented the unexplored north-west of America as the location of
'a fabled inland sea'. Americans have long used the same term to
describe the Great Lakes, a notable example being James Feni-
more Cooper's adventure novel *Pathfinder; or, The Inland Sea*
(1840), set on Lake Ontario. In fact, there are inland seas across
the world. In Japan, the placid Inland Sea forms the watery heart
of the country, where the three main islands interlock. Africa
has several inland seas including Lake Malawi and Lake Kariba.
Water historian Philip Ball tells us that, in 2297BCE, floodwaters
transformed Northern China into 'a virtual inland sea worthy
of any legend'.[2]

Two points arise from these examples. First, the idea of an
inland sea is not an Australian curiosity. Secondly, an inland sea
might be a concept infused with fantasy and myth. But it was
also a workaday word that could refer to any large freshwater
lake or to a landlocked stretch of ocean, like the Mediterranean.
Thus, Governor Richard Bourke described the settlement of
Melbourne as being 'at the head of the Inland Sea called Port
Phillip'.[3] So we should be cautious about assuming that every
reference to an inland sea is a reference to the mythic inland sea
that was supposedly the object of collective desire in colonial
Australia.

The notion that the Australian explorers were propelled by a
collective 'myth of the inland sea' has an impressive provenance.
In *Cooper's Creek* (1963), the popular historian Alan Moorehead
tells us 'the colonists dreamed that one day they would discover

an inland sea'. In *Riders to an Unknown Sea*, published in the same year, the bush writer George Farwell agrees: 'There were aboriginal legends about it. Escaped convicts brought back strange rumours. The first explorers riding west of the Blue Mountains were beaten by marshes they thought must be the edge of the sea.' In Frank Flynn's *The Living Heart* (1964), we read that in colonial Australia the 'legend of an inland sea was strong…Many men had set out to prove this theory'. Suzanne Falkiner's influential book *The Writers' Landscape: Wilderness* (1992) discusses the early explorers under the heroic and purposeful heading 'To the inland sea'. In her 444-page *Great Australian Explorers* (1979), Marcia McEwan throws caution to the wind and declares that 'all the explorers since the crossing of the Blue Mountains in 1813…believed in the existence of an inland sea'. Derek Parker's *Outback: The Discovery of Australia's Interior* (2007) goes one better, assuring us that, in the era of exploration, *'almost everybody* believed that somewhere in the centre of Australia there must lie a vast inland sea.'[4]

The recurring verb is significant. We are repeatedly told that the early nineteenth-century colonists *believed* in the inland sea as if it were somehow sacred or transcendent. It was, the historians tell us, a 'myth' or a 'legend'. It was Australia's El Dorado. It is frequently referred to as 'the fabled inland sea', and the search for it is regularly dramatised in contemporary writing as a 'quest'.[5]

All this is nonsense. The quest for the inland sea has become one of the received truths of Australian history. But it is a truth that is rarely supported by solid evidence.

One of the key texts to promote this myth is *The Inland Sea and the Great River: The Story of Australian Exploration* (1964). It was written in retirement by Dr J. H. L. Cumpston, the respected foundation director-general of the Commonwealth Department of Health. The book has been especially influential because it was published when the corpus of scholarly writing about Australian history could be stored in a modest bookcase. In its time, it was one of the key books on exploration. The subtitle raises the expectation that the book will show that the twin goals—the inland sea and the great river—were the driving force behind the exploration of Australia. In fact, the book is an engaging summary of key explorer journals, starting with the Dutch navigators. It contains very few references to the inland sea or to the great river—though when these do occur Dr Cumpston milks them with gusto. Furthermore, Cumpston leaves us with the impression that the inland sea was the true north of the colonial imagination and that the great river was a subordinate notion which never quite caught on.

Cumpston was certainly lured by the inland sea. It featured in two more of his books: a biography of the explorer Charles Sturt (who *was* looking for an inland sea), and a book about the explorer Augustus Gregory called *Augustus Gregory and the Inland Sea* (1972). Though this last book contains extensive quotations from the explorer's own writing, none indicates that Gregory had any fixation on an inland sea. Indeed, on the sole occasion he discussed the issue, it was to remark that the existence of 'inland lakes' was 'improbable'.[6]

Cumpston and others recruit the maritime cartographer Matthew Flinders and the buccaneer-explorer William Dampier into the league of true believers on the grounds that they both suggested that there was an opening on the northern coast which led to an inland sea. This attribution owes everything to Charles Sturt. In the introduction to his final published journal, Sturt wrote a short history of Australian exploration in which he represented Flinders as a father-figure who shared his own passion for the quest. In fact, as Flinders circumnavigated the Australian coastline in 1802, he was alive to any number of theories about the interior. Was it a vast desert? Or an immense lake, like the Caspian Sea? Perhaps some opening in the coast really would lead him to a new Mediterranean. Or perhaps there were undiscovered straits that divided this apparent continent into two or more islands. 'Such were the questions,' wrote Flinders, 'that excited the interest and divided the opinion of geographers.'[7]

True, as Flinders sailed across the Great Australian Bight, he speculated that its towering cliffs might conceal an inland sea. But he was equally alert for the opening to a great river. As he wrote at that time, 'Large rivers, deep inlets, inland seas, and passages into the Gulf of Carpentaria, were terms frequently used in our conversations of this evening; and the prospect of making an interesting discovery seemed to have infused new life and vigour into every man in the ship.'[8]

Flinders' open-mindedness was simply ignored by Sturt, and this misrepresentation had the desired effect on subsequent writers. Julian Tenison-Woods, in his *History of the Discovery and Exploration of Australia* (1865), made great play of Flinders' speculations about an inland sea, as if Flinders had fashioned an object of desire which lured later explorers. In *The History of Australian Exploration* (1888), Ernest Favenc tells us that, 'This was the goal of Flinders' ambition, the vision that haunted him always—the discovery of a mediterranean sea.' Favenc himself was a writer of Victorian melodramas: exactly the kind of man to be 'haunted by visions'. But Flinders was a sober professional—a painstaking maker of maps. He was not a man to be *haunted* by inland seas—or anything else.[9]

The continuing misuse of quotations to support the myth is exemplified by a website created by the South Australian Water Corporation. It makes the usual claim that the explorers went in search of the inland sea and tells us that they were spurred on by advice that Sir Joseph Banks gave to the British government in 1789: 'It is impossible to conceive that such a large body of land, as large as all Europe, does not produce vast rivers, capable of being navigated into the heart of the interior.'[10]

This has become a stock quotation—it has appeared in various history books to show that the inland sea was an idea supported by the highest authorities. Yet it is perfectly plain that Banks' pronouncement had nothing to do with an inland sea. He was predicting the discovery of *large rivers*. Banks went on to cite the experience of his protégé Mungo Park, the African explorer who had recently 'discovered an immense navigable river...which offers the means of penetrating into the centre of that vast continent', and proposed sending Park to Australia to repeat the performance.[11]

Yet the inland sea has entered our historical literature as an ideal that exerted an almost spiritual pull over the imagination of the early nineteenth century. As the literary historian Roslynn Haynes explains in *Seeking the Centre* (1998):

> The zeal with which the hypothetical inland sea was pursued,
> in the face of so many deaths and against all reason, indicates
> that its existence was more than just an economic advantage;
> it was an ideological necessity, reminiscent of the long-term
> European belief that a great southern continent must exist
> because it was 'needed' to balance the northern continents.[12]

Seeking the Centre is a virtuoso book, but on this point I have to disagree. There is no evidence of any such 'zeal'. Nor is there any basis for the claim that the quest was the cause of 'so many deaths'. Countless white men died in the outback. But by my reckoning, only one man died in search of the inland sea: Sturt's lieutenant, the ironically named Mr Poole, who died in 1845 of scurvy, cursing and sweating at Depot Glen.[13]

This myth is part of a larger fiction that maintains the colonists were drawn by a kind of cultural magnetism to the heart of the country—into 'the centre'—as if they yearned for consummation there. Thus the cultural historian Ross Gibson tells us that from the moment the settlers landed on the coastline they 'looked inland': their imaginations were *drawn* there, he says, by a 'centripetal impetus'.

> In front of them, immediately, was an enormity with which they felt compelled to relate. And because Australia is an island, regardless of where on the coastline settlers stood when they pondered the inland, they all looked toward one ultimate point of convergence—toward the centre—the endpoint of the spiral...Here, after the revolution of the American colonies, was perhaps the last practicable site for a European Utopia.[14]

It's an evocative pronouncement in which Gibson implies that this tug towards the centre began to assert itself even as the first convoy was settling into Sydney Cove.

In fact, all the evidence points the other way. The history of Australian exploration is notable not for any rush to the centre, but for an utter lack of urgency. Indeed, in the early years, grazing (which turned the colonial gaze inland) was outstripped by whaling and sealing, which required men to stand on the coast and scan the oceans. A decade after the first settlement, Sir Joseph Banks was protesting to the British government that 'discovery of the interior' had been 'neglected'. Thirty years later, the Colonial Office was still hearing complaints that 'only a corner of this immense island should have been explored'. In 1854, the Melbourne *Argus* lamented that the gold rushes had put all thought of exploration 'into the shade', while Julian Tenison-Woods rued that 'years of complete indifference' had delayed the exploration of the continent. The first priority of nineteenth-century exploration was not to occupy the inland, but to secure the coast—which is why, in 1803, the first breakaway party from Sydney headed, not inland, but for Port Phillip

and thence to Hobart—as far away from 'the centre' as it is
possible to get.[15]

Oxley and the great swamp

A key figure in the myth-of-the-myth of the inland sea is John
Oxley, the first of the land explorers who, we are told in a recent
history of exploration, was 'perfectly convinced of its existence'.[16]
Indeed, the only scholarly biography of Oxley, by the cartographer Richard Johnson, bears the triumphal title *The Search for
the Inland Sea* (2001). The publisher's media release assures us
that Oxley's expeditions were 'feats of dogged endurance and
persistence, as he pursued his dream of finding the mysterious
"inland sea" that he firmly believed lay in the Australian interior'.[17] But, for all its many footnotes, the book never documents
this claim. In the same vein, the relevant chapter in Michael
Cannon's exquisitely illustrated book *The Exploration of Australia*
(1999) is titled 'Oxley searches for a non-existent inland ocean'.[18]
In fact, Oxley was looking for a great river—and Cannon's lucid
text explains exactly that. If his four pages about Oxley were a
newspaper article, one could only conclude that the headline
was added by a subeditor who hadn't read the story.

John Oxley was a sharp-faced Yorkshire boy when he joined
the Royal Navy in 1799. He sailed for Sydney shortly afterwards
and, over the next decade and a half, transformed himself into a
gentleman of property. By 1817, he was farming 400 hectares of
prime grazing country at Camden near Sydney and held the
influential office of surveyor general. But this terrier of a man
was about to confront the geography of silence, an ordeal that
would shatter his optimism and ruin his health.

In the Aboriginal territories on the far side of the Blue
Mountains, government surveyors found the headwaters of two
rivers that flowed inland, which they renamed in honour of

Governor Lachlan Macquarie—the Lachlan and the Macquarie. So where did these rivers go? The eponymous Governor Macquarie—a Scottish officer of generous vision and grandiose self-regard—entertained the hope that one of his rivers might flow the entire width of the continent, 'all the Way to the Western Coast'. In 1817, he despatched his surveyor general, at the head of a splendid expedition, to discover whether the Lachlan was indeed such a river, or whether it merely flowed into some 'inland lake'.[19]

It's plain why a great river was such a desirable option. It was the key to understanding the continent. In a land where rivers were few, a great river would be the blueprint for colonisation. Farmers and graziers would settle on its margins. In time, towns and cities would rise and prosper on its banks, and the thrumming of engines would rumble across the water as riverboats transported produce and people across the country. Whether Macquarie knew it or not, in his commission to Oxley he was echoing the instructions that US President Thomas Jefferson had issued the previous decade to the American explorers Meriwether Lewis and William Clark. 'The object of your mission,' Jefferson wrote on 20 June 1803, 'is to explore the Missouri river.' He directed them to follow it westwards to discover whether it flowed to the Pacific, or connected with other rivers, to offer a 'direct & practicable water communication across this continent, for the purposes of commerce'.[20]

Like the iconic expedition of Lewis and Clark, Oxley's mission was a substantial undertaking propelled by great hopes. He was accompanied by a bush-hardened surveyor named George Evans, a tough young botanist named Allan Cunningham and a team of ten 'other Persons of Inferior Ranks'. Macquarie spared no expense: the expedition also included two boats and 'thirteen Strong Pack-Horses' loaded with enough provisions to support the team for five months.[21]

Oxley's party crossed the Blue Mountains in high spirits and began to follow the Lachlan downstream—some rowing the boats, others on horseback—as it flowed across a wide grassy plain. But this river was no Missouri. The further west the men laboured, the more downcast Oxley became. The weather that season was wet, and the ground was boggy underfoot. When the Lachlan broke its banks, Oxley's mood plummeted into despair. As water seeped across the country, the river lost itself in a great boggy swamp that stretched to the horizon. The horses wallowed in the water, while the oarsman fought their way through thick reeds and sandbanks. Sharing his contemporaries' horror of such country, Oxley reviled this as a place of 'sickly marshes, and unhealthy plains', where the turbid waters spread 'silence, death and desolation'.[22]

Today, there is a dam on the river, and much of the wetlands have been drained. The surrounding country is occupied by the prime sheep-and-wheat country around Condobolin and Forbes. But Oxley could guess at none of this. He and his companions became exhausted by the ordeal of urging their horses, wagons and boats through the sullen bog, and feared that poisonous gases were seeping from the marshes. At last, Oxley ordered his party to turn away to the south-west, where they found solid ground. But they had exchanged flood for drought. On the sun-blasted plains near today's West Wyalong, Oxley was unable to imagine 'a more desolate region'. A month later, he was still weighed down by despair. 'Nothing can be more melancholy and irksome,' he wrote, 'than travelling over wilds which nature has condemned to perpetual loneliness and desolation'. He had gone in search of the river of life, only to have his heart broken by the arid plains of inland New South Wales.[23]

By the time the exhausted party returned to Sydney, Oxley was a defeated man. With 'infinite regret and pain', he had come to the conclusion that 'the interior of this vast country is a marsh and uninhabitable'. It was 'useless for all the purposes of civilised men'.[24]

Governor Macquarie was devastated, telling Lord Bathurst that:

> The Result of this Tour leaves me to lament that the River Lachlan, of which the most Sanguine Hopes had been Entertained that it would in its course to the Sea have become of great and Important Magnitude for the purposes of Navigation and Commerce, loses itself over a large Extent of Morasses.[25]

But Oxley's pessimism was not universal. The ambitious W. C. Wentworth was confident that the Lachlan reformed somewhere beyond the marsh country and would yet be 'found to empty itself into the ocean on the north-west coast'. Writing in his book *A Statistical, Historical, and Political Description of the Colony of New South Wales* (1819)—a publication designed to persuade intending British migrants to choose New South Wales over America—Wentworth shared his dream that the Lachlan would yet be found to 'vie in point of magnitude with any river in the world'.[26]

Even the melancholic Oxley dared to hope. But then, he was a professional explorer: it was in his interests to believe that there was *something* out there worth discovering. As he was travelling back to Sydney along the headwaters of the Macquarie, he had formed the view that, unlike the boggy Lachlan, this was a vigorous river flowing through fertile country. Governor Macquarie seized on this assessment. In May 1818, the governor dispatched a new expedition under Oxley's command to explore the Macquarie River 'to its Embouchure'. The governor equipped Oxley even more fulsomely than before, allowing him fifteen men, a team of horses and carts laden with provisions for six months.[27]

On 22 June, Oxley sent a rider back from the banks of the Macquarie with word that he was confident that 'its termination would be either in interior waters or coastwise'. But a few days later, men, horses and carts were once again wallowing in swamp mud. Oxley was engulfed by the conclusion that both the Lachlan and the Macquarie spent themselves in the one vast, poisonous marsh.[28]

On 30 June he wrote, 'For all practical purposes, the nature of the country precluded me from indulging the hope that, even if the river should terminate in an inland sea, it could be of the smallest use to the colony.' It was the first time he had used the expression 'inland sea'.

'I was sanguine in my expectations of soon entering the long sought for Australian sea,' he wrote four days later, but 'it all at once eluded our farther pursuit by spreading on every point from north-west to north-east, among the ocean of reeds which surrounded us, still running with the same rapidity as before.' The 'long sought for Australian sea' is a startling expression. Clearly there were people in Sydney who espoused the idea—or this observation would make no sense. Not surprisingly, this is the passage that is quoted again and again to support the contention that Oxley was a 'champion' of the idea of *the* inland sea. This is a clear misreading. From Oxley's point of view, an inland sea was a second-best option. And, as he went on to explain (in syntax reeking with diffidence), if this was an inland sea, it didn't add up to much:

> To assert positively that we were on the margin of the lake or
> sea into which this great body of water is discharged, might
> reasonably be deemed a conclusion which has nothing but
> conjecture for its basis; but if an opinion may be permitted to
> be hazarded from actual appearances, mine is decidedly in
> favour of our being in the immediate vicinity of an inland sea,

or lake, most probably a shoal one, and gradually filling up by immense depositions from the higher lands, left by the waters which flow into it.[29]

In the days that followed, Oxley continued his dirge. 'Nothing could be more melancholy and dreary than the scene around us,' he wrote, as he faced the torment of advancing through this interminable quagmire. On the night of 11 August, 'an awful storm of thunder and lightning' hurled itself upon them, swamping their boats and soaking them in misery. Oxley felt irrelevant, unmarked either by the tempest or the Aborigines. 'The reverberation of sound among the hills was astonishing,' he lamented. 'The natives continue in our vicinity unheeded, and unheeding: even the noise of their mogo [stone axes] upon the trees is a relief from the otherwise utter loneliness of feeling we cannot help experiencing in these desolate wilds.'[30]

If this was a roaring wilderness, then it was a wilderness that held out no promise of conquest or salvation. Far from civilising the territory with his 'imperial eye' or 'ear', Oxley was tormented by a land that, in both its silences and its bellowing rages, was indifferent to him. By late August, the men and horses were toiling home through waterlogged country that concealed treacherous bogs of mud and quicksand in which a horse might easily drown. When the thunder retreated, it was the turn of the silence to oppress the explorer with its indifference. 'In our track we saw no signs of natives,' Oxley wrote on 17 August, 'and the country seemed abandoned of every living thing. Silence and desolation reigned around.'[31]

When their journey finally brought them back to the New South Wales coast, Oxley's relief was overwhelming: 'Bilboa's ecstasy at the first sight of the South Sea could not have been greater than ours, when on gaining the summit of this mountain, we beheld Old Ocean at our feet: it inspired us with new life: every difficulty vanished, and in imagination we were already at home.'[32]

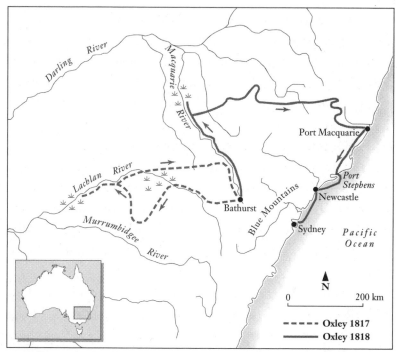

In the high rainfall years of 1817 and 1818, Oxley set out on separate expeditions to explore the Lachlan and Macquarie Rivers, hoping to find a river that flowed across Australia. Each time, he was beaten by marshes, leading him to the false conclusion that inland New South Wales was a vast swamp.

Despite the comparison, Oxley was no reincarnation of the conquistador Vasco Núñez de Balboa. In 1513, the Spanish general led a company of soldiers across the Isthmus of Panama—slaughtering hundreds of indigenous people and seizing their treasure—to become the first European to stand on the western coast of the Americas and gaze upon the Pacific Ocean. There on the heights of Darien, he claimed for Spain all the lands washed by the ocean. In contrast, when Oxley saw the Pacific, he was simply pleased to be home. His assessment of the lands he had crossed was bleak. 'It was with infinite pain and regret,' he wrote, 'that I was forced to come to the conclusion that the interior of this vast country is a marsh, and uninhabitable.'[33]

Wentworth had imagined silence as a mute giant fleeing before the advancing clamour of civilisation. But now the silence had ceased to retreat. The intruders, far from conquering the land with the crack of gunshots and the life-giving hum of industry, had entered into a zone where, as Oxley put it, 'silence and desolation reigned around'.

The Australian explorers' published journals followed a literary form that was already well established by explorers of Africa and North America. Oxley was a student of the genre: he had many such books in his personal library. The public demanded tales of discovery—of hidden lands, natural wonders, exotic tribes with savage rites, and of fabulous wealth ripe for exploitation. The explorer himself was expected to be a man of supreme daring, embodying the ideals of the white race and of empire. His mission was no less, as Mitchell later put it, than 'spreading the light of civilisation over a portion of the globe as yet unknown'.[34]

Most Australian explorers were keen to fulfil these literary expectations, characteristically beginning their published works with a self-promoting summary of their additions to the great field of endeavour laid out by their predecessors. Early in his own reports, Oxley tried to strike the pose of a great white explorer in the manner of Meriwether Lewis or Mungo Park. But, in the end, Oxley's exposure to the extremes of isolation, silence and thirst defeated his own sense of self. 'It is impossible to imagine a more desolate region,' he confessed, 'and the uncertainty we are in, whilst traversing it, of finding water, adds to the melancholy feelings which the silence and solitude of such wastes is calculated to inspire.' He wrote, not of triumph, but of his own 'pain', 'distress' and 'wretchedness'.[35] He was too lacking in bombast, too traumatised by his ordeals, to be the author of his own legend. His successors in the field of exploration—Sturt, Mitchell, Leichhardt, Stuart and Giles—wrote like heroes. Oxley wrote like the rest of us.

So, contrary to the claims made by the history books, Oxley did not found the myth of the inland sea. Rather, he was a key figure in articulating an attitude that runs counter to that optimistic longing—the Great Australian Melancholy. Many of the writers and explorers who followed Oxley wrestled with the same challenges and the same disappointments. Inland Australia refused to supply the key elements of the paradigmatic explorer story. The countryside was rarely exotic. The natives were rarely dangerous. The few triumphs rang out against a background of tedium, despair and sullen endurance.

Macquarie's secretary posted a brave notice commending Mr Oxley's 'zeal, talent, and attention'. His attempt to trace the Macquarie to its embouchure had not proved 'so favourable as was anticipated', yet 'the failure is in a great degree counterbalanced by other important discoveries made in the course of this tour'. Despite everything, they had encountered patches of excellent 'grazing country'. That was welcome. But the official notice was an expression of consolation. The venture was, at base, a failure.[36]

Myth makers, however, have little use for failure. Writing at the end of the century, Ernest Giles represented himself as the last of the great explorers. His best-selling journal fed a market thirsty for tales of pluck and endurance on the lonely frontiers of Australia. He ignored Oxley's bleak reflections and recast him as a hero—the man who 'founded the theory that in the centre of Australia there existed a great inland sea'.[37] The fact that Giles and the phalanx of historians who followed him have misrepresented Oxley's marsh as 'a great inland sea' is an indication of just how rare endorsements of the inland sea actually were. Contrary to the received wisdom—and the history books—Oxley did not go in search of 'the fabled inland sea'. Nor did he claim to have found it. Oxley's meanings are plain. He went in search of a great river—and he found a swamp.

8

RIVER OF DREAMS

Yes, as every one knows, meditation and water are wedded forever.

HERMAN MELVILLE, *MOBY DICK*

Phillip Parker King and the great river

While Oxley was scanning the plains of inland New South Wales for the banks of a great river, the sea-going Captain Phillip Parker King was searching for the mouth of the same river among the rocky inlets on the north-west coast of the continent. King was born on Norfolk Island, the son of Governor King, and was educated in the ways of the sea at the British Naval Academy, Portsmouth. According to family legend, at the age of seventeen the handsome young colonial met Matthew Flinders, the man whose work mapping the coastline of Australia he was destined to complete. On 22 December 1817, the liberal-minded King sailed out of Sydney Heads in command of a trim little cutter called the *Mermaid*, with a company of eighteen men. They included his assistant, twenty-year-old John Septimus Roe, the peripatetic botanist Allan Cunningham, and Bungaree, an Eora man who had already circumnavigated

Australia with Flinders and who was one of the bravest and funniest men in Sydney.

Sailing on the orders of the British Admiralty, King's mission was to refine the coastal map of Australia drawn by Flinders. One of his many tasks was to examine the fretwork of bays and islands in the north-west corner of the continent—the only substantial stretch of coastline that Flinders had left unexplored. King's official instructions required him to investigate whether there was 'any river on that part of the coast likely to lead to an interior navigation into this great continent'.

On 20 February 1818, the single-masted *Mermaid* was cruising along the Western Australian coast near the emerald blue waters of Exmouth Gulf, the nursery of humpback whales, dugongs and turtles. It was the wet season, when the tropical weather is hot, humid and sometimes wild. King reported that a blistering wind was blowing off the continent, which 'from its heat, and from the listless sensations it caused, resembled the hot land-wind of Port Jackson'. He saw immediately what this meant. If the offshore winds were hot on both sides of Australia, then 'the interior of this immense island' must be 'occupied by vast sandy deserts'.

In this oppressive heat, King and his companions investigated the sparkling bays, the mangrove swamps and the bushy promontories of that ancient red-rock country. From the deck of the *Mermaid*, they saw fat boab trees presiding along the cliffs like giant, white bottles. Holding their hands up to cut the glare of the tropical sun, they could see white sea-eagles hanging on the wind. Sometimes, when the men waded ashore, Aborigines came down from the cliffs to meet them. King sketched several of these people and drew their weapons and tools. But his main task was exploration. By the time he sailed away from that north-west coast, he had completed a detailed set of maps and topographical sketches that left him in no doubt. There was no great river.[1]

Though later mariners judged his maps of the region to be superb, the proponents of the great river theory were not dissuaded. They continued to believe that, somewhere in that tangle of bays, islands, creeks and mangroves, there was a major river disgorging the runoff of the vast interior into the Indian Ocean. The very notion that a continent the size of Australia could be in want of a river was too bleak a prospect for any self-respecting optimist to entertain. As an Englishman named Thomas John Maslen put it, it was impossible to contemplate the works of 'a Bounteous Creator' and believe that any imperfections could exist on the face of the planet. Australia *must* have an 'outlet for its waters'.[2]

Marvellous maps

Maslen was a retired officer of the East India Company. In the late 1820s he was living in Halifax, Yorkshire, where he pursued his many passions, including town planning, decimal currency, Bible study and Australia. He began to set out his theories about the future of the continent in a manuscript he called *The Friend of Australia*. Maslen had read reports from New South Wales that a prolonged drought had greatly diminished Oxley's impassable marsh. Pondering in his Yorkshire study, Maslen came to the same conclusion as Wentworth: the marshes must have drained into 'a river of the first magnitude'. He was as certain, he wrote, 'as if it had already been navigated'. This river was part of God's loving plan for Australia.[3]

To dramatise his point, he commissioned a lavish map of the continent on which he laid out God's plan. He imagined that much of Western Australia was occupied by mountains. In a flat open space further to the east, he placed an enormous lake. At the heart of his vision was a spectacular valley slicing through the region now called the Pilbara. Through this alpine gorge flowed the water that would determine the destiny of Australia. This was 'The Great River or the Desired Blessing'—a river forty kilometres wide discharging into the ocean on the north-west coast. Since the mouth of this blessed river had eluded maritime explorers, Maslen proposed that the government should fund a huge land expedition equipped with camels and elephants and 'subject to the articles of war'. These British soldiers of discovery would march from one side of the conti-nent to the other, establishing supply depots along the way until the entire topography of Australia—including its mighty river— was known.[4]

Maslen had both the manuscript and his lavish fold-out map printed in 1827. But, due to 'public indifference', the binding and publication of the book were delayed. It was during this delay that Maslen read a newspaper story that threw his ideas into turmoil. The newspaper reported that a squatter from Bathurst named Thomas Jamison had learned from local Aborigines there was a *great lake* several days ride to the west—a lake teeming with fish and aquatic animals similar to dogs. Jamison claimed that he had ridden into the interior of New South Wales with Aboriginal guides to investigate, but was forced to turn back just two days shy of his destination because he ran short of provisions. (If he had pressed on, the Aborigines would presumably have taken him to the Menindee Lakes, a network as vast as Sydney Harbour on the western banks of the Darling River.)[5]

On the face of it, this news accorded perfectly with the map. A great lake in eastern Australia left plenty of room for a river in the west. But this system could only work if the nation was divided into two principal catchments. It is clear from what happened next that Maslen thought, his map notwithstanding, that the great river and the great lake were mutually exclusive theories. In 1830, he had the map and the printed pages bound for publication, but he added both an introduction and an appendix in which he explained that contrary to the argument set out in the book, he was now convinced that the great lake theory was correct. So passionate was he in his reassessment that he prepared a revised version of the map, even though it was too late for inclusion in the book. On this new map, he erased the all-important words 'The Desired Blessing', and re-labelled the lake with the words 'Supposed Sea'. It was a muddle that made a nonsense of his claim to know the geography that existed in the mind of God.

But that was not the end of the matter. As we are about to see, the explorers Charles Sturt and Thomas Mitchell were embarking on major expeditions in eastern Australia. Their discoveries would create sufficient interest in Britain for Maslen to issue a second edition of *The Friend of Australia* in 1836. In a new appendix, he explained that discoveries made by the two explorers now convinced him that the great lake theory was wrong after all and that his 'great river' was still waiting to be discovered.[6]

Maslen's fanciful map has become part of the iconography of Australian history. It has been reproduced in several history books. The revised version is even featured on the website of the Library of New South Wales, rather beautifully animated so that its imaginary waterways gradually flood with the colour blue.[7] This enduring fascination might seem difficult to account for. After all, Maslen was a retired gentleman with eclectic interests, living in Yorkshire. He spoke for no one but himself. But the map is tantalising. It charts the dreams and speculations about inland Australia that were possible in the 1820s and 1830s. It is a map of the colonial imagination. And it is correct in this: while talk of an inland lake or sea bubbled to the surface now and again, it was the great river—a mighty watercourse draining the country—that dominated the landscape of desire in New South Wales.

Maslen was not the only Briton pondering the hydrology of faraway Australia at this time. In 1827, the same year that Maslen drew his map, James Ballantine of Glasgow became so agitated that he wrote to a powerful member of parliament named William Huskisson. It was totally unacceptable, declared Mr Ballantine, that after forty years of British occupation the waters of inland Australia were still a matter of conjecture. The land was 'not sparingly supplied with rain'. (Oxley had shown that.) It was simply ridiculous that the apparent absence of major rivers was still 'hypothetically attributed to an inland sea'. A thorough investigation might reveal a more satisfactory reality. Like Maslen, Ballantine urged the government to mount a military operation, equipped with camels, to sweep across the country and discover the truth.[8]

(Mr Huskisson forwarded the letter to the Colonial Office, channelling his own endeavours into the development of the British railway system. He would have been wiser to concentrate on the search for Australia's elusive river. Three years later, the honourable gentleman was run down by Stephenson's newfangled locomotive, the *Rocket*, making him the first man in history to be killed by a train.)

It was ten years since Oxley had announced the existence of the great swamp. Since then, the official exploration of inland New South Wales had indeed stalled. To Maslen and Ballantine in Britain, this tardiness was an affront to imperial prestige. But this was an entirely metropolitan assessment. For Governor Sir Ralph Darling, presiding over affairs in Sydney, the exploration of Australia was a costly instrument of the government's land policy: the leading explorers were, for the most part, government surveyors. In his decisions on whether or not to fund further expeditions, Darling was juggling two contradictory factors. Exploration of the inland would clearly advantage the squatters. And since the British government wanted to see the sheep industry prosper, it had an interest in locating well-watered grazing lands. On the other hand, the government was determined to keep the squatters within manageable administrative boundaries. Any discovery of grazing lands far from Sydney ran the risk of unleashing a land rush that the government would be hard pressed to administer. So exploration and settlement policy had to be managed carefully and jointly.

In September 1826, Darling issued a decree that set a boundary between the slice of New South Wales that the settlers were attempting to transform into English farmland and the great, uncharted 'wastes' beyond. With his customary imperiousness, Darling drew an arc on the map and pronounced it to be 'the Limits of Location'. In 1829, under the pressure of drought, His Excellency shifted his boundary a little further out. It was now an arc about 270 kilometres from Sydney. Any colonist, however noble his ambitions or lofty his family name, who ventured beyond those limits was a trespasser on the king's domain.

Darling did not care for the squatters' unruly arrogance—and was especially affronted by their richest and most impudent spokesman John Macarthur, a man of massive ambition who burned with an insatiable hatred for meddlesome governors. But this governor's wariness was not simply a matter of personal antagonism. Darling and his masters in Whitehall knew the squatters as a class of ambitious individualists they had encountered across the empire, and had good reason to try to hold them on a leash. British law was preoccupied with the rights of large landowners to exercise exclusive control over their holdings—which was why poachers found themselves transported to Botany Bay. To the law-makers in Whitehall, the colonial squatters—as their name implied—were freeloaders running their sheep and cattle on lands belonging to the king. Seen in the most hostile light, they were potential agents of lawlessness on the unpoliced frontiers of Australia. As the historian Keith Hancock put it in 1930, 'The English Government viewed their disorderly advance with distaste. These waste lands of the Crown were an Imperial patrimony, and it was an intolerable trespass that they should be occupied without leave.'[9] To the government, then, exploration was desirable only in so far as it assisted the orderly appropriation of the Aboriginal lands for grazing. It was possible, in short, to have too much of it.

In October 1827, the Colonial Office dispatched Mr Ballantine's letter to Darling. In fact, the need for further exploration was already on Darling's mind. So too was the subject of the inland sea.

Allan Cunningham gets his maths wrong

That year, the colony was in the grip of another cruel drought. Crops were withering in the ground, the creeks were running dry and the gardeners were struggling to keep their vegetable gardens alive. As in 1813, the sheep and cattle men were forced to drive their stock inland in search of pasture and water. But without success. Riders from the inland settlements were reporting that, there too, the creeks were empty and Oxley's swamps were drying up. 'The interior suffered equally with the coast', wrote Charles Sturt, 'and men, at length, began to despond under so alarming a visitation. It almost appeared as if the Australian sky were never again to be traversed by a cloud.'[10]

In May 1827, Darling sent Allan Cunningham to search for grazing country in the Aboriginal territories between the Hunter River (in northern New South Wales) and the country around modern Brisbane. Cunningham was a passionate botanical collector for the Royal Gardens at Kew, and a protégé of Sir Joseph Banks. After eleven years of exploring Australia by land

and sea, he had seen more of the continent than most. On this latest mission, he led his men northward on a course parallel to the Great Dividing Range—roughly seventy kilometres on the inland side of the range. The whole way, they were assaulted by the merciless heat of the drought. After eleven days of travel, they were, as Cunningham expressed it, 'on ground previously untrodden by civilised man'. For a further week, men and horses laboured through thick, dry bush. 'Through those gloomy woods, with scarcely a trace of either Indian or kangaroos,' Cunningham wrote, 'we patiently pursued our way until the 19th of May'. Over the next fortnight, they traversed many kinds of country. Sometimes they rode across fields of grass. Sometimes through thicker woods. But everywhere, the countryside was silenced by drought. The men were now tired and thirsty—presumably suffering the pounding headaches caused by dehydration. Time and again, they found the remains of campfires, empty gunyas and untended footpaths—signs that Aborigines normally used this country. But the travellers saw 'neither the wandering Indian nor any description of animal'. The world seemed to have been abandoned. About eighty kilometres east of the present Goondiwindi their ordeal grew worse. The men rode on to a heat-blasted plain, where cruel mirages of trees and water danced in the void. From the saddles of their hollow-eyed horses, the men scanned the surrounding solitudes for Aboriginal smoke—desperate for a sign that human life was possible here.[11]

But just a few days later, in early June, the weary party stumbled into the sort of country every explorer craved. Cunningham had found the lush valleys of the Condamine: 'downs of a rich, black and dry soil, clothed with an abundance of grass...constituting a range of sound sheep pasture convenient to water but beyond the reach of floods'.[12] He renamed this pasture-in-waiting 'the Darling Downs'. (Today, this is a prosperous pastoral and agricultural region centred on Toowoomba about 130 kilometres west of Brisbane.) The party returned to Sydney by a parallel route, having been absent for thirteen weeks. As an exercise in exploration, it had been an efficient and tough assignment. Routine—and extremely successful.

Cunningham was now ready to advance his own theory about the so-called riddle of the rivers. As he saw it, there were only two options. Either the inland-flowing rivers drained into 'a lake of considerable magnitude', or they converged to form one great river that flowed across the continent. By an ingenious use of altitude readings, Cunningham calculated that the journey from the inland side of the Great Dividing Range to the far north-west coast was all downhill—and far steeper than the fall over the length of the Mississippi, the Niger or the Nile. A drop of that magnitude pointed to a river, rather than a lake. His analysis is long-winded: it is easy to mistake his meaning. A reader who skipped the figures could come away thinking that Cunningham's acknowledgment of the force of the great lake theory was actually an endorsement of it. The chronically over-worked Governor Darling made exactly this mistake. He told Lord Goderich at the Colonial Office, 'I would observe that Mr Cunningham appears desirous to render the result of his expedition confirmatory of a favourite hypothesis—the existence of an inland sea.' Cunningham was desirous of no such thing. He believed that his calculations pointed to the existence of an Australian Mississippi.[13]

This is not to deny that the existence of an inland sea may have become, as Darling put it, 'a favourite hypothesis' around Sydney in 1827. There must have been *some* talk of the idea. On the other hand, I have trawled through the *Sydney Gazette* and the *Australian* newspapers for 1827 and 1828, and found nothing to indicate that an inland sea was the subject of popular speculation. Darling was notable for his haughty detachment from colonial life and his inability to read the popular mood. Perhaps he had simply registered that the inland sea was a 'favourite hypothesis' of his friend and employee, the explorer Charles Sturt, a regular guest at Government House. If anyone believed in the inland sea, Sturt was that man.

Charles Sturt on the Darling River, 1829

The historian Kathleen Fitzpatrick wrote of Sturt that for twenty years 'the vision of the inland sea had the power to lure him, again and again, into what he called "the heartless desert"'.[14] The truth was less dramatic. The idea of the inland sea crept up on Sturt over those twenty years. He explored it cautiously—sometimes championing it, sometimes abandoning it altogether.

But by 1829, he knew that Cunningham's figures were wrong. Sturt realised the survey data revealed that Australia was shaped like a saucer—that much of central Australia was lower than the coastal highlands on either side of the country. It was impossible for a river to flow into this bowl and crawl up the other side. This led Sturt to suspect that somewhere in north-western New South Wales there was an accumulation of water, amounting to an inland sea. But he also believed that this lake or sea might still be open to the ocean on the north-west coast.[15] If this was right, then the supposed channel from the coast to the inland was not a great river. It was a strait carrying sea water into the interior. Sturt's inland sea was salty.

In the searingly hot January of 1829, Governor Darling took advantage of the drought to send Sturt to re-investigate the Aboriginal country that Oxley had denounced as a swamp. When Sturt arrived in the place where ten years earlier Oxley's marshes had extended to the horizon, he found that the drought had sucked the water out of the country. The reeds and grasses were dead. The trees stood limp and weary in the heat.

The ordeals that Sturt and his party endured on this trip were appalling. Sturt described how he and his deputy Hamilton Hume tethered their horses for the night and made camp beside a waterhole. The mosquitoes were unrelenting and the men tried to drive them away with smoke. When this failed, Sturt rolled himself in a heavy cloak and perspired so heavily that his clothes were drenched. Hume, 'who could not bear such confinement' was 'most unmercifully bitten'. Three days later, on the banks of a trickle, which Sturt renamed 'New Year's Creek', they were attacked by swarms of stinging flies, presumably the ferocious March flies that are common in the swamp country. The horses reared and rolled frantically in the dust, driven almost to madness by the insects. The men attempted to cover their faces with handkerchiefs and swathed their hands in socks, but the flies bit through everything. 'I never experienced such torment', wrote Sturt, 'and only when the sun set, did these little creatures cease their attacks.'[16]

Tired, thirsty and sore, the men pressed on along the creek. Within a few days the waterway was almost completely dry. The few remaining puddles contained water so foetid that it was repellent to drink. Sturt became lost in Oxley's geography of silence:

> There was scarcely a living creature, even of the feathered race, to be seen to break the stillness of the forest. The native dogs alone wandered about, though they had scarcely the strength to avoid us; and their melancholy howl, breaking in upon the dead of night, only served to impress more fully on the mind the absolute loneliness of the desert.[17]

Sturt found that there were indeed marshes on the Lachlan and Macquarie Rivers. But they were now quite distinct, and separated by hundreds of square kilometres of arid country. His gruelling investigation of the region also convinced him that there was no flow of water into the inland beyond. 'It only required an examination of the lower parts of the marshes', he wrote, 'to confirm the theory of the ultimate evaporation and absorption of its waters, instead of their contributing to the permanence of an inland sea, as Mr. Oxley had supposed.' That was the option that only the pessimists had considered. The marshes did not drain into a river. Nor into a lake. They evaporated or soaked into the ground.[18]

Nevertheless, Sturt pressed on. Though his men were blistered by the sun, and near exhaustion, he led them even deeper into the torment. Then, to the men's relief, they found themselves standing in the shade of a line of river gums. The travellers had arrived on the steep banks of 'a noble river'. Though they could not see a single other person, Sturt noted that 'The paths of the natives on either side of it were like well-trodden roads; and the trees that overhung it were of beautiful and gigantic growth.' He renamed this river the Darling.

In the raw heat, the thirsty men scrambled down the steep banks and splashed into the Aboriginal river. They took deep, greedy gulps of the shallow water. Moments later they were gagging. Men who had been promised salvation now cried out in terror for their lives. The water was salt. Salt. They could not drink it. 'The discovery was certainly a blow for which I was not prepared,' Sturt wrote. 'The cup of joy was dashed out of our hands before we had time to raise it to our lips.' The desperate men threw sticks into the water to check the flow. But the sticks floated stationary on the oily surface. This 'noble river' had shrunk to a series of stagnant ponds.[19]

A couple of days later, the flagging expedition hobbled into a village of seventy huts. Sturt estimated that each hut could house ten to twelve people. The men dismounted and looked around. This seemed to be a permanent settlement. Each hut was surrounded by a trench to keep out rain. The floors were swept. A couple of beautifully made nets—one nearly ninety metres long—hung from the trees. There was accommodation here for 700 people. But the place was deserted.

A short distance further down the river, the party turned a bend and stumbled upon four Aborigines fishing with a huge net. The fishermen froze in horror. Sturt and his weary men stood still. No one moved. No one spoke. No one raised a weapon. Suddenly, the Aborigines gave 'a fearful yell' and ran into scrub. Twelve other Aborigines leapt up from the river and ran screaming for cover. Sturt and his men scrambled on to open ground, loaded their guns and prepared to defend themselves. Then they heard a crackling in the distance. The Aborigines had set fire to their country.

As the travellers' eyes began to sting with smoke, an old, naked man leapt screeching out of the burning scrub, and hurled himself towards the interlopers. He lunged and ducked. He crouched in the dust and lunged again. He shouted threats and abuse. And then the ultimate insult: he displayed his bottom. But Sturt and his men were armed—and they burst out laughing. Hamilton Hume attempted to persuade the old man that they meant no harm. Sturt joined in, and gave the man a tomahawk. And the old man's fear and aggression seemed to melt away.

But now Sturt saw that 'the old chief' was in the grip of a deep despair: 'his bosom was full even to bursting and he seemed to claim at once our sympathy and our affection'. As other Aborigines stepped warily out of the smoke, the elder gazed on his people sadly, and tried to explain the tragedy that had scoured his village. Many of his tribe had developed violent boils and lesions all over their bodies. And now they were dead. The elder called over several young men so that Sturt and Hume could see their deadly sores. 'Nothing could exceed the anxiety of his explanation,' wrote Sturt, 'or the mild and soothing tone in which he addressed his people, and it really pained me that I could not assist him in his distress.' The tribe was dying of smallpox.

And so the suffering explorers left the stricken Aborigines on their river bank—each group unable to help the other. The whites rode on downstream, deeper into the heat. Sometimes they found small pools of drinkable water away from the river. More often they went thirsty. But the salt water, which threatened their very lives, was reviving Sturt's fondest hopes. Furthermore, there were wild fowl and pelicans on the ponds, and the surrounding country was flat to the horizon. The signs were good. He was sure that they 'were rapidly approaching some inland sea'. Perhaps, after all, this salt river was pointing the way to a new Mediterranean.

But, in the very next paragraph of Sturt's journal, this inland sea evaporated. Hume noticed that salt water was seeping from the dry bed of the river. Sturt saw immediately what this meant. The pools in the river were not the backwash of an inland sea as he had hoped. They emanated from these 'brine springs' beneath the earth. There was no inland sea. His quest was hopeless and his blistered men had reached the limits of endurance. He decided to turn back.[20]

We now know what was happening. Whenever the water level in the Darling falls, salty groundwater leaches into the riverbed. In a serious drought like this one, the fresh water in the Darling dries up and is replaced by salty green puddles.

The horses were hollow-ribbed and trembling with exhaustion. The bullocks were about to drop. The men were facing death. Even in this desperate state, the animals refused to drink from the evil-smelling river. But Sturt and his men were in agonies of thirst. They lay down at one of the ponds, and gulped down belly-fulls of the salty swill. Within hours Sturt was racked by vomiting—spewing on to the steaming earth. Soon afterwards, Hamilton Hume and Mr Hopkinson were squatting miserably in the desert and squirting their boots with liquid shit. Only the tinker stayed fit for duty. And it was well that he was unaffected, since, according to Sturt, the thirst-crazed horses were desperate to escape this horror and would have left the distressed men to die had the tinker not restrained them.[21]

Incredibly, the men and beasts endured this torment for another day. The members of the party were scarcely able to speak when they limped into their base camp just before sunset. There they were greeted by other members of the party, who revived them with salted meat and pannikins of barrelled water. As they prepared to return home, Sturt knew the country with an intimacy born of suffering:

> There is no life upon its surface, if I may so express myself; but the stillness of death reigns in its brushes, and over its plains. It cannot, however, be doubted that we visited the interior during a most unfavorable season. Probably in ordinary ones it wears a different appearance, but its deserts are of great extent, and its productions are of little value.[22]

Here then was an act of capitulation. Charles Sturt, the explorer-soldier leading the advance party of empire, had retreated in the face of a country that refused to yield. He had turned his back on 'the stillness of death'.

On 4 March 1829, Sturt wrote to the governor from Mount Harris that he had returned to civilisation 'having been driven from the interior, in consequence of the extreme drought which prevails there'. Sturt enclosed a 4000-word account of the expedition, detailing his route, the demeanour of the Aborigines, his achievements and mishaps and his conclusions about the country he had encountered, especially its water. He ended:

> I fear our expedition will not pave the way to any ultimate benefit; although it has been the means by which two very

doubtful questions,—the course of the Macquarie, and the
nature of the interior, have been solved; for it is beyond doubt
that the interior for 250 miles beyond its former known limits
to the W.N.W., so far from being a shoal sea, has been ascer-
tained not only to have considerable elevations upon it, but is
in itself a table land to all intents and purposes. And has
scarcely water on its surface to support its inhabitants.[23]

So Sturt had rejected both theories of the inland sea—the
salt water and the fresh. Yet George Farwell, in his popular
history *Riders to an Unknown Sea* (1963), imagined this exchange
as Sturt returned to Sydney.

> 'Well, Sturt,' Governor Darling said, after they filed through
> the streets of Sydney Town. 'Had enough of it now? I warrant
> you'll waste no more time on your wonderful inland sea.'
>   'Not at all, sir. I want to go back. Just as soon as I can.'[24]

We may be sure that neither man said any such thing. When
Darling reported on the outcome of Sturt's expedition to
Viscount Goderich, he was certain that his lordship would find
Sturt's report to be 'in every respect highly satisfactory'. But he
said not a word about any inland sea. It was not on the official
agenda.[25]

Sturt had missed one feature that held the promise he longed
for. About thirty kilometres north of the river, in the very
stretch of the Darling along which his party had laboured (near
modern Bourke), there was an Aboriginal mound spring gushing
hot water from deep within the earth. To the Aborigines, the
place was sacred. Its name was Wee Wattah. Fifty years later it
would betray the existence of a vast subterranean water storage:
the Great Artesian Basin. By then this Aboriginal country would
be overrun by squatters.

As for the inland sea, Sturt abandoned the idea. His view

was that the Darling itself accounted for the runoff from that region of Australia. The course it followed downstream, and its intersection with the Murray, had still to be learned.[26]

Major Mitchell and the great river

Major Thomas Livingstone Mitchell arrived in Sydney in 1827, the same year as Sturt. Both men were in their mid-thirties. Both were tough and ambitious. Mitchell was a highly qualified military surveyor, and Darling duly appointed him surveyor general after Oxley died in 1828. The new man was appalled by the slap-dash arrangements in Oxley's office, which he set about knocking into shape. At the same time, he embarked on a thoroughgoing program of road building in the hinterland of the expanding colony. And it was while Mitchell toiled at this workaday task that Governor Darling announced that he was sending his military secretary Captain Sturt on the expedition beyond the Macquarie marshes. The war-toughened major was left seething with frustration, brewing a resentment of his subordinate that would poison their relationship ever after. But governors came and went. And in 1831, the imperious Darling sailed out of Sydney Harbour for the final time, with the jeers of the convict faction ringing in his ears.

With Darling gone, Mitchell seized his opportunity. The government had recaptured a runaway named George 'the Barber' Clarke, who had been hiding out with Aborigines on the Liverpool Plains. Faced with the prospect of execution, Clarke attempted to curry favour by claiming knowledge of a great river called the Kindur. It rose in central New South Wales, he said, and flowed north-west across the continent to the distant Indian Ocean. In November 1831, Mitchell departed—without Clarke—to investigate. Two months later, his party reached 'a noble sheet of water' in precisely the region

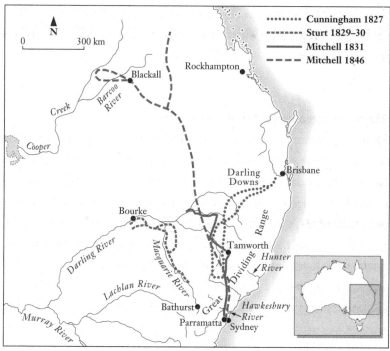

Some of the expeditions led by Cunningham, Sturt and Mitchell

the convict had described. But this river flowed south, and Mitchell soon realised that it was the Darling—the river already claimed by Sturt. Mitchell was about to push on when Aborigines attacked his base camp, ransacking his supplies and killing two of his men. Forced to retreat, Mitchell returned to Sydney convinced that Clarke had invented the story. If there was any such river, it lay much further north.[27]

Mitchell undertook another two significant expeditions, returning to England in 1837, where he enjoyed a deal of celebrity and received a knighthood. But his service in Australia was not yet complete. In December 1845, at the age of fifty-four, Mitchell departed from Sydney on his final venture. He set out at the head of a party of thirty men and several hundred stock, his mission to discover a route through the interior to the distant settlement of Port Essington on the north-western tip of

Arnhem Land. But as the cavalcade lumbered towards the north, he learned that the German explorer Ludwig Leichhardt had just robbed him of this prize. Mitchell decided, instead, to make a thorough survey of the interior of the region we now call Queensland. During the next nine months, he found and mapped thousands of hectares of potential grazing country. All the while, thoughts of the great river played on his mind and he began to search for it in earnest. In September 1846, he rode over a range near present-day Blackall in central Queensland and found himself looking down on a river 'as large as the Murray'. It appeared to be flowing towards the distant Gulf. Surely, the discovery of this long-anticipated river would be the crowning achievement of his career.

> It seemed to me, to deserve a great name, being of much importance, as leading from temperate into tropical regions, where water was the essential requisite,—a river leading to India; the 'nacimiento de la especeria,' or *region where spices grew*: the grand goal, in short, of explorers by sea and land, from Columbus downwards. This river seemed to me typical of God's providence, in conveying living waters into a dry parched land, and thus affording access to open and extensive pastoral regions, likely to be soon peopled by civilised inhabitants. It was with sentiments of devotion, zeal, and loyalty, that I therefore gave to this river the name of my gracious sovereign, Queen Victoria.[28]

With his provisions running low, Mitchell was forced to return to Sydney. But his triumphal declaration was wrong. The following year, Edmund Kennedy, a member of Mitchell's team, went back to the region. He soon found that the Victoria was actually a river that the Aborigines called Barcoo. Not far from the point where Mitchell left it, the Barcoo turns south and joins Cooper Creek. Mitchell's great river led, not to India, but to the dry saltpans of Lake Eyre. Not for the first time, he had allowed his desires and enthusiasms to override his professional prudence.

In fact, Mitchell prided himself on the precision of his surveys. As far as he was concerned, Oxley and Sturt crawled along the valleys drawing maps that were little more than lines of travel surrounded by a void. Mitchell saw himself as a man of the high places—a climber of hills and trees—from where he laid down a grid of the surrounding countryside. He was measuring up the real estate for occupation.[29] The irony is that Mitchell, for all his insistence on military precision, had a more active imagination than Sturt. Sturt was repeatedly defeated by the country he found. But Mitchell was uplifted by his visions of what the land might soon become.

Mitchell's judgments of country were firmly expressed. While he praised the grasslands west of Port Phillip as a new Eden, he dismissed the stony country between Parramatta and the Hawkesbury River as 'barren…unprofitable and worthless'.[30] But for all his meticulousness, Mitchell sometimes described wonders that simply were not there. On one occasion, his reports reinvented a dry, stony hill as a pasture thick with grass. Other times, muddy lagoons became wonderful lakes. On the Port Essington expedition, he transformed a swamp in Queensland into 'Lake Salvator'; his journal even tempted aspiring settlers with a picturesque illustration of a noble body of water over-hung by shady trees, like some dreamy mere in the English Lakes District. The colonists who took his bait were soon broken by poor soil and inadequate water. Writing in the 1960s, the historian Lyndsay Gardiner concluded that, at Lake Salvator, Mitchell's desire for glory 'defeated his scientific honesty'. But Paul Carter disagrees. In his characteristically oblique language, he argues that Mitchell was not attempting to deceive. Rather, he was implementing 'a strategy for translating space into a conceivable object, an object that the mind could possess long before the lowing herds'. These inventions were Mitchell's way of 'rendering the country habitable'.[31]

It comes down to this. Very occasionally, Mitchell's passion for engineering caused him to draw no clear distinction between *describing* the country and *designing* the country. In his mind, the land was waiting to be shaped by the 'art' of engineering. Indeed, he was frustrated that so many squatters would only settle beside lagoons, without realising they could be building reservoirs where none had been before. As he crossed the empty Plains of Mulluba (near Tamworth in New South Wales), he imagined man-made channels draining the country during downpours and filling the reservoirs of busy farms. His inspiration was the transformation that was already unfolding on the Liverpool Plains, where 'herds of cattle, browsing at a distance, added pastoral beauty to that which had been recently a desert'.[32]

I do not want to overstate this tendency. Like his fellow explorers, Mitchell was searching for grass, water and routes of communication. But Mitchell's habit of scanning the land for potential engineering projects made him more mentally robust, some might say more arrogant, than Oxley or Sturt. Ultimately, those two were at the mercy of the climate and the terrain. The silence undid them.

Though Mitchell championed the transformative power of engineering, by the late 1840s he was tormented by the impact that his civilisation was having on the Aborigines. Aboriginal men, he wrote after one encounter, were pictures of physical perfection. They were living in paradise, free from sin, free from drudgery and utterly content.

> The only kindness we could do for them, would be to let them and their wide range of territory alone; to act otherwise and profess good-will is but hypocrisy. We cannot occupy the land without producing a change, fully as great to the aborigines,

as that which took place on man's fall and expulsion from Eden. They have hitherto lived utterly ignorant of the necessity for wearing fig leaves, or the utility of ploughs; and in this blissful state of ignorance they would, no doubt, prefer to remain. We bring upon them the punishments due to original sin, even before they know the shame of nakedness.[33]

Mitchell, for all his toughness, was capable of a disarming tenderness and sensuality. In his published journals, he reveals that when he shot a female kangaroo, he was distressed by the cruel way she died—and by the fact that she had a joey in her pouch, confessing that, 'thoughts of the young kangaroo did obtrude at dinner, and were mingled with my kangaroo-steak'.[34] But, of course, Major Mitchell kept on hunting. And he continued surveying.

At heart, Mitchell was a robust pioneer of an ethos of development and productivity that, in the following century, would become known as 'Australia Unlimited'. Whatever his misgivings, Mitchell was erecting signposts for the squatters, as they drove their stock across the country, devouring the grasslands, and commandeering the waterholes of Aboriginal Australia.

Squatters

Whereas the explorers' success depended upon them broadcasting their discoveries, the canny squatter was more likely to keep his discoveries to himself. The squatters were moving beyond the frontier, and beyond the reach of recorded history—often known only to each other and to the Aborigines.[35] By 1840, the banks of the westward flowing rivers, particularly the Namoi, the Macquarie and the Lachlan, were occupied by stations extending as far as 500 kilometres beyond the Blue Mountains. The squatters had seized country to a similar distance inland of Moreton Bay, which we know today as Brisbane. At the same time, they were swarming across the grasslands of the Port Phillip district in such numbers that it seemed to the Scots settler John William that every location with a 'due supply of water is now in occupation'.[36]

These economic adventurers were given a legal status quite new to British law. The government was not prepared to surrender control of the inland to the squatting class, and refused to sell or lease the lands beyond the limits of settlement. Instead, the squatters were required to apply for a licence to graze, for which they paid a small annual fee plus a levy based on the size of their flocks and herds. These licences were issued and enforced by the local commissioner of crown lands. Often living in the same rough, isolated conditions as the squatters themselves, these officials exercised sweeping powers. In addition to arbitrating boundary disputes between settlers and enforcing the licence fee, the commissioner was chief magistrate of the district and commanded a small force of armed irregular mounted police. The system was an attempt to rein in the squatters, many of whom were, in effect, operating beyond the law.

In December 1839, there were just 694 licensed stations in New South Wales. But the real number of sheep and cattle stations was much larger, with many graziers living as nomads, driving their stock from one grassland to the next. As Governor George Gipps confessed to the Colonial Office, 'The rapidity with which Stations are pushed into the interior, is very great; and they are frequently formed without the permission or even the knowledge of the Commissioner.' Often it took 'some accidental occurrence (perhaps an unfortunate collision with the Aborigines)' before the authorities even knew of a station's whereabouts. 'The exposure to the hostility of the Aborigines' was 'one of the greatest drawbacks' faced by the settlers. But 'of these or the dreadful consequences which follow from it',

Gipps wrote, 'it is not now my purpose to speak'.[37]

The squatters did more than any other single group—except perhaps the gold diggers—to shape the destiny of inland Australia and its peoples, and to build the colonial economy. But the great irony of this revolutionary impact is that the squatters—both because they were such private men and because they lived by hard physical work incompatible with writing books or journals—did little to shape the attitudes or culture of the majority of the settlers, who lived in towns and cities. Indeed, several of the books that have come to stand as first-hand accounts of the early squatting era were actually written by the children of squatters, based on interviews with their parents.[38] The first draft of the history of expansion into the hinterland was written by the official explorers—an elite who in number were about the size of a football team. It was they and the colonial writers, painters and poets who did most to shape the mythologies that dominated the Australian imagination.

No explorer, except Charles Sturt, consistently wrote about an inland sea, let alone *the* inland sea, as the object of his quest. As we've seen, Thomas Mitchell was equally passionate—and equally susceptible to folly—in his quest to find Australia's great river, its 'El Dorado' as he called it. So how did the inland sea ascend to the mythic status it now holds? That is the next phase of the story. On his final expedition, Sturt did indeed embark on a gruelling search for an inland sea—a search that shaped a powerful national mythology and ended in a victory for silence.

9

SILENCE VICTORIOUS

Farewell happy fields,
Where joy forever dwells: hail, horrors!

JOHN MILTON, *PARADISE LOST*

Sailing to the centre

Ayers Rock did not appear in the centre of Australia until around
1960. Between 1910 and the 1950s, the centre of Australia was
located in the vast salt wastes of Lake Eyre, the so-called 'dead
heart'. And, before 1840, Australia did not have a centre at all.
No one had thought to invent one.

One of the first explorers to name the 'centre' as his objective was an affable English naval officer named John Lort
Stokes, the principal surveyor on Charles Darwin's old ship, the
Beagle. During his adventures around the lush tropical north-
west coast in the late 1830s and early 1840s, Stokes was
entranced by the spectacular red-rock country of the Victoria
River (which he named after 'her most gracious majesty the
Queen'). He reported it as a paradise, filled with exotic birds and
a limitless supply of fish, and where the Aborigines were people
of 'fine manly bearing'. One balmy night, the travellers became

so jovial around their blazing camp fire that it seemed to Stokes that the hills themselves 'echoed back for the first time the laugh and the song of civilised man'. It was as if the land itself were welcoming them. As if the high red cliffs were speaking English. Here, Britain had an opportunity to 'subdue the wilderness' and continue its mission to 'civilise the world'. Though the *Beagle* advanced no more than eighty kilometres up the Victoria, Stokes wrote that he was convinced that it was the highroad into 'the heart' or 'centre of this vast continent'.[1]

Word of this marvellous discovery soon reached the fledgling settlement of Adelaide on the distant south coast, in the lands of the Kaurna people. Here, on the banks of the Torrens River, churches 'belonging to sects of almost every denomination in the known world' graced the town—some still smelling of paint and varnish. The settlers already knew that the Aboriginal territories immediately beyond the Adelaide Hills were hot, arid country that held no hope for English-style agriculture. But being free immigrants, rather than convicts, they were optimistic and adventurous people. They seized on Stokes' ebullient reports from the distant north as if, as the *South Australian Register* put it, they were a boost to the 'spirit of enterprise'.[2]

Living among these newcomers was the veteran explorer Charles Sturt, his health, eyesight and financial security broken by his ordeals. In a bid to make money, he had driven a herd of cattle overland from Sydney, but had stumbled into such difficulties that his young friend Edward Eyre had to rescue him from the bush. In Adelaide, the evangelical Governor George Gawler welcomed Sturt with a senior public service position, while the fresh-faced settlers afforded him the status of elder statesman. As Eyre noted, Sturt appealed so effectively to their optimism that the inland sea became 'a common and popular theory' in Adelaide, albeit one to which Eyre himself was 'decidedly opposed'.[3]

In May 1840, Sturt yoked together his two key ideas—the *centre* and the *inland sea*. That month, he addressed a 'respectable audience' of some sixty gentlemen in Bentham and Nonmus' salerooms to help raise public subscriptions to fund an expedition to the north. Sturt stirred the emotions of his crowd, invoking such noble explorers as Columbus, Cook, Humboldt, La Pérouse, Clapperton and Sir John Franklin. Thanks to these brave men, he told the eager young settlers, the coast of every continent had been mapped, and the centre of every continent had been penetrated—save that of Australia. 'Its recesses, whether desert or fertile,' he told them, 'are unsought and unexplored. What is known of the interior is due rather to private enterprise than to public energy.' Now, here in Adelaide, there was a mood to carry on that work. Sturt's voice was ringing through the room as he laid down this challenge. 'Let any man lay the map of Australia before him and regard the blank upon its surface, and let me ask him if it would not be an honourable achievement to be the first to place a foot at its centre.'[4]

So enthusiastic was the response that just three weeks later Gawler was hosting a lavish public function to farewell Edward Eyre on the 'Exploratory Expedition to *the Centre* of New Holland.' The existence of the centre was now official. The ladies and gentlemen of the colony chattered and laughed as they enjoyed 'an elegant *déjeuner à la fourchette*'. Soon, they were crowing and clapping and raising their glasses as Sturt bestowed upon his young friend a Union Jack, sewn by some of the young ladies in the Government House circle. In stentorian tones, Sturt charged Eyre to carry the flag 'to the centre of a mighty continent, there to leave it as a sign to the savage that the footstep of civilised man has penetrated so far'. Oh, how the people of Adelaide cheered and sang.[5]

On his first night in the bush, as his men slept, Eyre was struck by the silence that now enveloped him. 'From the crowded

drawing-room of civilised life,' he wrote, 'I had in a few hours
been transferred to the solitude and silence of the wilds.' It
seemed to Eyre that nature itself was 'buried in deep repose'.
Having once before been as far north as dry Lake Torrens, he
had a fair idea of the furnace that lay between him and this
newly proclaimed 'centre'. This venture had been partly his idea.
He had arrived in Adelaide to find men talking about an expedition to link Adelaide to Perth—traversing land he suspected to
be desert. He convinced them that the plan was 'utterly imprac-
ticable' and urged them to set their sights on the north. But now,
he was doubtful the land would justify their optimism.[6]

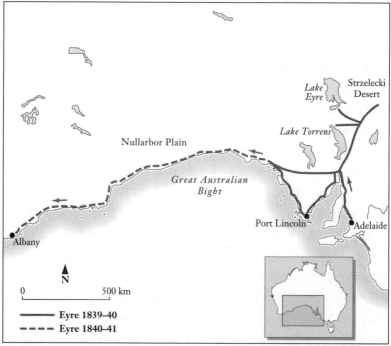

*On three expeditions in 1839–40 Eyre explored north of Adelaide and the
triangle now known as the Eyre Peninsula. In 1840, he led an expedition
westwards hoping to find a fertile route leading north into the centre of
Australia. In fact he and his Aboriginal companion, Wylie, walked to
Albany.*

Sturt too had doubts. Shortly after the farewell dinner, he wrote to his friend Charles Campbell, a wealthy New South Wales pastoralist, saying, 'I really sometimes tremble for Eyre's safety'. Sturt predicted that a vast body of water would force the young man eastward of his intended course into a desert.[7]

Eyre did find his way blocked, but not by water. He was unable to find a way beyond the arid salt flats of Lake Torrens and the vast salt lake that now bears his name. Aridity, in fact, drove him *westward*—so far west that he and his Aboriginal guide Wylie crossed the barren coastal edge of the Nullarbor Plain in an epic of endurance ending in Albany in July 1841.

Charles Sturt's divine mission

Meanwhile in Adelaide, Charles Sturt, now aged forty-six, was no longer in favour at Government House. The Colonial Office had recalled Gawler for being too open-hearted with the British government's money. His replacement as governor was a proud army captain named George Grey—a colonial careerist, seventeen years younger than Sturt and already an experienced Australian explorer.

Under orders to cut costs in the fledgling colony, Grey removed Sturt from his handsomely paid position as Assistant Commissioner for Lands, and offered him a routine post on two-thirds the salary—a still very generous £400. Already in debt to his brother Evelyn and to his friend Charles Campbell, Sturt walked the dusty streets of Adelaide in a cloud of fury and despair. Surely he deserved to be appointed surveyor general, or even governor. He had certainly earned a knighthood to match the one so recently bestowed on his preening adversary Major Thomas Mitchell.[8] But no. His sufferings on the frontier, his standing as an officer—these counted for nothing.

Sturt, however, was born into that English class which

associated easily and graciously with people of influence. Men of his degree did not make decisions, but they knew the people who did. In March 1844, Sturt began writing to his old patrons Sir Ralph and Lady Darling in London. Grey had misused and humiliated him. He could no longer support his wife Charlotte or educate their two sons. He was determined, as he put it, to 'elevate myself to that position amongst my friends in England from which my limited means have hitherto kept me'. Sturt wooed the Darlings with his conviction that the Darling River would prove to be 'the key to the Centre of this immense Continent'. Would Sir Ralph talk to his friends in Whitehall? [9]

Sturt would later claim that he returned to the ordeals of the desert 'only in the cause of humanity'—a declaration that has warmed the cockles of his admirers' hearts ever since.[10] But his private letters tell the story of a man preoccupied by financial insecurities, and seething with a sense of injustice. His determination to plunge back into the heat and the silence was not motivated by public duty. It was the brooding fantasy of a man whose reason had given way to proud and dark thoughts. As he later wrote to Charles Campbell, 'I was unhappy, Campbell, very unhappy, and I sought this service in despair.'[11]

Sturt's approach to Darling came at a time when the colonial governors were cautious about funding further exploration. It was expensive, and Eyre's ordeals had produced no discoveries of commercial value. But Sir Ralph Darling did not let his old friend down. The Colonial Office agreed to finance Sturt in a well-resourced expedition into the countries beyond the Darling River. To Sturt's satisfaction, it fell to Grey to convey the government's decision. Sturt was to lead a major expedition into 'central Australia', and he could have whatever men and equipment he needed.[12]

The official instructions were concise. Sturt was to examine the soil, vegetation and topography of 'the country near the central portions of the continent'. He was particularly to investigate whether there was a mountain range running across central Australia, and whether this was the source of any rivers flowing towards the west or north. The hypothesis behind these orders was clear. The Colonial Office imagined there might be a fertile catchment to the west of the Darling River. In short, Sturt was to continue the core mission of Australian exploration—he would travel through the Aboriginal territories in search of rivers and grass. These instructions contained no mention of an inland sea. Not a hint.[13]

But Sturt was in the grip of an obsession. He would stake his reputation on a theory in which no authority believed.[14] He would return to the merciless desert that he hated so profoundly to search for his inland sea. In part, his speculations about the nature of the inland were based on physical evidence. He had watched birds migrating west from Sydney, and, more recently, had seen birds flying north from Adelaide. He reasoned that there must be well-watered country where the two flight paths intersected. But beyond this ingenious logic, the birds had become auguries, instruments of a deeper mysticism.[15] Sturt wrote to George Macleay who had been his cheerful companion on the 1829 expedition down the Murray:

> I have a strange idea that there is a central sea not far from the Banks of the Darling in 29° L. I should go fully prepared for a *voyage*. You I am afraid will condemn this, but there is a destiny for us all, and unconsciously we are the instruments in our own hands of its fulfilment.[16]

He told Macleay that his expressions of good will at the farewell dinner for Eyre four years earlier had been half-hearted. He had never believed that Eyre would succeed. 'With the best wishes for his success, I never for a moment anticipated that Eyre would succeed in his attempt to penetrate to the Centre,'

Sturt confessed. 'I have had for years a presentment that that task was reserved for me.' Or, as he told the pious Lady Darling, 'I have had a presentment on my mind for years, that the task of exploring central Australia would be mine and we are often unconscious instruments ourselves for the fulfilment of our allotted destinies.'[17]

This belief in the power of predestination or Providence was characteristic of evangelical Anglicanism, a form of Christianity that was both respectable and influential in England in the nineteenth century. As Sturt indicated repeatedly, he believed that his personal ambitions reflected the plans of that 'all Good and Powerful Being, who orders events according to His unfathomable wisdom'. God had guided him in the past, wrote Sturt, 'and I should trust His goodness if I should be again placed in equal difficulty and danger'.[18]

So the quest to discover an inland sea was the brave, tragic and lacerating obsession of an aging and vision-impaired British officer. As he confided to Charlotte, his own 'credit or reward' was 'the only object for which I sought and undertook this tremendous task'. Sturt's devoted biographer Michael Langley confessed that he was dismayed to read these words, unwilling to believe that Sturt was risking the lives of his men 'solely to realise a personal and selfish ambition'. But that was exactly how a Victorian military officer, imbued with a sense of his own divine destiny, thought about the men under his command. If God willed it, then it was their fate to lay down their lives in the service of a higher purpose. Indeed, this same elitism and sense of honour would produce the suicidal Charge of the Light Brigade just ten years later. And let's be clear: Sturt was also prepared to sacrifice *himself* in this quest for recognition. It would be 'better for me to run the risk of letting my bones blanch in the desert,' he told Sir Ralph Darling, 'than to remain where I am without prospect of advancement'. He would win back his respectability and make his fortune, or die in the attempt.[19]

On the afternoon of 10 August 1844, a crowd gathered in dusty King William Street to farewell the expedition. It was a sunny spring day. There were ladies in long dresses. Labourers and bushmen in their working clothes mixed with gentlemen in top hats and fine coats. These good people of Adelaide chattered and waved as the cavalcade of men, with seven carts and drays, horses, bullocks and sheep, rumbled past them in a great river of noise—and disappeared into the Aboriginal north.[20]

Sturt's chosen companions were his assistant James Poole and the expedition doctor John Harris Browne. Also present was Edward Eyre, who had agreed to travel with them along the Murray where he enjoyed amiable relations with the Aboriginal people. This group were styled 'the officers'. There were also fourteen others referred to simply as 'the men' who included a stockman named Robert Flood and a skilful young bushman named John McDouall Stuart. These men were the instruments by which Sturt would pursue his own God-given destiny.

A few days from Adelaide, the party rested at Moorundi on the banks of the Murray to repack the carts in a more orderly fashion, and to pick up their Aboriginal 'attachés', Camboli, Nadbuck and Tampawang. It was here that Sturt assembled the white members of his crew and outlined their responsibilities. They were to be cheerful, cooperative and to obey his orders. They were not to have any private relations with the Aborigines, 'more particularly the native women'—a practice which, he told them, was a cause of 'many of the acts of violence that had been committed on the river'. Sturt then read some prayers, the men secured their loads, and the expedition was under way. 'The silence which had prevailed', wrote Sturt, 'was broken by the cracks of whips, and the loud voices of the bullock-drivers. The teams descended one after the other from the bank on which they had been drawn up, and filed past myself and Mr. Eyre, who stood near me, in the most regular order.'

Sturt watched the long line of carts rumble across the Moorundi flat, and wondered how many of those men would return alive from the desert. He wondered too whether he himself would succeed in his quest to reach the centre, outshining Eyre 'who shrank from the task I had undertaken'. As the men and horses disappeared into the scrub, Sturt turned to address his companions. But he was alone. 'Mr. Eyre, and the other gentlemen who had been present, had left me to my meditations.'[21]

In the solitude of command, Sturt sought comfort every Sabbath by writing a series of letters to his 'dearest wife' Charlotte in the form of a weekly journal. These pages have been woven together and bound in blue cloth—presumably by Charlotte herself—to create a little book. This fragile document is kept in the library of Rhodes House in Oxford. To my eye at least, its pages, covered with Sturt's handwriting, are stained by the red earth of central Australia. This 'Charlotte Diary'—part journal, part love-letter, part confessional—reveals that Sturt was tormented by a crisis of faith right from the outset. Perhaps he had misread the divine plan. 'Was it decreed,' he wondered, 'that I should return baffled and disappointed from these gloomy and inhospitable regions?' Sturt had journeyed into this country of despair before. He knew that even if he found Eden he would first endure terrible agonies. He was returning to country that he had already described as a lonely place 'over which the silence of the grave seemed to reign'. It was, he confessed to his wife, a 'doubtful enterprise'.[22]

While Sturt brooded in his tent each evening, a gunsmith named Daniel Brock sat alone under the stars. Brock was the expedition's shepherd and collector of bird specimens. He was a God-fearing Methodist and had nothing in common with the other men. To him, they were brutalised old convicts who spent every drunken night sitting around their campfire, swearing, blaspheming and telling dirty stories. (The doctor Mr Browne agreed. They were 'a great set of ruffians'.) Brock too was keeping a secret, intimate diary, anticipating that it would be read only by his 'revered parent', and presumably by his 'dear wife' Delia. To Brock, he and Sturt were two brothers in Christ labouring in the company of sinners and fornicators. But the Old Harrovian Captain Sturt was not about to engage in Bible study with his Methodist bird shooter. So Brock read his Gospel under the stars and dreamed of salvation in the great hereafter, while Sturt knelt in his tent and prayed for his earthly rewards. Their private diaries both remained unpublished for over one hundred years.[23]

Sturt's journey to central Australia has been retold countless times by historians and educators determined to conjure a founder-hero worthy of a national history, a Sturt of 'untiring zeal, a consideration for others, and forgetfulness of self'.[24] This is the image perpetuated by Michael Langley in his indispensable but one-eyed biography, *Sturt of the Murray* (1969). A backlash was led by Edgar Beale's scholarly *Sturt, the Chipped Idol* (1979). Fired by the rediscovery of Brock's journal, Beale pilloried Sturt as an arrogant British officer unhinged by his obsession with a non-existent sea. Beale, it seems, was dismayed to discover that this Victorian military officer was neither an altruist nor a modern liberal and that he was driven by personal ambition. More recently, feminist and postcolonial scholars have damned Sturt as a propagandist for the imperial project.[25] I want to break free of this argument, to rediscover the complexities and contradictions of a man who was at once brave, ambitious and in the grip of an extreme state of mind.

Set against Sturt's official writings, Brock's secret journal is a subversive document. Far from seeing the empire as a blessing for the indigenous people, Brock wrote that 'an Englishman is a curse to the Aborigines of any country'. 'The white man,' he wrote on the depopulated banks of the Murray River, 'has been here cruel, more cruel, than any savage.' Brock's diary breaks open the conventions under which the explorers wrote as if they struggled and suffered more nobly than their crews. It puts the men at the forefront of the story, recording how these forgotten toilers drove the carts, manhandled the stock across rivers, measured out every mile of the journey with heavy lengths of chain and shot animals for food or study. At the end of each day's weary travel, these men erected a marquee for Sturt and a bell tent for the officers, complete with camp stools, tables and bedding. They penned the sheep with nets, fed and watered the horses and bullocks, cooked the meals and got drunk. When they finally went to sleep, they rolled out their swags on the back of a cart or on the cold earth—while one or two of their number kept watch through the night for hostile Aborigines.[26]

In Sturt's accounts, these activities are scarcely mentioned. He was *the explorer*. Like all explorers, he was heroically alone, even when he was in the midst of his men. It was he—he alone—who had traced almost every inland river to its termination. And now he felt the mysterious inland beckon—uncertain whether it was summoning him to victory or luring him to his death. But he declared himself sure of this: no man had a greater claim to undertake this quest. Surely it was his destiny to plant his foot 'in the centre of Australia'.[27]

With such ambitions pounding in his chest, Sturt led his mounted party upriver until they reached the confluence of the Darling. Here, Eyre bid his companions Godspeed and returned to Adelaide. Sturt was reflective as he and his party lingered at this powerful intersection where two very different rivers mix. The broad, cool Murray rises in the Alpine country of New South Wales and flows even in the fiercest summers. As Sturt had experienced on that expedition with Macleay eleven years earlier, the country around the Murray often looked barren to the European eye, though the river itself is always a place of life. By contrast, the Darling, which snakes on a diagonal down the entire length of New South Wales, is a temperamental master. A traveller could die of thirst on its steep and dusty banks.

As the expedition turned north along the Darling, Sturt had no idea what this river, whose upper reaches he knew so well, had in store. He wrote as if he had passed through a gateway into the grim interior, noting that 'the same death-like silence pervaded this spot, as with the other parts of the river on which I had been'. But water and grass changed his mood instantly. The grasslands along the Darling were 'park-like' and 'as verdant a lawn, and as beautiful a spot, as ever was seen'. Five days later, a deluge of water came surging towards them. Somewhere, far to the north, rains had fallen. Sturt was delighted by the way the Darling was transformed 'into a broad and beautiful river, dashing and foaming along'.[28] But, as the travellers pressed on, the cheering sound of water gave way to the hot, dry emptiness of the inland. Sturt's hopes were tested by the reality that now seemed to claim him—the repellent 'death-like silence' of the 'gloomy scrub'. (The word 'gloomy' occurs twenty-one times in his *Narrative* of this expedition. He associates the silence of the land with death six times in his published journals.[29]) The men were grumbling as the little party toiled further along the Darling through Barkindji country, where they had a series of intense encounters with the local people.

Sturt's theories are a tangle, but in essence he had adopted a hypothesis proposed by Matthew Flinders that a depressed band of country running from the Gulf of Carpentaria to Spencer's Gulf had once been beneath ocean, separating the eastern and western sides of the modern continent. Sturt knew that this central region was now arid—and yet he persisted in the belief that somewhere in central Australia there was a sea—a *salt* sea—fed by a strait flowing in from the north-west corner of the continent.[30] He apparently believed that some of the inland rivers of eastern Australia also drained into this salt lake, although this part of his theory is very vague. It is also unclear what the benefits of this lake would be. Indeed, he wrote in one unpublished draft of his journal that 'as I have always thought, so I still think, that the difficulty of gaining the Shores of that Sea will be almost insurmountable'.[31] It is a fatalistic pronouncement suggesting that, after all, he did not anticipate that there was a river highway into the inland sea.[32]

Brock, too, was reading the land. Dune by dune. Creek by creek. As they advanced deeper and deeper into the heat, he was scathing of Sturt's refusal to accept the obvious:

> 15th [October]. About noon Mr. Poole and Stuart returned bringing encouraging intelligence, they had fallen in with water, and had observed a large body in the distance. This has made Sturt all alive—he fancies we shall soon come upon the great waters of the interior...Nothing is heard but about the boat.[33]

This sighting—like others—was a mirage. A month later Sturt was still at it. On 10 November, they found water by digging. It was a sign from God. 'The Providential supply,' wrote Sturt, 'will enable us to go on thirty miles further, and it may be that we may find the means of reaching a latitude sufficiently high to determine the existence of an inland Sea.' But he was now lost. He no longer gazed on the land with an 'imperial eye'. Or if he did, the land returned his gaze. Among wild and rocky hills, surrounded by heat and silence, Sturt looked up into the sky and saw a black kite gazing down *at him*, examining 'what we were, in evident astonishment at such an apparition in his lonely and silent domain'. There was no hint here that the timeless spirit of the land, the deathlike silence, would ever retreat. It was as if he had passed into a parallel dimension.[34]

The hills gave way to bleak, stony plains. As the travellers approached the Barrier Ranges, Sturt found himself looking across a grim blue-green expanse of 'the universal scrub' stretching to the distant rocky wall of the ranges. The land was taunting him. 'One might have imagined that an ocean washed their base,' he wrote, 'and I would that it really had been so.'[35] Such imaginary oceans would rise and fall in Sturt's mind again and again. They were not, as some commentators suggest, ideological tides designed to wash away the claims of Aboriginal Australia. Sturt's oceans spoke only about him. He experienced the sand dunes, the blue expanses of the bush and the mirages as 'seas' because he sensed that he, the explorer blessed by Providence, was being toyed with—both by the land and by Providence itself.[36]

But how quickly his mood could swing. On 17 November they saw in the distance dark clouds massing over the country, and it began to rain. Sturt became excited. Surely those clouds formed a watery canopy over the inland sea. Brock was contemptuous: 'It is really amusing to hear the Captain asserting that he has been *very near* a large body of water because they saw large clouds, as if pending over some such body; however he did not see it.'[37]

By January 1845, Brock noted that Sturt's delusions were worse and that the men had started pandering to them. 'If any body wants to please him, they have only to tell him they heard swans, which seem to pass to the NW.' Mr Flood had begun seeing things 'that nobody else sees, and the Captain swallows greedily such information'.[38]

By now, the outback of New South Wales was, in Sturt's words, a 'molten desert'. The heat, wrote Brock, 'passes through every nerve'. The men were tortured by hordes of stinging flies by day and voracious mosquitoes at night, and thirst was their merciless companion. They could travel for days through the flat, indifferent country without seeing a soul. On the Pinnacle, the highest point of the Barrier Range, Sturt saw that God's Providence was less assured than he had believed: 'We stood, as it were, in the centre of the barrenness: we were gradually and steadily working our way into the interior: I had hoped, by this time, with God's blessing, that we should have raised the veil that had so long hung over it.'[39]

Lifting the veil

Relying on such imagery, the cultural historian Kay Schaffer asserted, in a hugely influential section of her book *Women and the Bush* (1988), that Sturt and his fellow explorers habitually represented the country as if it were a woman they had set out to ravish and possess. There was a precedent for this suggestion. The US feminist literary critic Annette Kolodny showed in her brilliant and now classic study *The Lay of the Land* (1975) that the British often envisaged North America in precisely these terms. Thus Roger Wolcott, a colonial governor of Connecticut, wrote of an ardent mariner pressing 'upon the virgin stream who had as yet never been violated by a ship'. In the USA, colonial imagery was panting with talk of virgin soil begging to be ploughed, fertilised, cropped and possessed. As Kolodny explained, according to the patriarchal logic of imperialism, 'to make the new continent Woman was already to civilise it a bit'.[40]

The American-born Schaffer claimed that the same imagery shaped the ideology of exploration in Australia, adding the idea that the bush was also sometimes represented as a vengeful mother. But it is the 'virgin bush' idea that has become the orthodoxy, reappearing in Ross Gibson's *South of the West* (1992). As the writer Suzanne Falkiner informs us 'the historical imagery of the landscape as the body of a woman waiting to be conquered is so ingrained that it is no longer noticed'. The notion that nineteenth-century settlers thought of the land as a woman whom they were destined to conquer has been repeated many times, most recently by Catriona Elder, in her Australian studies textbook *Being Australian* (2007).[41]

But what is the evidence? Gibson introduced the claim by informing the reader that when Major Mitchell lorded over the grasslands of Australia Felix he declared, 'Of this Eden it seemed I was the only Adam; and it was indeed a sort of paradise to me'. So, asks Gibson, 'Where is Eve? It seems plausible to say that she is the landscape itself.' Schaffer also used the Mitchell quotation and drew the same induction, based as it is on nothing more than the principle that every Jack must have his Jill.[42]

Fatally for this argument, Mitchell said no such thing. The passage that Schaffer and Gibson quoted appeared in a Victorian school reader in 1928, in which an editor silently merged two entries from Mitchell's journal and then added Adam. What Mitchell actually wrote was this: 'Of this Eden, I was *the first European* to explore its mountains and streams.' Not an Adam in sight. And so—by this logic—no Eve either.[43]

The stunning feature of these commentaries is how unpersuasive are the few quotations offered as primary evidence, and how these same quotes are recycled from one text to the next. All these commentators rely heavily on the fact that Sturt repeatedly spoke of 'lifting the veil' on central Australia, asserting that he was metaphorically exposing the face of a bride or an oriental woman. According to Schaffer, for Sturt, 'the land takes on the features of a veiled, seductive, exotic, unknown, but desired maiden'. Simon Ryan likewise claims that Sturt represented the land as 'coquettish' and tempting 'a specifically male viewer to lift the veil'. Gibson grandly refers to this as part of the 'subliminal drama of divestment'. The allegation is that

Sturt was guilty of symbolic rape. Indeed, these commentators also detect a sexual threat in the way explorers sometimes described their expeditions as having 'penetrated' country. But the metaphor here is not sexual, it is military. As we've seen, Sturt was one of those explorers who most often experienced the land as gloomy and repellent. He did not violate it. He felt threatened by it.[44]

In any case, the veil in Sturt's writing simply does not imply the presence of a woman. 'Veil' was the standard colonial term for a fly net. As the colonial writer J. D. Hennessey explained, in the bush the flies were so bad that 'All the men wear veils'. Sturt himself reported, on this very expedition, that the flies were so relentless on Cooper Creek that 'I continually wore a veil'.[45]

Sturt did use a feminine metaphor on one occasion. Talking of the 'veil' which hung over central Australia, he speculated that it was hung there by the hand of Nature who 'had intentionally closed it upon civilised man, that she might have one domain on the earth's wide field over which the savage might roam in freedom'. As Simon Ryan observes, this is 'the best known' example of 'the persistent metaphor of the land as female'.[46] But, it is not the land that is being gendered. It is Nature—a fact that reinforces my point. Because the inland was arid, the explorers were not inclined to endow the land itself with a gender precisely because they felt 'Mother Nature' to be absent. (Furthermore, Sturt's language is respectful of this liaison between nature and 'the savage' rather than triumphal.)

In fact, for Sturt, face veils were rarely the issue. In the religious tradition that permeated his writing, the veil (if it represented anything at all) generally referred to the veil that covered the Holy of Holies in the temple of Solomon. For the Christian explorer, the veil that hung over Australia hid, not a woman, but 'a mystery'—which it was his destiny to reveal to the world. The veil, in short, was almost always imagined by

Sturt as a curtain. That's precisely how we hear the term when Sturt uses it: 'Over the centre of this mighty continent there hangs a veil...' Some*thing*—not some*one*—was hidden. Likewise, Edward Eyre was clearly imagining a curtain when he admitted that he had 'not been able to lift the veil which is drawn before the centre of this still mysterious continent'. Any doubt on this point is vaporised by Daniel Brock who tells us that Sturt's expedition was an 'attempt to lift off *the curtain* which has hitherto been so impenetrable on this interesting country'.[47]

What is so striking about the Australian frontier is how *rarely* it produced the American-style rhetoric of the 'virgin land'. Indeed, the religious historian Roland Boer argues that when it came to gender most Australian explorers actually saw the land as harsh, unforgiving and 'manly'. Most often, however, colonial writers experienced the desert in elemental terms. In the poem 'Australia' (1848), Samuel Prout Hill mirrors Wentworth's fleeing Austral giant. But in Hill's Australia, it is the explorer and not the land-spirit who has been put to flight. 'The Desert,' Hill writes, had awed Sturt 'with *its* sterile majesty of space,/And warn'd him backward from the fatal place.' The arid zone tested the explorers. It mocked them. It remained *it*.[48]

The explorers experienced alienation in arid Australia more often than they drank in the euphoria of domination. The writer Patrick White had a profound sense of this. In his novel *Voss* (1957)—a book which, in some circles, is discussed in tones of awe as if it holds the key to the 'Australian condition'—he has his fictional explorer Voss say, 'I do meet scarcely a man here who does not suspect he will be unmade by this country. Instead of knowing that he will make it into what he wishes.'[49] The land did not whisper seductive entreaties into the ears of the explorers. In fact, it often repelled them with a mighty and 'death-like silence'—a vast indifference that threatened to reduce the men themselves to silence, or to bone.

Yes, the explorers strove to achieve mastery over the interior—to conquer it by knowing it. But they were struggling, not with a 'female other', but with an inhuman world of sullen elements—of rock, sand and silence. Indeed, they soon learned that water was *their* master. As John McDouall Stuart explained, 'I must go where the water leads me.'[50]

So Charles Sturt did not woo the desert. In his heartbreaking search for water, the arid country taunted him with the illusion of lost oceans that evaporated into sand.

Sturt and silence

The critical phase of Sturt's expedition occurred when his team was trapped for a mind-rotting six months in an oasis, sheltered from the surrounding arid country by rocky walls of slate. Inside this little world, the daytime temperature was generally near 40°C, but the walls enclosed deep, cool gullies where birds gathered in the white gums beside deep pools of water. Sturt thanked Providence for their deliverance, and named this sanctuary 'Depot Glen'. He had not yet discovered anything.

One airless day, as the bored men were bickering, Sturt escaped on a walk with Mr Browne. About five kilometres along the creek, they came to a place where a flood had dumped great piles of rubbish, stones and timber. The surge had uprooted entire trees and hurled them into the branches of other trees, where they remained lodged—bleached and silent in the heat. 'Perhaps,' wrote Sturt, 'the death-like silence of the scene at that moment led us to reflect, whilst gazing on the ravages made by the floods, how fearfully that silence must sometimes be broken by the roar of waters and of winds...The country must on such occasions have the appearance of an inland sea.'[51]

After one month of this confinement, Sturt left most of the men in the safety of Depot Glen and walked into the inferno outside, with Stuart, Flood and a boy named Joseph Cowley. The four headed north across an ocean of sand ridges and gloomy scrub to a waterhole they had visited several weeks earlier. Here Flood and Stuart established a base camp, while Sturt and the boy Joseph pressed even further north into the heat, with the poor horse Punch straining at a cart laden with barrels of water. Soon the two travellers and their horse were scrambling, sliding and clambering over one red sand ridge after another. When they reached the crest of each sand ridge, there before them another identical dune was waiting. Finally Punch broke down. But Sturt would not stop. He and Joseph abandoned the horse, 'took a quart of water and a piece of damper', and continued to struggle over sandhill after sandhill. As the heat began to take possession of them, it seemed to Sturt that once again the land was mocking him: sand ridges rose and fell around him 'like the waves of a tempestuous sea'. He was set upon reaching 'the meridian of 28°', the latitude where the Colonial Office hoped to find a mountain range and the edge of a whole new catchment. When the angle of the sun told Sturt they had arrived, the man and the boy stopped.

'There we stood, Dearest,' Sturt wrote to his wife. In that terrible desert, it appeared as if they were 'the last of creation amid the desolation and destruction of the world'. There was a 'solemn stillness' all around them, and not a living creature to be seen in that 'dreary and monotonous wilderness'. Sturt felt that he and Joseph were 'the last of the human race left to witness the destruction of our Planet'. According to Sturt, young Cowley agreed. 'Oh Sir,' said the poor boy. 'I was never in such a place as this before. It is a dreadful place indeed.'

The man and the boy turned away from the great nothingness and struggled back across the dunes, collecting the stricken horse on the way. In a blistering ordeal across one hundred kilometres of burning sands, they made it back to the waterhole where Stuart and Flood were waiting.

To a modern traveller, it would be clear that this fearful journey led deeper into desert, and further away from water. But Sturt was now driven by a faith beyond reason. He confided to Charlotte that he believed they were 'within 150 miles of an inland sea'. To Charles Campbell, he wrote: 'I am quite sure that we are within 150 miles of an inland sea or a large river, and I have a splendid boat, so that I am prepared for flood or field'. (On the question of an inland sea, even Sturt was hedging his bets: he was now prepared to countenance the existence of a great river.)[52]

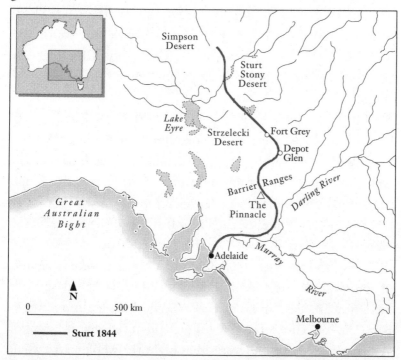

Sturt's final expedition on which his dreams of an inland sea evaporated in the Simpson Desert

The four men returned burnt and exhausted to Depot Glen. There, the party languished beside the dwindling water supply, waiting for the rains. The birds left for 'a better and more hospitable region', and 'a gloomy silence pervaded the camp'.[53] As game became scarce and their rations started to fail, Poole succumbed to scurvy. His legs turned black. The roof of his mouth came away, and he died, cursing and blaspheming—a man who had lost all respect, wrote Sturt, even for himself. Brock was made 'sick at heart' by the callousness with which the other men buried him. Sturt read the funeral service, but he confessed to his journal that 'I was in truth glad that Mr Poole was gone, for he was a mischief-maker in every sense of the word'.[54]

Now that the rainy season was about to commence, Sturt was determined to resume his progress into 'the heart of the Interior' and plant the flag 'in the centre of this continent', obtaining 'the object for which I undertook this long and desperate journey, the means of putting myself square with the world'.[55]

They established a new depot at Fort Grey, one hundred kilometres north-west of Depot Glen. Throughout August, September and October, Sturt led small sorties into the wild country—sometimes stumbling on to a tiny creek, a lonely Aboriginal waterhole, or a silent plain of dry grass. But inevitably, the desert dunes or the flinty furnace of the Stony Desert blocked his way. By mid-October, Sturt's horses were living skeletons, and the men, including Sturt himself, were in agonies of scurvy and thirst. At last, he looked on to the desert and recognised defeat. 'In no direction could I see a glimmering of hope,' he told Charlotte. 'I felt quite convinced that if I went on and that we did not find water that night the whole party would perish.' Brock was almost blind and expected to die, declaring: 'I throw myself and all my sins upon Jesus.'[56]

Sturt's published journal, *Narrative of an Expedition into Central Australia* (1849), is not a tale of discovery, but an epic of suffering, endurance and failure. Despite a few trickles of hope,

Sturt experienced inland Australia as a desolate emptiness where 'the stillness of death reigned round us'.[57] Though Sturt would maintain a shy hope for another decade that somewhere in central Australia there was an inland sea, his rhetoric lost all optimism. Back in England, he expressed his views, he said, 'with diffidence and hesitation', knowing that his faith was 'contrary to the experience of other travellers'.[58] Finally, in 1858, he conceded. The explorer Augustus Gregory had entered a great central desert from the north of the continent. Sturt saw that this was the same desert he had entered from the south. He advised the Colonial Office that any further 'exploration of it would end in disappointment'.[59]

10

MAPPING THE SILENCE

An absolute silence leads to sadness: it is the image of death.

JEAN-JACQUES ROUSSEAU, *REVERIES OF A SOLITARY WALKER*

Contours of defeat

The colonial dream now faced a crisis. Sturt had been one of the last officials to cling to the ambition that inland Australia would one day succumb to the sounds of civilisation and the hum of industry. But the land had answered back. The colonists now knew the worst. There was no great river in central Australia. No inland sea. As the skies grew hotter and the landscape drier, and as rolling fields gave way to scrubby plains and arid ranges, the settlers found that the geography of silence was no longer in retreat. It was all around them.[1]

It is only slightly fanciful to say that we can map this silence, that we can draw a line on the map and say the colonial traveller who crosses that frontier is entering the zone of silence. The factor that determines this frontier is water: on a map of average annual rainfall, the 500-millimetre (or 20-inch) isohyet marks the country beyond which the silence becomes challenging. We need to make two qualifications. Unlike Europe, Australia has a climate characterised by extreme variability. What the rainfall map cannot show is how unpredictably the rainfall levels—and therefore the regions of silence—shift from season to season and year to year. We should also allow that, in the tropical north, the boundary retreats and advances in response to the dry and wet seasons. As the rainfall varies, so does the silence. When the rain falls, the frontier came comes alive with sound. As Ludwig Leichhardt explained, the calls of birds and frogs transformed despair into hope, because they indicated that 'water is at hand'. Mitchell was exhilarated when the 'dry and silent' Macquarie River was brought to life 'by the rushing sound of waters and loud cracking of timber'. In contrast, in May 1862, John

The settlers experienced the dry inland as a place of silence. We need to imagine this map of average rainfall as a living organism on which the regions expand and contract from year to year.

McDouall Stuart found no such relief in the dry north of South Australia. 'No rain seems to have fallen here for a length of time,' he wrote. 'We have not seen a bird, nor heard a chirrup of any to disturb the gloomy silence of the dark and dismal forest— thus plainly indicating the absence of water in and about this country.'[2]

The silence of Australia was no longer in retreat. It was a zone you entered, and from where you returned if Providence was merciful. This was country so indifferent to the white man's presence that it refused to be colonised by time. As Mr Pringle observes in Patrick White's novel *Voss* (1957), when the explorer Voss sets out on his fateful journey, 'It has been shown that deserts prefer to resist history and develop along their own lines.'[3] The challenge became, not to break the silence, but to survive it.

Throughout the history of Australian colonisation, this frontier of silence has been more than a matter of poetics. It has determined who made their fortune and who failed. Who lived and who died. During a merciless drought in 1865, George Goyder, the surveyor general of South Australia, drew a line across the southern regions of the colony that more or less followed the 250-millimetre isohyet, well beyond the frontier of silence. North of 'Goyder's Line' lay saltbush country where the drought had reduced farmers' dreams to dust. As always Mr Goyder was precise: this region would never be suitable for cereal crops or other agriculture. It was a warning to anyone who passed that way not to be deceived if the creeks were flowing or the grass was green. The rainfall here was too variable for crops. Only the margin of the colony south of the line could safely be sold off to small selectors for agricultural development. But in the mid-1870s, South Australia enjoyed a run of years with higher than average rainfall. Ambitious men with an appetite for hard work began planting wheat, raising sheep and building homes further inland. The rain kept falling; the deserts bloomed, and the South Australian government encouraged small farmers to settle and build almost to the shores of Lake Eyre. As the sun-blackened settlers bagged their harvests, they ridiculed Mr Goyder and his line, and bolstered each other with the nostrum 'rain follows the plough' and with the theory that rain was stimulated by newly planted crops and trees. But they had all missed Goyder's point: do not be deceived when good rains come. Within ten years the rains had retreated, and families who had invested everything beyond the frontier were driven back towards the coast by heat and death. Today this dry interior is occupied by large pastoral runs, and dotted with ruined homesteads and ghost towns—the silent follies of that decade of rain.[4]

The calculations made by Goyder mattered because in the 1860s the new democratic parliaments in Victoria, New South Wales and South Australia began to break up many of the old pastoral leases and sell them off, at favourable terms, to small 'selectors'. The politics of selection were radical and democratic. Selection was a blow for 'land justice'. It was designed to smash the monopoly of the squatters and permit poorer folks to set themselves up on modest farms. But country that had been adequate to sustain grazing was often too dry to sustain the thirstier business of small-scale agriculture. The hardship and alienation that many of these selectors faced—toiling on allotments that were too small and too dry to pay their way—would soon become part of the mythology of the great Australian bush.

This victory for melancholy was tempered somewhat by the discovery of gold in eastern Australia in 1851 when a torrent of high-spirited and youthful newcomers overwhelmed the old order of convicts and sheep. Many of these fortune hunters expressed a Wentworth-style optimism in the future of the land. As well they might. The Victorian diggings were in rolling fertile country well supplied with rivers, and the gold rush soon produced a rich vein of nationalist writing and art.

But, away from the goldfields, the voices of pessimism or inertia dominated, producing such images over the next hundred years as:

> A sultry haze broods o'er the silent bush,
> And horse and ox move slow through streaming dust.[5]

Or the melancholy of the plains near Hay:

> Flat to a lowering cloud-dun sky
> The mute, still plains stretch drearily.[6]

Or consider the nihilism of Thomas Heney's 'The Boundary Rider', in which a young stockman rides alone 'in the wilderness', where all 'human effort' is lost in the great 'immensity'. The land is 'empty as heaven and silent, smit with a vast despair'. In the final stanza, we are told that every day he risks his life as the stockman rides through the waterless land:

> Alone in a vast still tomb, cruel and loath to spare,
> Death waits for each sense and slays whilst the doomed
> wretch feels despair.[7]

The melancholy is repeated in Roderic Quinn's 'Noon on the Barrier Ranges'.

> The saltbush steeped in drowsy stillness lies,
> The mulga seems to swoon,
> A hawk hangs poised within the burning skies,
> And it is noon.[8]

These lines are significant, not because they are famous, but because they are not. They are typical and interchangeable descriptions of 'the bush' or 'the outback' that came to stand as a kind of geographical metonym for—as people still say today—'the real Australia'. Despite the ecological diversity of the continent, it was this silent bush, or outback, that, during the second half of the nineteenth century, established itself as the great challenge to the colonial dream and provided the key preoccupations of an emerging literature. Alexander Boyd, a school inspector and enthusiastic geographer in northern Queensland, described the sensation of waking early before his companions. 'A deep silence reigns over the camp,' he wrote. 'I feel a great sense of loneliness and solitude, and for want of anything better to do I begin to soliloquise. My soliloquy ends with inquiry, "What on earth is to be done with this wretched Never-Never country?"'[9]

The colonists now faced a new challenge. They had to make sense of this silence—with all its connotations of timelessness, Aboriginality, death and nothingness.

11

NECRONATIONALISM

When the legend becomes fact, print the legend.

The Man Who Shot Liberty Valance

Dead heroes

The nameless dead inscribed a history on to the silence of the outback. They declared by their tell-tale silence that the land now had a story. I call this ethos *necronationalism*—a nationalism based on death. This is the spirit that shaped the story the writers told about Ludwig Leichhardt, the explorer who in 1841 declared that the 'interior, the unknown core of the continent, is my goal, and I will never give up until I reach it'.[1] Seven years later, he vanished during his attempt to cross the continent from Brisbane to Perth.[2] For decades afterwards, search parties and imaginative writers went in quest of him, in quest, not so much of his bones, as of some revelation about his mystery.[3]

Leichhardt-the-man became lost in Leichhardt-the-myth. He was transfigured by death in the wilderness, sanctified by mystery and elevated to high art as the model for Patrick White's fictional explorer Voss. He had become, as the poet Randolph

Stow put it, one of the 'sand-enshrined lay saints', as if the dead explorer had been inducted into the silent mystery at the heart of Australia. [4]

Leichhardt's trail to oblivion and sainthood was unwittingly followed by two adventurers named Robert O'Hara Burke and William Wills when they crossed the continent from Melbourne to the northern coast in 1860–61 only to die needlessly in the Aboriginal country near Cooper Creek.

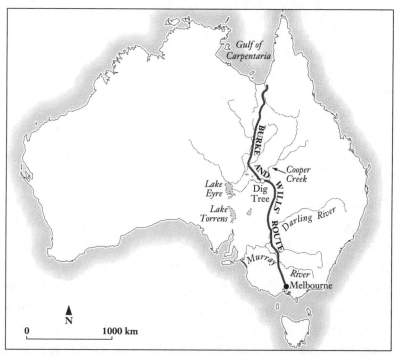

In mid-1861, Burke and Wills died on Cooper Creek having returned from the Gulf of Carpentaria. Despite the folly and waste of the expedition, the Victorian government hailed them as heroes.

By any reasonable measure, their expedition was a debacle. It cost a staggering £57,840 (compared with £3000 for Sturt's final expedition), and resulted in tragic and avoidable deaths. The burgers of Melbourne were determined to claim the expedition as a success: after all it doesn't do to lose a king's ransom on a folly. The government's line was that the duo had accomplished 'the great objective in view of crossing the continent of Australia for the first time'. In 1863, the grieving citizens of Melbourne venerated the two men in a macabre and extravagant show of mourning. It began when 100,000 Melburnians filed through a gloomy, candle-lit room adorned with black drapes, ostrich feathers and heraldic symbols. In the middle of this Arthurian chamber, two glass-topped coffins were placed on an ornate platform so that the citizens could gaze on the mangled bones of the two dead heroes. Wills' skull was missing, as were Burke's hands and feet, apparently eaten by dingos. This display of colonial excess did not, however, meet with universal approval. Melbourne's *Examiner* complained that the spectacle was 'anything but an edifying one'. The *Age* called it 'indescribably disgusting'.[5]

The climax was a funeral procession in which volunteer regiments, plumed horses and carriages paraded along streets lined with 40,000 weeping people. Houses and shops along the route were draped in purple and black. A tale of folly, hubris and misadventure had been rescripted as a patriotic epic in which the two dead leaders were mourned and venerated as fallen heroes of the empire. As the popular historian Alan Moorehead explained a century later, death had raised Burke and Wills 'to another and higher plane, one might even say a state of grace'. That most mystical of Australian historians, Manning Clark, agreed. Wills, he declared, was sanctified by death in the desert: 'A fine son of humanist civilisation, a man with a dream of glory, and a great delight in life, faced the silence with a nobility that transfigured the sandy waste in which he lay into a mausoleum fit for a hero.'[6]

The common view is that Burke and Wills died of thirst somewhere near Cooper Creek, in what amounted to a parallel, timeless dimension. It was a limbo mythologised by Moorehead as 'the ghastly blank', and which Sidney Nolan painted in *The Burke and Wills Expedition* (1948), where the stupefied travellers gaze at us, unseeing, from a void—from a great empty silence.

In her thoroughgoing study of Burke and Wills, the English writer Sarah Murgatroyd was determined to dispel this impression of the Cooper.

> Today, the same hot wind still rustles through the branches of the old coolibah at Depot Camp 65 on the banks of Cooper Creek...The creek still murmurs as it sweeps past the cracked red earth, and the air is filled with the chattering of the parrots and the raucous shrieks of the cockatoos. The Cooper was never a silent place.[7]

As Murgatroyd points out, contrary to the myth, Burke and Wills crossed Australia in an unusually wet season. Their failure to return in time to the base camp at Cooper Creek—the delay that cost them their lives—was caused by an excess of rain. They were detained, not by burning desert sands, but by muddy bogs.[8] But the weather does not suit the myth. If Burke and Wills were to be elevated into legend, then legend required that they die of thirst—in the waterless silence.

Weird melancholy

By the mid-1870s, this necronationalism was a pervasive sentiment in Australia, especially in artistic circles. As he wrestled with this notion, the Melbourne journalist and novelist Marcus Clarke wrote his famous celebration of the 'weird melancholy of Australia'. As a pronouncement about the nature of the country, this manifesto could be challenged, but it could not be ignored. Clarke begins in the mountains, where even the most savage sounds simply reinforce the silence:

The Australian mountain forests are funereal, secret, stern. Their solitude is desolation. They seem to stifle in their black gorges a story of sullen despair. No tender sentiment is nourished in their shade. In other lands the dying year is mourned, the falling leaves drop lightly on his bier. In the Australian forests no leaves fall. The savage winds shout among the rock clefts, from the melancholy gums strips of white bark hang and rustle...From a corner of the silent forest rises a dismal chant, and around a fire, dance natives painted like skeletons. All is fear-inspiring and gloomy.

The country is in thrall to the primal forest, where a solitary traveller is at one with the strangeness and the timelessness.

The lonely horseman, riding between the moonlight and the day, sees vast shadows creeping across the shelterless and silent plains, hears strange noises in the primeval forests, where flourishes a vegetation long dead in other lands, and feels, despite his fortune, that the trim utilitarian civilisation which bred him shrinks into insignificance beside the contemptuous grandeur of forest and ranges coeval with an age in which European scientists have cradled his own race.[9]

This was no retreat. Indeed, it was an affirmation of an ancient principle: it is in stillness, solitude and silence, say the great spiritual teachers, that we discover truth. Clarke was insisting that the solitary individual knew himself only when he experienced the silent and howling vastness of Australia. 'In Australia alone,' he continued, 'is to be found the Grotesque, the Weird, the strange scribblings of Nature learning how to write.' This weird, inarticulate land was coming into being— and in the process it was transforming the migrants into a new kind of people. 'The dweller in the wilderness acknowledges the subtle charm of this fantastic land of monstrosities,' Clarke declared. 'He becomes familiar with the beauty of loneliness.' Clarke was asserting that the colonists had reached a new and perilous relationship to country. They were poised between monstrosity and humanity, between alienation and belonging, between loathing and love.

In some ways, Clarke's forests were not so different from the gloomy woods that Wentworth and his kind were so keen to clear from Sydney Cove. But Clarke did not see himself as an enemy of the forests. He spoke for Australians whose melancholy relationship with the land was now an expression of reverence. At the same time in the USA, voices that spoke of the aesthetic and environmental value of the trees were challenging the triumphalism of the colonial axemen. George Perkins Marsh's crusading *Man and Nature* (1864) issued a resounding plea to Americans for the values and majesty of nature. 'Man is everywhere a disturbing agent,' warned Marsh. 'Wherever he plants his foot, the harmonies of nature are turned to discords.'[10]

In Australia, too, writers were counting the cost of the fallen trees. As early as 1828, the native-born poet Charles Tompson had lamented the destruction of his boyhood woods around Castlereagh, bemoaning 'The rude invasions of the spoiling axe,/ That chased the dryads from th'affrighted glade'. By the 1860s, such views were multiplying. The great German-Australian naturalist Baron Ferdinand von Mueller contrasted 'the magnificence of a dense forest' with the barren expanses left treeless by 'the destructive hand of man'. 'The silent grandeur and solitude of a virgin forest,' he wrote, 'inspires us almost with awe.'[11]

This was not mere talk. In 1866, the government of New South Wales set aside leafy country in the Jenolan Caves district of the Blue Mountains as 'a source of delight and instruction to succeeding generations' and as a lure for tourists from across the world. Thirteen years later, the colony's government followed the example of America's Yellowstone National Park by

establishing the world's second national park in the lush valleys
and forests of Port Hacking, south of Sydney. These were examples that other colonies would soon follow.[12]

A silence that can be heard

But such reserves were in fertile, wooded country—clearly
worth preserving. The colonists' relationships to great 'wastes'
of Australia were more complex. 'The awesome silence of the
Australian bush is one of the first things to impress the obser-
vant traveller,' wrote the novelist David Hennessey in 1896:

> Animated nature near at hand is, of course, never quiet, but
> there are no distant sounds, as in African and Indian jungles.
> The warm dry air, fragrant with the peculiar odour of myriads
> of gum and other eucalyptus trees, is perfectly voiceless; in
> fact, the silence is remarkable, for, except near a water course
> where a current of air is always moving, there is no 'sound of a
> going' in the topmost branches of the trees. The perfect still-
> ness is death-like; as though nature stood around
> compassionating your hardihood in having penetrated into
> those vast monotonous solitudes, where so many thousands
> have died raving mad of thirst and hunger.[13]

The same necronationalist preoccupations infused the
writing of Ernest Favenc, a bushman who spent years in the
saddle searching the inland for rivers and Aboriginal grasslands.
The silence, he explained, was the voice of Australia:

> If there is such a thing as darkness which can be felt, then the
> Australian desert possesses a silence which can be heard, so
> much does it oppress the intruder into these solitudes...Repel-
> lent as this country is, there is a wondrous fascination in it, in
> its strange loneliness and the hidden mysteries it might

contain, that calls to the man who has once known it, as surely as the sea calls to the sailor...A land such as this, with its great loneliness, its dearth of life, and its enshrouding atmosphere of awe and mystery, has a voice of its own, distinctly different from that of the ordinary Australian bush.[14]

A. G. Stephens, a writer and subeditor on the *Bulletin*, believed that the proximity with death stripped Australian bushmen of their sense of self. 'The Universe presses very closely upon a solitary or semi-solitary dweller in the Bush,' wrote Stephens. The bushman loses all sense of his individual humanity, feeling instead that he is but 'an atom in the grand scale of Nature'. True, the bush can sometimes be 'an ecstasy and an inspiration'—when the night stars burn so brightly that you might touch them, or the cool air of the morning is alive with the tang of eucalyptus. But more often, the bush is 'a desolation and a despair'—when the sky is molten brass and the stock are dying by the hundreds. If humanity seems 'puny' in the face of the bush, then it is utterly extinguished 'where the Bush joins hands with her terrible sister the Desert'. And yet, declared Stephens, a man instinctively revolts against this 'submergence of individuality'. Which is why, he said, so many colonists—men and women—write poetry and ballads. A man writes in verse, said Stephens, 'because the creation-act reassures him of his strength' in the face of desolation.[15]

Out where the dead men lie
This region, where time was an enigma and the self was undone, became known as 'the Never-Never'. One theory about the origin of this term comes from a stockman named Frederic Cooper who reported that in the 1840s drovers in northern New South Wales spoke of taking cattle to 'Nievah vahs', which

he believed to be a local Kamilaroi term meaning 'unoccupied land'. This, he said, was later transmuted to 'never nevers'. Although the name came to be identified with the top end of the Northern Territory, the setting for Jeannie Gunn's *We of the Never-Never* (1908), it was commonly used by the 1880s to endow any remote part of the interior with dimensions of emptiness, Aboriginality and a sense of national mystery. This Never-Never nationalism reached its logical, suicidal conclusion in the writing of a young Sydney man named Barcroft Boake. Two decades younger than Favenc, Boake spent his early twenties droving in the pastoral regions that Favenc had helped to wrest from the Aborigines. Boake's youthful desolation is palpable in the one poem for which he is remembered, his gloomy necronationalist classic 'Where the Dead Men Lie' (1891). Here, 'the wastes of the Never-Never' are a bleak wilderness inhabited only by the corpses of failed bushmen. As the poem insists in its dirge refrain, it is the land 'Out where the dead men lie'—a line that still permeates the emotional geography of white Australia.[16]

We can taste this dark brew of nationalism, silence and death as it percolates through the many 'lost child' stories in Australia, notably in Marcus Clarke's own short story 'Pretty Dick' (1869) in which a child dies in a transcendent swoon, lost 'in that awesome scrub, silent and impenetrable, which swallow[s] up its victims noiselessly'. These are not kidnap stories. They are tales of sublime death, in which the land itself takes the children, or else the children surrender themselves to the all-embracing nothingness of the country, leaving their parents to suffer unspeakable anguish.[17]

The menacing force that kills these children also claims Patrick White's Voss. At the end of the novel, Voss's soul mate, the orphan Laura Trevelyan, tells us what the death of the explorer has been about. 'Knowledge was never a matter of geography,' she says. 'Quite the reverse, it overflows all the maps that exist. Perhaps true knowledge only comes of death by torture in the country of the mind.' By then, the novel has entered a kind of delirium: the topography of Australia and the torments of the human soul have become indistinguishable. In death, Voss has achieved his apotheosis by surrendering to a toxic metaphor.[18]

A nationalism that longs for stories of defeat, death and the sacrifice of the young later found its apotheosis in the story of Gallipoli—a tale so sweeping and so tragic, so open to being told as if carnage were a sacred experience, that it has usurped the place of the explorers in the Australian imagination. But Marcus Clarke's weird melancholy and the legend of the child transfigured by death in the silent bush have continued to seduce Australian artists. Joan Lindsay's novel *Picnic at Hanging Rock* (1967) and the iconic film of the book directed by Peter Weir (1975) took necronationalism to new extremes. They tell the wistful tale of a group of dreamy schoolgirls—all bare legs and flowing locks—who go for a walk up the weird, timeless slopes of Hanging Rock. In the key scene, a fat girl named Edith realises that her friends have vanished: '"Miranda," she called..."Miranda!" In the breathless silence her voice seemed to belong to somebody else..."Miranda...!" There was no answering voice. The awful silence closed in and Edith began, quite loudly now, to scream.' There is a hint that her schoolmates have been sexually abused and murdered. But the story lays that ugly possibility aside. They have been chosen, while poor Edith has been rejected. Like Leichhardt, Burke and Wills, Voss, and Pretty Dick, the lost girls have been immortalised by the silent mystery of the land itself.[19]

The era of the explorers had begun—as exploration always begins—in a mood of high optimism that rivers and lakes and fertile plains awaited discovery. The era ended in resignation, melancholy and disappointment—a mood of rejection and defeat, which some artists elevated to a form of spiritual surrender. At least now there was a story to tell—a white man's dreaming to fill the void. As the nationalist writer Vance Palmer put it, the literature of the 1890s was a 'quickening' when 'the dumb continent…began to voice'.[20]

The song of the river

But you cannot water the vegetables with ballads or fill a dam with short stories. Writers might conjure stories out of aridity, death and silence, but the song that was most refreshing was the song of the river. The commonplace European trope of water as chattering, burbling or even singing became the music of salvation in Australia. In Australian poems and stories, rivers are forever bubbling out of the silence, bringing life and song to the lethargy, and time to the timeless land.

The poet Arthur Bayldon heard the birth of a stream as 'She sang her first faint song'. The poet H. E. Boote found a creek 'deep in the hush of the dreaming bush' which 'sings a song, its reeds among,/That thrills my every sense'. Major Mitchell slept beside a river where he enjoyed sweet dreams of discovery brought on by the 'welcome murmur of its rippling waters'. The writer Furnley Maurice heard the silence retreat 'into the shadows' as the 'ripple music' of fresh rain caused 'soaking noises' to fall 'upon the meadows'. The novelist Miles Franklin wrote that her first lullaby was the song of the Jounama River rushing down from the Bogong High Plains to join the Tumut River. And the *Picturesque Atlas of Australasia* (1886) described the headwaters of the Yarra River 'singing' through the upland valleys of tall trees and ferns before it plunged on to the plain below, where it 'bubbles into eddying bays, and babbles on the pebbles'.[21]

Water was not merely a relief from the heat and the silence. It held out the sweet, cool promise that things could be otherwise. In the relentless heat of the Barrier Ranges in central Australia, the poet Roderic Quinn imagined a time when the land was different.

> Here stood tall mountains when the world was young,
>   Their peaks uplifted high;
> Here was the song of many waters sung
>   In days gone by.[22]

So, suppose the water were to return. What then? The nationalism of defeat was (and remains) an enduring tradition in Australia, but it has not been universally endorsed. At the end of the nineteenth century, a new spirit of optimism was stirring, alongside the bush nationalism of the *Bulletin* school, among lesser-known poets, writers of pulp fiction and engineers. The search for water—and the struggle to dispel the geography of silence—was not yet done. The water dreamers were about to come into their own.

12

THE GREAT ARTESIAN BASIN

'What makes the desert beautiful,' said the little prince, 'is that somewhere it hides a well.'

ANTOINE DE SAINT-EXUPÉRY, *THE LITTLE PRINCE*

Groundwater dreaming

Aboriginal Australia is gurgling with wells—each with its own story and cultural authority. In the Simpson Desert, traditional Aborigines maintained an extensive network of wells, including water tunnels up to ten metres in length, which they dug at an angle to reach underground supplies. In the 1920s, elders of the Murgin people in Arnhem Land told a young Californian anthropologist that in their country the spiritual life of each individual flows from a watering place—a well, a lake, a billabong, a river or the sea. Each of these places is linked to a realm of subterranean waters that is the home of the ancient ones who lived in the days when the world was created.[1] By investing their springs and rivers with such life-giving spiritual power, the Murgin are expressing a common human impulse. From the healing waters of Lourdes, to the spring of the goddess Ragnya Devi at Tula Mula in Senegal, to the ancient 'holy wells' of

Britain and Ireland, traditional civilisations are soaked in sacred springs—all honouring an axiom attributed to the Roman philosopher Seneca: 'Where a spring rises or a river flows, there should we build altars and offer sacrifices.'

The industrial revolution, however, produced a new kind of spring—a wonder fashioned, not by gods, but by human ingenuity. In the 1820s, England saw the harvesting of groundwater on an unprecedented scale as drilling rigs, usually operated by a man walking in a circle, opened gushing bores of artesian water. These wonderful discoveries provoked intense speculation, not about the sacred, but about where this water originated. Following a theory first proposed by the Greek philosopher Anaxagoras (500–428 BCE), people in England and Australia commonly held that there was a region within the earth—a great subterranean chamber—filled with pressurised water. According to this view, water from this underground ocean sometimes forced its way to the surface as springs, and it was these springs that were the principal source of all rivers. Enthusiasts imagined that any bore, if sunk deep enough, was certain to liberate an inexhaustible flow of water: you simply had to drill. London's powerful Institution of Civil Engineers, however, was wary of such schemes. 'That the bowels of the Earth contain Springs of Water in abundance there can be no doubt,' the Institution conceded to one English proponent of drilling in 1830; but drilling for subterranean water was a waste of money. The water would percolate to the surface anyway, filling the rivers. As the Institution pointed out, in England there was 'scarcely a city or town of any magnitude but what has some fine river or copious brook in its immediate neighbourhood'.[2]

In thirsty Sydney, where fine rivers and copious brooks were in short supply, the patriotic *Australian* newspaper seized on reports of the new English drilling technique to urge the government to commence immediate drilling in New South Wales to liberate the 'large masses of water, or rather immense rivers rolling through the bosom of the earth'.[3] However, experiments at Homebush produced disappointing results, and, in any case, the search for rivers was a more immediate priority for the government's official surveyors.

In the southern township of Adelaide, the water supply was in peril. The colonists founded their settlement in 1836 on a tree-lined river they called the Torrens and which local Kaurna people knew as Karra Wirra-Parri. During the long, hot summers, the river transformed itself into a string of deep cool waterholes separated by thick reeds, beneath which the water continued to flow. But the settlers stripped the river bare. They cleared the river gums from the banks, and carted away the gravel to make their roads. As the banks eroded, the fish died and the ponds filled with silt. Within a few years, the water was 'scarcely fit to drink', and, in the summer of 1860, the river dried out completely. As the settlers slaked their thirst on tepid beer, their talk turned to groundwater. One member of Adelaide's Philosophical Society 'startled' his learned colleagues when he asserted that beneath South Australia there was 'a vast underground sea heated by underlying volcanoes, causing the springs to pierce the surface of the earth at favourable points'. The language sounds fanciful, but in all probability the speaker had stumbled on the steaming mound springs near Lake Eyre. In any case, the Torrens was ruined and the *South Australian Register* was clear that the time had come to investigate the 'applicability of the artesian principle for securing a permanent supply of water'.[4]

Meanwhile in England, artesian bores now fed several cities including Nottingham, Liverpool, Birkenhead and London, and scientists were fashioning the modern understanding of underlying principles of both the hydrological cycle and of artesian basins. Most significantly, they now recognised that all groundwater originated as rain, and that it was the seepage of this groundwater into rivers that explained why the rivers continued to flow long after the rain stopped falling. This new understanding shaped a scientific paper delivered in 1879 by the luxuriantly bearded Henry Chamberlain Russell, an eminent astronomer and meteorologist based at the Sydney Observatory. According to Russell's statistics, less than 2 per cent of all the rain that fell in the arid country north-east of Bourke ended up in the Darling River. He estimated that another 48 per cent evaporated in the extreme heat. That left 50 per cent unaccounted for. So where was it? To Russell, the answer was obvious. It had seeped into the ground, and was draining through underground channels into the distant waters of the Great Australian Bight—just waiting to be tapped.[5]

Russell's paper caused such a swell of interest that it was reprinted as a small book and later won him credit as the first person to predict that a huge store of artesian water lay beneath inland Australia. But this may be overstating his perspicuity: the groundwater that Russell anticipated does not enter the deep artesian system. That same year, 1879, an intrepid young professor of palaeontology from Adelaide University named Ralph Tate got closer to the mark. Tate travelled to the usually waterless shores of Lake Eyre, in the traditional lands of the Arabunna people in remote South Australia. To the outsider, this can be a fierce inferno of a country. It appears like the surface of an abandoned planet, where a white crust of salt stretches to the horizon, and fossilised beaches are strewn with pebbles and shells washed smooth by prehistoric tides. In the hot, sandy scrub on the western edge of the lake, Tate visited the sacred Arabunna mound springs. The biggest of these mineralised mounds is over two metres high and contains a steaming pond with a surface area of hundreds of square metres.

Hot water from this miniature lake trickles over the edge of the
mound creating a scorching habitat for gnarled crustaceans and
tenacious little plants that grow nowhere else on earth. When
the young scientist saw this water bubbling on to the floor of the
desert, he recognised what it was: artesian water. He could point
to no other source than the rains of tropical Queensland—
falling 1500 kilometres away.[6]

By some measures, the Great Artesian Basin is the largest
artesian supply in the world. Most of it lies deep beneath
Queensland, but it also extends into the Northern Territory,
New South Wales and down into South Australia. A few scientists believe that this water was captured at the beginning of
time, when the world was formed. But most say that this is rainwater that has been accumulating for millions of years in a layer

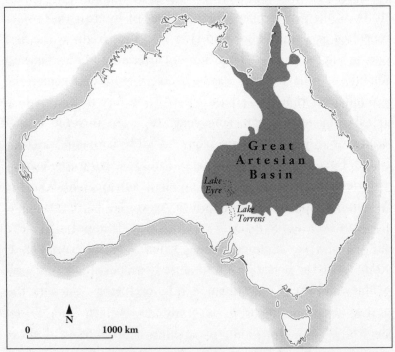

*The world's largest collection of artesian water, the Great Artesian Basin,
lies beneath one-fifth of the continent.*

of earth, an *aquifer*, sandwiched between layers of impervious rock. As Tate surmised, this rainfall enters the basin in Queensland on the inland side of the Great Dividing Range, where the aquifer touches the surface. The highest of these intake beds are over 700 metres above sea level. From here, the water percolates down through the earth—mostly in a south-westerly direction towards Lake Eyre. Tate was standing on the outer edge of the basin where ancient rainwater gushes back into the daylight.[7]

While the professor was making his field notes, the Officer brothers were running cattle on scrubby Aboriginal land 900 kilometres to the east at a place called Killarah, near Bourke. Although they did not know it, the Officers were near the very centre of the Great Artesian Basin. The most notable hydrological feature of their run was an Aboriginal mound spring called Wee Wattah. Before long, the squatters' thirsty cattle had trampled the mound into a muddy slough. But in 1878, the station's enterprising manager David Brown used a mechanical rig to drill five fifty-metre bores close by. Four of these clogged almost immediately. But a year later, the fifth was still producing a steady spout of 58,000 litres per day. Brown sank another bore beside 'an old native spring' where, to his great satisfaction, he released a smaller spout at a depth of less than six metres. Inspired by Brown's success, stockmen on neighbouring Aboriginal country appropriated by the cattle king Samuel McCaughey drilled their own shallow bore and also struck water. This was the very country where, thirty years before, Charles Sturt had found 'no life', writing in despair that 'the stillness of death reigns in its brushes and over its plains'. These were interior wastes, he wrote, 'whose character and soil must change, ere they can be available to any good purpose'. Now the character of this part of the interior *had* changed. There was artesian water beneath the earth.[8]

Since the 1860s, Queensland had been a magnet for the pastoral industry. While the new legislative assemblies in the other eastern colonies attempted to curb the power of the squatters by resuming pastoral runs and auctioning them off to small selectors, Queensland actually increased the legal size of a squatting run and lowered the rent that squatters had to pay. But Queensland squatters could not simply peg out an area of Aboriginal territory. If they failed to occupy and stock the country, then their lease lapsed and another squatter moved in, or else the tenure of the Aborigines lasted a little longer.

The early 1880s were drought years in central Queensland. As many squatters struggled to hold their land, the government took responsibility for water conservation. Beside the dusty stock routes of the outback, government workers laboured to build tanks and dams. In 1882, in the isolated settlement of Winton, government engineers, using American drilling rigs, found groundwater at 100 metres. But the water was insufficient to supply the town, and by 1884 the government was carting in additional supplies. Almost everyone thought of 'water conservation' as the responsibility of the colonial governments, an attitude that prompted the engineer John Wright to castigate the squatters for being so unwilling to invest in their own water engineering.[9]

Simon Fraser (the grandfather of future Australian prime minister Malcolm Fraser) was an exception to this neglect. In 1865, Fraser joined the rush of Victorian graziers and land speculators to develop pastoral runs in Queensland when he joined with 'several other gentlemen' to form the Squatting Investment Company. As the drought of the early 1880s tightened its grip, Fraser's brother-in-law told him about the three-metre-high mound springs on his own run, containing pools of water seven metres across. News of this water, bubbling out of the bowels of the earth, persuaded Fraser that 'an artesian supply might yet be found to spread its benefits over the thirsty pastures of Western Queensland'. He engaged a Canadian well-borer named J. S. Loughead (pronounced Lockheed) to drill in the Cottonbush Paddock on the company's Thurulgoona Station, fifty kilometres from Cunnamulla. Loughead's towering 'Canadian pole tool' could penetrate 600 metres into the earth—about six times deeper than the American drills used by the government.[10]

In the summer of 1886, after weeks of pounding powered by a clanking steam engine, Loughead's drill broke into the main body of water at the unprecedented depth of 512 metres, releasing a roar of 2.1 million litres (the capacity of one Olympic swimming pool) per day. Fraser later claimed this as 'the beginning of the artesian water supply of Australia', telling the story as a triumph of free enterprise over the small-mindedness of government. In fact, Australia's first documented artesian bore was Wee Wattah. But Wee Wattah tapped into an aquifer that was uncharacteristically close to the surface. Fraser's well was typical of the bores that followed. It was ten times deeper than Wee Wattah, and produced forty times more water. Water was now a raw resource—to be drilled, piped and exploited for private profit. As Fraser delighted in pointing out, the government engineer followed his lead by engaging Mr Loughead to drill at Barcaldine the following year. Loughead struck a major flow at 196 metres, and in January 1888 sank a second gusher at Blackall.

Artesian water allowed marginal grazing to extend into thousands of square kilometres of previously hostile country. The flood of squatters into the inland of Queensland, New South Wales and South Australia was now unstoppable. The Queensland pastoral industry boomed, the value of animal exports increasing from £366,000 in 1872 to £859,000 in 1896. That same year, the rapidly expanding wool industry in the colony was worth £1 million.[11] For the Aborigines, the results were devastating. Aridity had been their greatest defence against the white man and his guns. Now water was gushing out of the earth. But the environmental transformation should not be overemphasised. The deserts did not bloom. On the contrary, Aboriginal grasslands and other fragile ecosystems were soon trampled into dust by sheep and cattle. The bores made a few graziers exceedingly rich. But they did not open the country to more intensive settlement nor produce cities in the wilderness. Indeed, in the twentieth century, the pastoral holdings grew fewer and larger, while the surrounding country remained as arid as ever.

Beyond silence

As the colonial period was drawing to a close, the great emptiness at the centre of the continent still haunted the Australian mind. There were several responses to this apparent triumph of silence over colonial ambition. The first—generally represented in the textbooks by the *Bulletin* writer 'Banjo' Paterson—was a cheerful celebration of life in the bush that had no truck with the notion that silence had won any sort of victory at all. Paterson's ballads rattled along with the good humour typified by his classic 'The Man from Snowy River' in which the canter of horses and the cracking of whips 'woke the echoes' in a land that, anyway, was filled with life.[12]

A much darker response, famously typified by Henry Lawson, was to experience the inland for all its humour and folly as a place of alienation. Though Lawson professed an empathy with bushmen as 'the men who made Australia', it was an empathy for their sufferings and strangeness. Lawson's bush was, in his iconic phrase, 'the nurse and tutor of eccentric minds, the home of the weird, and of much that is different from things in other lands'.[13]

In popular memory, Lawson's melancholia and Paterson's triumphalism have been synthesised into that paradox of fear and affection that Australians have identified ever since as 'the bush'. But in the 1890s, Australians' sensibilities were informed by a more complex conversation than this dualism suggests. A third group, many of them lyric poets, embraced the death-like silence as the core spirituality of Australia. This attitude, which I have identified as necronationalism, produced some sweetly melancholic writing, such as this meditation on Australia by the Queensland poet George Essex Evans:

> Her song is silence, unto her
> Its mystery clings
> Silence is the interpreter
> Of deeper things.

But this manoeuvre leads to an imaginative dead end: the poet who declares that his song is 'silence' is soon out of a job. Inevitably, Evans was left longing for change.

> O for sonorous voice and strong
> To change that silence into song,
> To give that melody release,
> Which sleeps in the deep heart of peace
> With folded wings![14]

But there was a fourth response. In his trance poem 'A Vision Out West' (1897), the young Barcroft Boake describes a drover (not unlike himself) alone on a hilltop where 'silence reigns supreme'. As night closes around him, he looks down on to a plain of Mitchell grass which is rippling in the moon-light, and he sees it transform into an ancient 'spectral sea'. Before his eyes, great sea monsters and Asian battleships ride past on a tumultuous surge of history. This heaving pageant gives way to a calm and prosperous future created by the hydro-engineer. It is a paradise where

> Man hath taught Nature how to bring a mantle of perennial
>   green—
> Hewing canals whose banks are fringed by willows bending
>   deeply down
> To water flowing yellow-tinged beneath the moon toward the
>   town—
> Filling from mighty reservoirs, sunk in the hollows of the
>   plain,
> That flood the fields without a pause though Summer should
>   withhold her rain.

The drover has seen the destiny of British Australia: an irrigated utopia rising from the bed of an ancient inland sea.[15]

Boake's appetite for fantasy was fed by his devotion to the stories of the British novelist H. Rider Haggard, notably the empire-wide bestseller *King Solomon's Mines* (1885), an adventure story of lost tribes and derring-do set in Africa. But as Boake revealed in a heartfelt letter to his father, his empathy with Haggard's hero, Allan Quatermain, also contained the seeds of his own destruction. Like the fictional Quatermain, Boake was prey to suicidal despair.[16] It was no melancholic pose. In 1892, the author of 'Where the Dead Men Lie' hanged himself from a she-oak on Folly Point, on Sydney's Middle Harbour. He was twenty-six. The noose that strangled him was fashioned from his own stockwhip. The symbolism could not have been plainer.

These two works by Barcroft Boake—one embracing death, the other longing for time, energy and life—illustrate the choice that faced nationalists at the end of the nineteenth century. To politicians and patriots who longed for a prosperous future, the necronationalist tradition had become intolerable and unhealthy.

The young poet William Gay, writing in the 1890s, vented his frustration that the bold dreams of the explorers had given way to morbid despair: 'How long, O Lord, shall this my country, be/A nation of the dead?' This fixation, he declared, doth 'My country hinder from her destiny'.[17]

Civil engineering, particularly the building of pipelines and great water projects, had become the means by which Europeans sought to bring progress to lands they colonised. In Egypt, the French engineer Ferdinand de Lesseps used forced Egyptian labour to rebuild the Suez Canal (opened in 1869), while engineers completed the first Aswan Dam in 1902. In India, British engineers began expanding the ancient systems of irrigation. In Tunisia in the 1870s, French engineers even planned to flood the Chotts—the great saltpans that run from the Mediterranean into the heart of the Sahara—to create 'an inland sea' covering 6700 square kilometres, around two-thirds the size of Lake Eyre.[18]

In this new imperial era, the engineer had reinvented nature: 'harnessing' it, or setting it free. Indeed artesian water was a life force that only existed because of modern technology. Banjo Paterson, as always, was exuberant. 'We're sick of prayers and Providence,' he wrote in his bumptious 'Song of the Artesian Water' (1896). Drought was no longer to be feared.

> As the drill is plugging downward at a thousand feet of level,
> If the Lord won't send us water, oh, we'll get it from the devil;
> We'll get it from the devil deeper down.

The drill thumps and rams into the earth until, suddenly, the bore hole is spouting water.

> And it's clear away the timber, and it's let the water run:
> How it glimmers in the shadow, how it flashes in the sun!
> By the silent belts of timber, by the miles of blazing plain
> It is bringing hope and comfort to the thirsty land again.

Flowing down, further down;
It is flowing further down.
To the tortured thirsty cattle, bringing gladness in its going;
Through the droughty days of summer it is flowing, ever
flowing—
It is flowing, ever flowing, further down.[19]

That was the promise. Hydro-engineering would triumph over the shortcomings of nature. It would bring life and prosperity to the arid cattle and sheep stations of inland Australia.

As the Sydney poet Clarice G. Crosbie saw in a vision, a land of brown earth and stunted trees was being transformed by the life-giving music of water:

And the fountains' laughter is sweet with singing
As they rise and fall in fantastic play...
A lovely vision of fountains playing—
Fountains playing on a windy day.[20]

Lawson agreed. Tormented and possessed by his ordeals in the drought country around Bourke in 1892 and 1893, he too dreamed of salvation for his native land. To those doubters who believed that 'Australia was done' he retorted, 'We'll lock your rivers, my land, my land' and 'Dig lakes on the furthest run'.[21]

13

DICK HARDWICKE TO THE RESCUE

The European has only been able to become a man through creating
slaves and monsters.

Jean-Paul Sartre, Preface to Fanon's *Wretched of the Earth*

Lemuria

Suppose that beyond the deserts of Australia, artesian water had
allowed a mysterious civilisation to survive for thousands of
years. That was the premise of the Lemurian novels. The
concept of Lemuria (the land of the lemurs) was coined in
Britain in the 1860s, when several leading scientists proposed
that a lost continent once joined India to Madagascar, thereby
explaining biological similarities between the two places,
including the presence of lemurs. A decade later, the German
race-theorist Ernest Haeckel declared in his *History of Creation*
(1876) that this Lemuria was actually the birthplace of the first
primitive humans and that the Australian Aborigines were their
direct descendants.[1]

As the turn of the century approached, a thirst developed in
Europe, Britain and Australia for metaphysical theories about
the past, the future and the supremacy of the white race. At the

same time, some members of the intelligentsia, including the British biologist Alfred Russel Wallace and the visionary Australian politician Alfred Deakin, were persuaded that this new scientific age might explain the mysteries associated with spirits, astral travel and the afterlife.[2] These were no longer the preserve of priests, mystics and gypsies. There was nothing in the cosmos—nor in our darkest imaginings—that might not be susceptible to scientific explanation. In a time of wonders, it was wise to be both sceptical and open-minded in equal measure.

In a culture where a fascination with the paranormal had become respectable, Lemuria and spiritualism were conjoined in a heady mixture by the charismatic Madame Blavatsky, the co-founder of London's Theosophical Society. Blavatsky's principal work was an indigestible two-volume compendium of mystical research called *The Secret Doctrine* (1888), which claimed to be a 'synthesis of science, religion and philosophy'. In it, Blavatsky revealed that the lost continent of Lemuria had once spread, not across the Indian Ocean, but across the Pacific. No longer a continent of cute little mammals, her Lemuria was a land of bestial pre-humans who dominated the earth before the arrival of modern people. Her occult investigations revealed that Lemuria had sunk in a great volcanic cataclysm, leaving a few fragments above the waters. The largest was the land now known as Australia. Even in the current age of modern humans, she wrote, 'there are, or rather still were a few years ago, descendants of these half-animal tribes or races…The world knows them as Tasmanians (now extinct), Australians, Andaman Islanders, etc.'. The 'Australian savages', she went on, are:

> a very low sub-race, begotten originally of animals, of monsters, whose very fossils are now resting miles under the sea floors, their stock has since existed in an environment strongly subjected to the *law of retardation*. Australia is one of

the oldest lands now above the waters, and in the senile decrepitude of old age, its 'virgin soil' notwithstanding. It can produce no new forms, unless helped by new and fresh races, and artificial cultivation and breeding.

In short, Australia could only be redeemed by modern humans (the 'higher intellectual Races') who practised irrigated farming.[3]

Most of the Lemurian novels are permeated by Blavatsky's white supremacist theories. Indeed one of the earliest, written by George Firth Scott, was actually called *The Last Lemurian* (1891). Other books in this genre include J. F. Hogan's *The Lost Explorer* (1890), Carlton Dawe's *The Golden Lake* (1891), J. D. Hennessey's *An Australian Bush Track* (1896), Ernest Favenc's *The Secret of the Australian Desert* (1896), Rosa Praed's *Fugitive Anne* (1902), Alexander MacDonald's *The Lost Explorers* (1906), and William Sylvester Walker's *The Silver Queen* (1908).[4] There are also Lemurian elements in Simpson Newland's *Blood Tracks of the Bush* (1900), Ernest Favenc's *Marooned on Australia* (1905), and Erle Cox's science-fiction story *Out of the Silence* (1925).

In order to imagine a prosperous future for inland Australia, the Lemurian novelists invented a fantastic past—a time before the Aborigines. They evoked a feeling about the land best expressed by the novelist Rosa Praed who, having migrated to England, recalled the Australian bush as a 'primeval survival'. It reminded some people of Atlantis, she wrote, 'But before Atlantis was, old books say that the world had shaped itself into a great and different land, which was Lemuria.'[5]

Unlike the nationalist bush literature of the *Bulletin*, the Lemurian novels were quite explicitly imperial stories. Their heroes were mostly stalwart British Australians with such manly Anglo-Saxon names as Bright Hartley, John Holdfast and—most upright of all—Dick Hardwicke. Like hundreds of similar 'lost world' novels written throughout the empire during this period, notably in Africa, these books were propelled by themes, conventions and storylines established by Rider Haggard's *King Solomon's Mines* and *She* (1885). These hugely popular romances were steeped in imperial values, underpinned by theosophical notions of race and history, and were avidly read in Australia.[6]

But the Lemurian novels were also distinctively Australian stories. Since the earliest years of settlement, there had been speculation about the fantastic countries and peoples awaiting discovery in some remote part of the continent. Convicts imagined that China lay beyond the Blue Mountains. Matthew Flinders wondered if inland Australia might contain 'a superior country' inhabited by 'a different people'. As late as 1854, the Melbourne *Argus* speculated that explorers might yet find 'natives of a different order' from the Aborigines, or 'traces of primaeval civilisation' in some corner of the far north.[7]

Civilisation presupposed water, as the Lemurian writers themselves made clear by the most gung-ho acts of authorial intervention. Their novels were works of water dreaming. In *The Golden Lake*, Dick Hardwicke is standing by an oasis when he expresses the hope that permeates all these books: 'No fear of starving here,' said Dick. 'Ah, what a country this could be if only it had more water.'[8] Likewise, in *The Australian Bush Track*, an Englishman assures his colonial companions that, as in the United States of America, every portion of Australia will one day be settled and cultivated:

> 'This continent contains all the natural conditions necessary
> for the formation of a great and productive country; but they
> need to be manipulated artificially by the intelligence and
> industry of man. You have a splendid land, but in many parts
> no water, except by boring for it.'[9]

The same confidence occurs in Ernest Favenc's *The Secret of the Australian Desert*, where one character informs us that 'if the artesian water is found to extend throughout the interior it will change the whole face of the Australian earth in time…I believe the end of the century will see it settled from east to west throughout.'[10]

These tales of hydraulic civilisations beyond the deserts are assertions of optimism. As Dick Hardwicke says when he discovers the fabulous treasures of a lost race:

> 'Who knows what the people of this island might not have been? Their past is dead. The world shall never know their history, therefore it doubts whether they ever had one, forgetting that if events repeat themselves, as they say they do, what is to-day might have been thousands of years ago…'[11]

As the literary historian John Healy observes, the Lemurian tales 'open up Australia as a continent *in* space and time, as a continent *of* space and time'.[12] If the water dreamers could imagine a civilised past—before the listless Never-Never of the Aborigines—then it was possible to imagine a civilised future.

The set-up for most of the stories is more or less the same. The searing desert has isolated the inhabitants of a fabulous lost world for thousands of years. Now a group of white travellers sets out in search of this ancient civilisation, lured by the promise of gold and treasure. The lost races are usually a people whose civilisation was at its peak long before the arrival of the Aborigines. In *Fugitive Anne*, they are an elegant red-skinned people called the Aca, who have a flair for architecture and sculpture, and a penchant for human sacrifice. Sometimes, as in *An Australian Bush Track* and *The Golden Lake*, the lost races are the remnants of an advanced Aboriginal civilisation, prompting the hero of *The Golden Lake* to reflect that 'the Australian black' was not always a 'demoralised brute'. Heaven only knew what the blacks might have been in those far off times when the 'civilised world was a howling waste'. Sometimes, there are two rival tribes. In *The Secret of the Australian Desert*, one of the lost races is a technologically advanced Aboriginal group; the other is a superior Asiatic people.[13]

But in all cases, the lost tribes are living amid the remnants of customs, occult beliefs and a sophisticated, water-powered technology created in the distant past. Always, the tribe's civilisation has atrophied, degenerating into warfare, superstition or cannibalism, as the heroes of *The Golden Lake* discover to their horror when they witness a frenzied savage ritual.

> The she-fiends had ceased their infernal gyrations only through sheer exhaustion, and were led or dragged back to the circle...In a few moments a strong smell of burning flesh assailed our nostrils.
>
> *'My God, they're cannibals!'*
>
> It was Dick's voice, and he bounded like a rocket from his seat...[14]

Along the way, the white heroes deal with evil witchdoctors, beautiful white women who are captives of the tribe, degenerate half-castes, hidden chambers filled with gold, human sacrifice and volcanoes that erupt in the nick of time to scare off native armies.

Time and the inland sea

The Lemurian novels placed the lost inland sea of Charles Sturt at the heart of the Australian imagination; they reinvented one man's obsession as a national myth. Their ideological effect is to expose the apparent timelessness or silence of inland Australia as an illusion. Thus, at the outset of *The Golden Lake*, Dick's cousin, Archie, senses that spiritual forces are stirring in this wilderness:

Major James Taylor's idealised view of Sydney in 1821.

'The Tank Stream' by J. B. Henderson. By 1852
the stream had become the town drain.

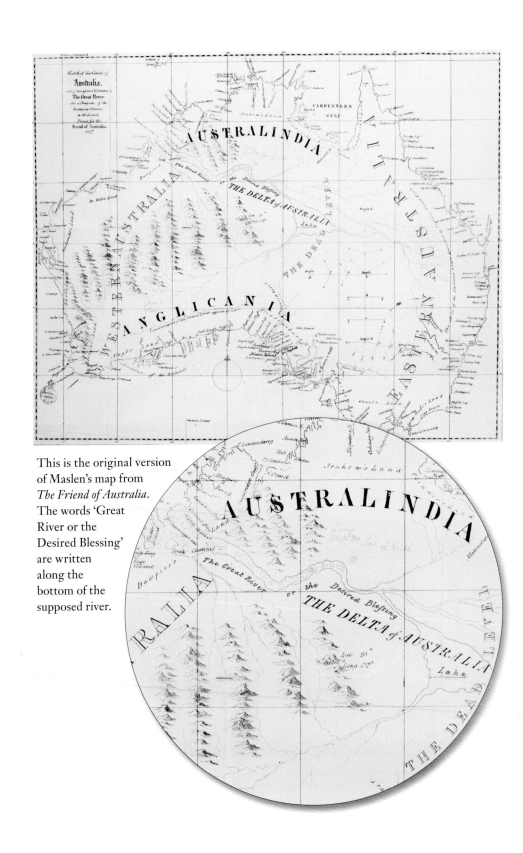

This is the original version of Maslen's map from *The Friend of Australia*. The words 'Great River or the Desired Blessing' are written along the bottom of the supposed river.

Major Mitchell represented the Salvator River
as a noble stream bordered by parkland.

Charles Sturt painted Depot Glen, the sanctuary
that saved the lives of all but one of his party.

PUBLIC FUNERAL AT MELBOURNE OF THE AUSTRALIAN EXPLORERS BURKE AND WILLS.—SEE PAGE 462.

Forty thousand people lined the streets of Melbourne
for the funeral of Burke and Wills.

In Sidney Nolan's painting of Burke and Wills, the stupefied
explorers gaze at us from a great empty silence.

In the Lemurian novel *The Secret of the Australian Desert*, the heroes wipe out the Warlatta tribe.

A Canadian pole tool strikes water in Barcaldine, Queensland, 1893. It is driven by the steam engine with the long chimney at the right-hand side of the photograph.

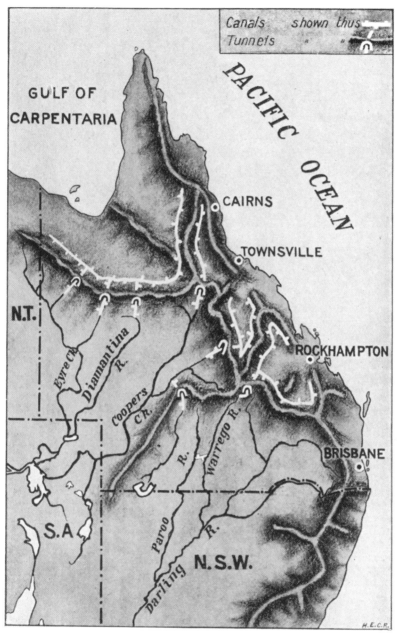

In his plan to transform central Australia, Ion Idriess
proposed that canals would collect water from the rainy
side of the Great Dividing Range. Tunnels would carry
the water into the rivers of the Lake Eyre catchment.

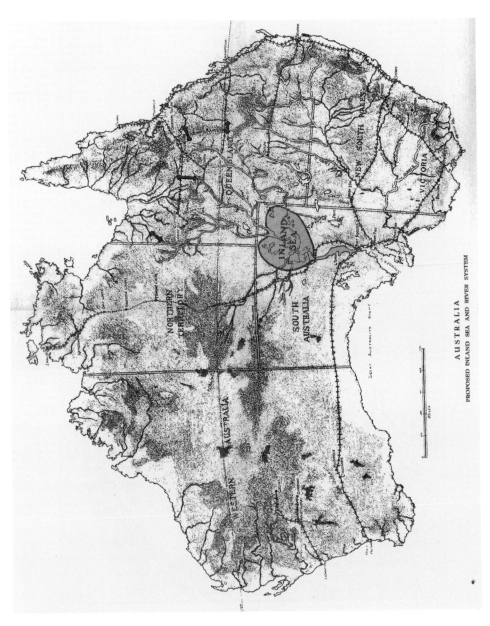

In 1945 L. H. Luscombe proposed a canal linking Spencer Gulf
with Lake Eyre to create a salt-water (heart-shaped) inland sea.

I often wonder if the desert through which the Israelites marched was half so weird and solemn, half so beautiful in its magnificent desolation. For there is a weird and terrific beauty in these vast stretches of loneliness; they seem to bring you nearer to Him, and the fate of all earthly things.

This is still recognisable as the 'weird melancholy' of Marcus Clarke. But as dawn breaks in the wilderness, Archie feels his mind swinging in the tide of history. 'Like a blood-red sea the desert lay before us, weirdly, horribly solemn; a sea over which the ghosts of ships and the ghosts of men might revel for eternity.'[15] This ancient inland sea (which prefigures Barcroft Boake's vision by six years) belongs to an epic age before the Aborigines, when heroes and monsters roamed the earth.

Never before had the inland sea been a preoccupation of writers or artists. It is in the 1890s, the age of irrigation and artesian water, that the inland sea first flows into the Australian imagination as a potent object of desire, drowning the old longing for a great river. By now, it was clear that much of central Australia was occupied by a depressed desert, a void, an absence of nature. But the Lemurian novels held out the possibility that things had not always been thus. They invented a past based on one tantalising fact. At some unimaginably distant time, there really was an inland sea in central Australia. Now, in the era of Victorian engineering, that sea was a blessing that the civil engineer could recreate. With this hope in mind, visions of this ancient inland sea swirled through the pages of the Lemurian novels.

In *The Secret of the Australian Desert*, the sea appears to another three white adventurers (again aided by an Aboriginal tracker). As they battle through the arid scrub, they discover an ancient carving of an anchor on a tree and ask excitedly, 'are we going to reach the much-talked-of inland sea and find a race of sailor men in possession?'

In *An Australian Bush Track*, our heroes have ridden for days through the unforgiving bush until they arrive at a homestead on the shores of a great lake. For Sir Charles Dawson, 'The sight of that cool inland sea, after the long journey through the bush', stirs memories of England. Towards the end of the book, when the adventurers escape from the lost tribe, they find that their getaway is blocked because rain has transformed the surrounding desert into a 'strange, temporary inland sea'.[16]

In *The Golden Lake*, the heroes know they are on the right trail when they discover a cave gleaming with golden sculptures and conclude that they were carved by a superior race of people who once dwelt on the shores of an 'idyllic inland sea'.[17] And when the explorers reach their goal, they find a lost tribe living beside a spectacular inland sea called the 'Golden Lake'. The name equates the nation-building power of water with the transformation that gold had already caused in the eastern colonies, and had just sparked in Western Australia where the novel is set. In *Fugitive Anne*, Praed tells us a dozen times that the arid desert across which her heroes are battling was once an inland sea. On the far side of this vanished sea, a lost civilisation still flourishes.[18]

But before they can restore the inland sea to central Australia, our British adventurers must be tried by ordeal, just as the real-life struggles with the arid inland were testing the colonists themselves. Thus, in *The Golden Lake*, Dick Hardwicke and his companions are assaulted in the desert by poisonous bull ants, by a wild grassfire, by blood-thirsty Aborigines, and by a dust storm that engulfs them 'as though it bore on its dusky wings millions of infernal spirits'.[19] But these threats come and go. The abiding and greatest threat to each of the parties is the lack of water.

The apostle of silence: Ludwig Leichhardt

Deep in the burning wastes of the desert, Dick and his companions are about to die of thirst, when they stumble into a small oasis (a fictional version of Sturt's Depot Glen). They drink deeply and find food. But they realise that death awaits them in the enfolding desert when they see a chilling signature blazed on a tree: 'L.–1849'. They have stepped into the tracks of the lost explorer Ludwig Leichhardt. As our narrator Archie gloomily reflects: 'There was something ghostly in the knowledge that he had trodden that very spot so many years before, and that the sole relic of him was the half-obliterated carving on the tree.'[20]

Leichhardt haunts these stories as if he were the animus of the desert, sacrificed and sanctified by the deadly lack of water that our heroes are determined to overcome. Thus *Fugitive Anne* opens with Anne escaping her violent husband when she flees a coastal steamer ominously named the (misspelt) *Leichardt*. When the heroes of *The Lost Explorer* rescue the elderly Mr Leichhardt himself from the clutches of a lost race, it is as if they have reclaimed an element of the Australian soul from the zone of death and restored it to civilisation. Meanwhile, the heroes of *The Secret of the Australian Desert* discover Murphy, the sole survivor of Leichhardt's party. Lacking the civilised mental armour of the British, Irish Murphy has gone native, degenerating into a Mr Kurtz figure whom the Aborigines revere as Mur-Fee. Another sole survivor of Leichhardt's expedition materialises in Simpson Newland's melodrama, *Blood Tracks of the Bush* (1900). This time-ravaged refugee from the Never-Never is an old man named John Smith—the Australian equivalent of Everyman. On the edge of death, this lost Australian tells our British hero that, thirty years earlier, he and Leichhardt discovered a mountainous pillar erupting with water in the middle of the desert. Smith reveals that there is a cave filled with the artefacts and gold of a 'lost race' at the base of the pillar. That cave is Leichhardt's final resting place. What is more, the water that spouts from the pillar drains away into the earth, feeding the Great Artesian Basin. In this literature of water dreaming, it is this splendidly phallic mound spring, rather than the morbid legend of Leichhardt, that symbolises the essence of the Australia that is coming into being. Leichhardt and Australia are reclaimed from the silence. In this revitalisation of the myth, the 'hum of industry' takes on a new voice—the voice of water gushing from the earth.

Artesian transformations

So it is no accident that when the heroes of *Fugitive Anne* enter the hidden city of the Aca, the first sound they hear is a subterranean river bubbling to the surface. This city lies beneath a great stone tortoise called Aak, which is sacred to the Aca—and which we, as readers, understand is the spiritual legacy of the lost inland sea on whose shores their civilisation once flourished. It is here that our heroine Anne comes face to face with the future. Beyond the tortoise, there is a hidden valley, watered by a river that has 'forced its subterranean way beneath the desert sands' and worked a miracle in the desert.

> It wandered through fields of Indian corn, hemp, flax, and vegetables, and irrigated plantations of cocoa, bananas, palms, and many other tropical products, including a species of aloe, from which they learned later that fibre cloth and a spiritous liquor, similar to Mexican mescal, were obtained...Along the river banks were belts of scrub, and in the clearing nestled wooden homesteads, the dwellings of goatherds and farmers.[21]

This power of groundwater to sustain a civilisation also saturates *The Last Lemurian*, in which a lost tribe worships a

half-man, half-lizard named the Bunyip—the 'last Lemurian'.
The Bunyip lives in a sacred pool in central Australia. This
proto-inland sea is the heart of a network of underground rivers
through which the Bunyip can swim to Aboriginal waterholes
right across the continent. It is beside this pool that our heroes
climb a tree and lie in wait. The moment they see the Bunyip
emerge from the water, they shoot him dead. Soon, an army of
malformed pygmies emerges from a city hidden behind a nearby
cliff and swarm to the pool, where they mourn their slain god.
Our heroes press home their advantage. They destroy the giant
yellow woman who has enslaved these pathetic beings and claim
the lost city's vast store of gold. The ideological point is clear.
The white man has liberated the waters and the wealth of the
continent from the thrall of inertia and superstition. The exploitation of inland Australia is about to start.[22]

White optimism

In his influential book *Writing the Colonial Adventure* (1995),
Robert Dixon argues that the exuberance of the Lemurian
novels actually masks a deep colonial anxiety about race, miscegenation and the perils of going native. For him, these are
stories in which both the Aborigines and the lost races threaten
white Australia's confidence in its own racial superiority and
destiny. My own view is that the anxieties and contradictions
that Dixon detects are a residue from Rider Haggard's *She* and
King Solomon's Mines, the clear models for these stories. But the
fin de siècle clash between imperial triumphalism and self-ques-
tioning that is the key to Haggard's stringency is swept away by
the simple exuberance of the Australian narratives. As the historian Melissa Bellanta observes in a penetrating essay on the
books, the weight of Dixon's postcolonial theory overpowers the
Australian context. Far from being expressions of anxiety, she

writes, the novels in fact affirm an 'optimistic belief in the miraculous'. The writers treat 'the lost race as inspiration for their nationalist endeavour' to use irrigation to create a 'fertile utopia'.[23]

The Lemurian novels belonged to a world of Boy Scouts and of tales about Francis Drake and the Charge of the Light Brigade. They affirmed an uncomplicated optimism about the future of a British Australia, a confidence that death and melancholy could be washed away by irrigation and the exploitation of the Great Artesian Basin. Indeed, the swagger of these novels makes a bold contrast with the anxiety that Europeans could be overpowered by the country that is so evident in Patrick White's *Voss* and that recurs in his *Tree of Man* (1957). We've seen this anxiety too in Nolan's 'Burke and Wills' series. It's a hallmark of his 'Ned Kelly' paintings, where Ned is represented as a black, soulless force in the desert—a figure of both menace and folly. In his epic *A History of Australia*, Manning Clark repeatedly speculates about whether 'civilisation' can ever triumph in a land that seems to render people 'savage'. In the same spirit, the painter Albert Tucker represents white explorers and the Kelly Gang as if the hostile bush has denatured them, transforming them into mute hunks of stone or wood.

The Lemurian novels display no such nihilism. True, an Irishman (or, as in *Fugitive Anne*, a Scandinavian) might be numbed by the land or corrupted by the savagery of its people. But not a British man or woman. Never. They triumph over the silences of the desert and are impervious to the carnal temptations of the lost races. They embody the superiority of the white race as a self-evident truth. Thus, when Dick Hardwicke and his companion finally reach the Golden Lake, they see a muscular native warrior about to ravish a young white woman in a canoe far across the water. Dick raises his rifle, shoots the native dead and rescues the girl. (And, yes, his rifle shot 'breaks the stillness'.)

The grateful girl, whose name is Ada, looks at Dick with 'admiration and awe'. The greatest delight is the colour of her rescuers' skins.

> 'I am white too,' she added, and as if to prove the truth of her words she rolled up her sleeve and showed a beautiful milk-white arm...She looked at Dick and smiled. 'I am very different from the other women of the village,' she said. 'Their faces are black, as black as the sky when there is no moon, when there is no star. I used sometimes to wish I was like them,' she continued; 'but now I have seen you two, I am glad my face is white.'[24]

These are tales of deliverance, of a lost land brought into history and prosperity, of a white race dreaming of triumph over the silence, believing, at last, in an inland sea.

The battle for the waterholes

So what of the Aborigines? In these stories, several of our gold-hunting heroes are travelling with Aboriginal guides who have uncanny tracking and hunting skills. But the white men are always better riders, better rifle-shots and less prone to blood-lust in battle. Furthermore, the novels draw a clear distinction between these 'loyal' Aborigines who have thrown in their lot with the settlers and the troublesome 'wild' Aborigines who are destined to be killed in the white man's quest to gain control of the waterholes and civilise the country.

I suspect that most readers will be startled to learn that such a literature exists in Australia. In many of the colonial African stories that followed the Haggard model, the slaying of natives was commonplace, and the moralities that accompanied such killings were various and complex. Similarly, the battles on the frontier in the USA produced the layered mythologies of the

Wild West. Thanks to story books and movies, Australian children have learned of gunfights and scalpings, of valiant native warriors like Sitting Bull and Crazy Horse, and of 'Indian fighters' such as Daniel Boone and General William Sherman. But, while the conflicts of the American frontier were mythologised, the frontier conflicts in Australia were so completely forgotten that my generation of urban Australians grew up playing 'cowboys and Indians', not 'squatters and Aborigines'.

There were good reasons for this. As we've seen, the dominant mythology of colonisation in Australia represented the Aborigines as the quiescent casualties of white settlement. Indeed, the doctrine of *terra nullius* depended upon this interpretation. If white memory acknowledged that Aborigines resisted the incursions of the graziers, then the fiction that the Aborigines were wandering tribes with no connection to place would begin to unravel.

There was also a quite contrary reason for the lack of wild-west action in Australian stories. Some white Australians had no stomach for it. In fact, the chief justice of New South Wales hanged seven convict stockmen in 1838 for the brutal killing and incineration of twenty-eight Aborigines, mostly women and children, at Myall Creek sheep station in northern New South Wales. The execution of these white men was a startling event. The Myall Creek case demonstrated that in the cities, particularly in government and the judiciary, there was a powerful liberal faction who were incensed by such slaughter. In a dimension of the city–country divide that is rarely acknowledged, there were hard men in the outback who learned to keep their own counsel after Myall Creek—literally on pain of death. In the bush, the slaughter of Aborigines was knowingly referred to as 'dispersal', or acknowledged with a wink.[25] Witness the Queensland bullocky W. H. Corfield who recalled how in the 1870s he once carried a gun to protect himself against

Aboriginal robbers. As it turned out, he was not molested on his journey across the frontier, because, he explained, 'Lieutenant Wheeler with his troopers was at that moment busy among the blacks'. Mr Corfield's tone is jocular. And his meaning is crystal clear.[26]

One of the most murderous of these policemen was the notorious Constable William Willshire, based at Alice Springs in the 1880s. (The conservative commentator Ray Evans calls him a 'criminal sadist'.)[27] Recalling one confrontation, Willshire rejoiced at the way his guns scattered the Aborigines in all directions and challenged the hold of silence over central Australia. His squad's Martini-Henry carbines, he wrote, 'were talking English to the silent majesty of those great eternal rocks'.[28]

The Lemurian novels were part of a wider body of popular literature that tried to dramatise the battle for the waterholes, both as a form of shoot-em-up entertainment, and as a way of reflecting on the moral implications of the bloodshed. The most candid of these books is the South Australian novel *Paving the Way* (1893), a frontier adventure story written by a tough squatter and politician named Simpson Newland. In an abrupt interruption to his own tale of gun fights on the frontier, Simpson drops his narrator's voice to observe that it is difficult to see 'what could have been done to prevent the bloodshed between the squatters and aborigines'.

> It is generally assumed that the blacks were the aggressors. No doubt they were so, by stealing sheep and cattle; but that was in retaliation for their country having previously been taken possession of and in this respect it cannot be disputed that the white man was the aggressor.

Newland was a passionate advocate of inland development. But he wanted urban Australians to understand that the prosperity of the pastoral industry was paid for in Aboriginal blood. It was a highly sensitive revelation. As he explained in a short preface, 'the time has not yet arrived in the life of Australia when the historian or novelist can write with an untrammelled pen'.[29]

Another writer who insisted that his story of frontier violence was 'true to life', was H. K. Bloxham, a long-time mayor of Bourke on the Darling River. In the preface to his novel *On the Fringe of the Never-Never* (1909), Bloxham tells us that each of his characters is recognisable as a pioneer who was well known in the district in the 1870s. They include 'William Gray', a rugged bushman who had already 'administered drastic punishment with rifle and revolver' to Aborigines in the Gulf country. As Gray joins an expedition to search for Aboriginal waterholes around Bourke, he warns his two tenderfoot companions that 'The only way to deal with wild blacks in a new country is to shoot down all the bucks on sight. The gins and piccaninnies can be tamed all right, afterwards.' Gray is vindicated when a horde of Aboriginal warriors attack the three would-be squatters, forcing them to open fire.

> Two—six—ten—fifteen of the rushing savages tossed up their arms and dropped headlong, or sprang into air and fell on their backs. Still the rest of the howling devils flung themselves forward. Five more were laid low. Suddenly, one or two of the survivors seemed to realise that half the attacking party had been killed or disabled.[30]

They surrender—and the brief and bloody battle has been won by the whites. In return for sugar, flour and tobacco, the defeated Aboriginal chief immediately betrays his people and leads the three gunmen to his tribal waterholes. Unlike the troubled Simpson Newland, Bloxham betrays no misgivings. He writes as though the question of who controlled the grasslands and the all-important waterholes—the Aborigine or the white man—could only be determined by violence. That was the hardnosed truth. As Ann McGrath explains in her history of black–white relations in northern Australia, the waterholes were strategic centres—for both settlers and Aborigines. This is where the violence started, she writes. And this phase of the conflict was short-lived: 'some clans fought to the death while others did not even have time to consider retaliation...They were killed because the white men feared their physical danger or resource competition.'[31]

In the Lemurian novels, too, the white man who enters Aboriginal territory does well to carry a gun. In *The Golden Lake*, the wild Aborigines (or 'niggers') are blood-thirsty demons who stand between the heroes and their prize. In the midst of a furious battle, our hero Archie is about to be speared by a terrifying Aboriginal warrior when the redoubtable Dick Hardwicke intervenes:

> Bang!
>
> With a wild cry the savage fell dead upon me. Dick had shot him not a moment too soon.
>
> I disencumbered myself of the objectionable carcase.
>
> 'I am once more your debtor, Dick.'
>
> 'A close shave, old chap...'[32]

There is no parody here. These are British heroes who have taken on a ferocious foe and won. In a similar scene, closely modelled on Rider Haggard, the adventurers in *The Last Lemurian* ambush a party of Aboriginal warriors, shooting them down in a fury of bloodlust which the next day gives way to 'a hideous nightmare' as our hero Dick Halwood (yes, another manly Dick) surveys the bloodied corpses of his victims.[33] It is almost as if Halwood, and not the treacherous Aborigines, is the true victim of the clash.

The Lemurian novel most preoccupied with frontier violence is Rosa Praed's *Fugitive Anne*. It is also the only book in this series to recognise the Aborigines as the white man's moral and intellectual equals. In this tale, the heroine Anne and her Aboriginal companion Kombo flee into the desert to escape a squad of enraged white vigilantes who are bent on avenging the ghastly massacre of Anne's relatives by members of Kombo's own tribe. The story derives from Praed's childhood in central Queensland, where local Yiman tribesmen killed, and some reports say mutilated, seven members of the neighbouring Fraser family and three of their employees. According to Rosa, her father led a squad of uniformed vigilantes who slaughtered somewhere between 150 and 500 Aborigines in reprisal.[34] Keith Windschuttle, a writer who is usually loath to believe that any such slaughter took place, concedes that the pursuers 'needed very little provocation to shoot most they caught'.[35] But the fictional Anne is in no doubt that such Aboriginal attacks were provoked by murderous squatters. 'Was it any wonder,' she asks, 'that afterwards white men were speared from behind gum-trees, and that there were murders on the lonely stations?'[36]

Part of what makes these stories so resonant today is the fact that these tales of frontier violence come from writers who, in the main, were not associated with the left-leaning, republican politics of the *Bulletin*. On the contrary, their enthusiasms were mostly imperialist and capitalist, and placed a premium on daring entrepreneurialism. This tradition lived on in Hudson Fysh, the tough, quietly spoken Anzac who founded Qantas. In 1933, he wrote that the occupation of Australia was 'a continual tale of warfare with the blacks'. Certainly, it was 'disastrous for the inferior race', he conceded. But it was 'in keeping with the history of the world's conquest and colonisation'.[37] Today, some right-wing polemicists deny that much of this bloodshed occurred. It is 'a fabrication', they say. Their predecessors were made of tougher stuff.

The Lemurian novels may have been divided on the morality of killing the natives in the name of possessing the waterholes and civilising the land. But the books spoke with one optimistic voice about the future of Australia. The builder of that future would be the hydro-engineer.

14

CHANGE OF HEART

At length the hardy pioneers
By rock and crag found out the way,
And woke with voices of today
A silence kept for years and years.

<small>Banjo Paterson, 'Song of the Future' (1902)</small>

Waters of empire

The arches of the Pont du Gard stride across the valley of
Remoulin in the south of France. I was just seventeen when I
first swam in the crystal waters of the Gardon River and gazed
up at the graceful stone bridge, as lofty as a cathedral. Anyone
who did not know the origins of this structure might reasonably
suppose it was created by some audacious nineteenth-century
engineer to carry trains high across the ravine. In fact, the Pont
du Gard is the most dramatic section of an aqueduct built two
thousand years ago by the Roman engineer Marcus Vispanus
Agrippa. The system transported water fifty kilometres in a
channel not much wider than a modern bath. You can still
follow it from a spring in the mountain village of Uzès to the
Roman settlement at Nîmes. To ensure the flow of his water,
Agrippa defied the rise and fall of the terrain with a succession
of bridges, trenches and tunnels, achieving an average decline of

just thirty-four centimetres per kilometre. This is the technology that irrigated Roman civilisation.

Today, environmentalists mistrust large-scale engineering projects, chiefly because some of the world's most imposing dams, such as Egypt's Aswan Dam, have inflicted serious damage on their catchments and robbed whole communities of their lands and their livelihoods. But water engineering—whether we are talking about a Roman aqueduct, an Aboriginal well in the Great Sandy Desert, the Hume Weir, or the tanks on the Tank Stream—is an essential act of human settlement and survival. It is also a statement of ownership, power and belonging.

Irrigation

As the nineteenth century drew to its close, most Australians thought of the arid inland as a place where nature was absent. To some, the desert had always been a big bowl of nothing. To others, it was a garden that had been reduced to desert by the rapacious squatters. Just where this great nothingness began was a little hazy. But somewhere out there, beyond the lively 'bush' of Banjo Paterson, beyond the picturesque rural landscapes painted by Eugene von Guérard and Louis Buvelot, or the sun-filled canvases of the emerging Heidelberg School, lay a great void—a land that was empty—because it was dry.

In this arid country, the hydro-engineer was the liberator of nature. Today, we tend to think of engineering as an impost on nature. But in colonial Australia, engineering was the art by which the raw elements of Australia were refashioned into a civilised, natural landscape. As early as the 1830s, Major Mitchell announced that the 'abundant waters' of the Murray River were 'sufficient to irrigate the whole country' (by which he meant the whole region) and looked to the day when its flow might be 'turned into canals' both for irrigation and transport. To him, nature in Australia, even in the fertile zone, was crude and unformed. It lacked the 'art' by which dams, canals, fences, houses, farms and bridges transformed raw country into a harmonious and productive order. He described an Aboriginal grassland in tropical Queensland, for example, as 'still unculti-vated and unoccupied by man', as a 'great reserve' where 'economy, art, and industry might suffice to people it with a peaceful, happy, and contented population'. In essence, Mitchell was aligning himself with the emerging heroes of the Victorian age, the civil engineers. His allies were the great canal builders—the likes of Thomas Telford and Ferdinand de Lesseps. They were remaking the surface of the planet in a mission summed up by the 1828 charter of Britain's Institution of Civil Engineers as '*the art* of directing the great sources of power in nature for the use and convenience of man'.[1]

The scope of engineering to bring order to the land was equally evident to anyone who contemplated floods—especially those inundations that periodically submerged enormous tracts of inland Queensland and then filled the Darling River. If the floods were extensive, then even the Diamantina and the Cooper overflowed. And very occasionally—perhaps once or twice in a lifetime—water surged all the way to Lake Eyre, transforming that salty wasteland into a magical sea teeming with birds and fish. Year by year, the cycle of drought and flood was played out on rivers and creeks throughout the country. In the rainy seasons, water surged down rivers when the farmers did not need it. During the long dry spells, the farms and townships along the river were crying out for water that had long since run out to sea.

In the 1890s, the country was awash with talk of 'conserving' these floodwaters by 'locking up the rivers' with dams and with the promise of an 'apparently unlimited artesian supply' in

Queensland. This was the crescendo of a new song of nationalism. The interior would be 'opened up' and populated. Men of vision would begin 'tapping the undeveloped resources of the land'. As Ernest Favenc declared in the conclusion to his history of Australian exploration, hydro-engineering would overcome the geographical divisions of the colonies, and fulfil 'the desire of every true Australian—a Federated Australia'.[2]

In Victoria, where the search for artesian water had produced disappointing results, the talk was all about irrigation, particularly on the Murray. The enthusiasts included the Anglican Bishop of Melbourne, the spry, pipe-smoking James Moorhouse. In 1882, Bishop Moorhouse was caught in a whirlpool of controversy—a situation he appeared to enjoy tremendously—after he castigated his parishioners who were beseeching the Almighty to bring them rain. 'Don't pray for it,' he told them. 'Dam it.'[3]

One of Victoria's most seductive advocates of irrigation was an amiable Scots water dreamer named Hugh McColl. In 1874, McColl had become the secretary of the Grand Victorian North West Canal Company, which tried, unsuccessfully, to finance the construction of a massive irrigation and transport canal through the heart of the colony's northern sheep country. Now, in a revival of the ideology that informed the selection policies of the 1860s, McColl told the Victorian parliament how state-run irrigation would open channels to radical social reform. Water would transform marginal grazing country into a patchwork of wheat fields, market gardens and orchards heavy with fruit. Irrigation would break the land-monopoly of the squatters by giving poorer citizens the opportunity to run their own farms. Contrary to the modern-day stereotype of engineers, McColl and the hydro-engineers were not prepared to sacrifice the environment to concrete and steel. In fact, in both Australia and the USA, proselytisers for irrigation argued that their water projects would help to repair the damage done to the natural world by decades of exploitation by squatters and ranchers. Irrigation would not merely reinstate the old environment, it would transform a man-made wasteland into a glorious garden where farmers and their families would prosper and grow.[4]

In the Victorian parliament, where the ideological chasm between protectionists and free traders cut across party lines, McColl's dreams of a government-funded utopia aroused some passionate opposition. But the mood in the colony was flowing against free trade. In any case, a key purpose of irrigation was to increase the population through immigration—traditionally a government responsibility.[5] In 1884, the government established a royal commission presided over by the young and charismatic liberal, Alfred Deakin. He was a vitalist—part of a generation of bright young people throughout the west who, at the turn of the century, believed that science gave men the power of life. His famous preoccupation with spiritualism was motivated by a defiant optimism that science could show that life did not end with a person's bodily demise. Irrigation, likewise, promised to reveal the life force that was 'veiled' or 'shrouded' by the melancholy silence of inland Australia. On the political front, irrigation's promise to open the land to small farmers appealed to Deakin's Jeffersonian notions of equality of opportunity, and he wasted no time in setting off to America to investigate the miracle of irrigation in California.

To his delight, Deakin found that American hydro-engineers had transformed deserts with 'the water of life' bringing 'life to the grass and flowers, to the loaded tree, to man and to the city of men whose homesteads and harvests follow its wake'. As the agricultural economist Bruce Davidson has shown, Deakin ignored two critical differences between Australia and America. First, the Californians did not require the huge water storages that would be necessary for irrigation in Australia, where the key objective was to 'drought proof' the dry country.

Secondly, American irrigators depended on Mexican workers to whom they paid starvation wages, a form of exploitation that was both impossible in labour-hungry Australia and unacceptable to Deakin's own egalitarian temperament.[6]

There were, however, other differences between California and Victoria that did have a profound impact on the young liberal. He was repelled by the self-interest of Americans' frontier individualism, especially by the way irrigators engaged their neighbours in acrimonious litigation over riparian rights (property rights in the river water itself). Nor was he impressed by the number of government officials who cheerily declared that they saw irrigation as a private interest and knew little about how it worked.

In 1886, the Victorian economy was booming, and the ladies and gents who strolled under the gaslights of Melbourne's fashionable Collins Street had every reason to be pleased with colonial life. Deakin himself was brimming with ideas and self-confidence as he steered the *Irrigation Act* 1886 (Vic.) through the parliament. In a fundamental break with English and US law, the Act decreed that no private individual could own a river or control the use of its water. Instead, control of rivers was vested in the Crown. The underlying principle was clear. In Australia, water was so precious that individuals should not profit from its control—the prospect of water becoming a private monopoly was unthinkable. Water policy should be decided, not by the strong-arm tactics of the money men as was the case in the (now notorious) 'water wars' of California, but by the democratically elected parliament. The logic of this new liberalism was so appealing that other states introduced similar provisions soon afterwards.[7]

Boom-time Victoria was in love with schemes. And irrigation was scheming on a visionary scale. Anticipating the philosophy that would characterise his prime ministership nearly two decades later, Deakin set up irrigation as a three-way partnership of private enterprise, state authority and community responsibility. At the same time, he supported the Chaffey brothers, two Canadian entrepreneurs who swept into Australia to develop their own 'irrigation colonies' at Mildura and at Renmark in South Australia—just as they had done in California. The government took responsibility for the construction of the most expensive elements of the scheme—the large dams and weirs. The construction of the smaller dams and channels was financed by government loans to local trusts, which also managed the system. The trusts were to repay the loans by a levy on the growers once their farms came into production. The trusts and the Chaffeys' private projects ran in parallel with each other.[8]

The initial results were stunning. Within six years, orchards, vineyards and green pastures were blooming in what had once been dry bush country adjacent to the Murray at Mildura. It was as if the barrier of silence had finally been breached. As Deakin declared when he launched the project, the 'gloomy legends of interior wastes' had been disproved. Charles Sturt had described this region as 'sandy and sterile'. But Deakin would have no such talk. 'The more we learn of our country,' he went on, 'the more we are led to believe that the first fearful impressions of its discoverers will all be falsified.' Sun-blasted wastelands, once shunned 'even by the kangaroo', were now flowing with channels, 'and out of the heart of once withered wastes have burst flowing rills'.[9]

But in the final decade of the century, rampant speculation, which had been driving an economic boom in eastern Victoria, boiled over. As the economy collapsed in a ruin of foreclosures and unemployment, irrigation was exposed as a drain on public money. The trusts were principally operated by the local growers, which put them in the position of having to collect debts from themselves. These moneys were rarely forthcoming. Furthermore, many farmers had treated irrigation merely as a supplementary water supply. They failed to comprehend that irrigation would never be profitable unless they adopted crops that were suitable for more intensive methods of farming. In any case, the channels were often poorly built, storages were pitifully inadequate and the entire dream had been costed on the assumption that the mighty Murray was an unfailing supply of water. A chronic drought from the mid-1890s to 1902—the notorious Federation Drought—exposed this confidence as folly. Groundwater leached into the wretchedly depleted river, sending salinity levels soaring and exposing the Murray as a temperamental and unreliable master. In December 1895, the Chaffeys filed for bankruptcy amid allegations that they were a 'gang of swindlers', a pair of North American 'land boomers' who had shaken down the government and ransacked the scheme for their own private profit. By 1903, Deakin himself was describing irrigation as 'an ideal which had failed'. But it was a judgment Victorians simply refused to accept.[10]

By now, there was a popular thirst for irrigation. This was combined with a growing belief that governments had a moral duty to conserve the precious waters of Australia by building dams. In 1905, the Victorian government yielded to the popular will by bailing out the Mildura scheme. Thereafter irrigation on the Murray became a highly centralised system, quietly subsidised and closely managed by the state.

Pipedreams in the west

Meanwhile in Western Australia, government enterprise was also at work. Here, the Irish-born civil engineer Charles Yelverton O'Connor—known as C. Y.—was transforming the geography of Perth and its hinterland. At the head of the colony's powerful public works department, the dapper and meticulous chief engineer built and ran both the Fremantle Harbour and a growing railway network. The initiator of these titanic projects was Western Australia's first democratically elected premier, a bear of a man named John Forrest—himself a government-trained surveyor and explorer.

Free British settlers had established the settlement of Perth in Noongar country in 1829, but the progress of the colony had been retarded by a lack of pastures and by a drain of population to the gold rushes in the eastern colonies. When prospectors' shovels unearthed gold at Southern Cross near Coolgardie in 1892, Forrest saw the opportunity for his colony to make up lost ground. But the old explorer knew that the gold-seekers were toiling in desperately arid scrub country.[11] Indeed, the want of clean drinking water was soon exacting its toll. Miners lay in hospital tents, dying of typhoid in the dry inland of the colony, while others continued to make the fearful journey in search of their fortunes. In response, O'Connor's men enlarged Aboriginal wells along the route to the goldfields. You can still see the mighty tanks that they quarried at Cunderdin, Kellerberrin, Merredin and Parkers Road, cunningly designed to collect millions of litres of rainwater as it flowed over great, buckled sheets of natural granite. When these tanks did not suffice, the government sent regular trains laden with water thundering into the remote diggings. But even these costly methods were not enough to satisfy the deadly thirst of the miners. The solution was a massive civil engineering project.[12]

In 1896, Forrest introduced a Bill to raise a staggering £2.5 million loan in England to lay a pipe. This was an age of audacious pipelines: the longest to be built in Britain at this time carried water from rural Wales to industrial Birmingham—a distance of 119 kilometres. But O'Connor's proposal was staggering. It would be the longest water-pipe yet constructed anywhere in the world, designed to convey water from Mundaring Weir near Perth uphill to the goldfields. At 530 kilometres, it would more than double the length of the Catskill Aqueduct commenced a decade later to supply New York and promoted ever since by the Americans as 'the world's greatest aqueduct'.[13] As workmen began laying the pipes through the baking interior and erecting great pumping stations in the wilderness, private contractors and free traders attacked the project as a mad waste of money—or more simply because this potentially profitable work was monopolised by O'Connor's own government department. Forrest stood firm. He had already seen speculators build slipshod railways that the government had later to demolish or improve. He would not allow the pipeline to fall into the same greedy hands, declaring in parliament that he was 'opposed to handing over this great enterprise—for it is a great enterprise—to private persons'. To critics of his budget deficit, he insisted that these costly projects—the harbour, the railway and the pipeline—would stimulate the development needed to pay off the loans. They were investments in growth.[14]

In 1901, with the great pipeline two-thirds complete, Forrest resigned as premier to take up a seat in the new federal parliament. With Forrest gone, the free-trade press unleashed itself on O'Connor, accusing him of professional incompetence, exploitation of his workers and corruption. He was a 'crocodile impostor', thundered the *Sunday Times*, guilty of 'reckless extravagant juggling with public funds'. Slander piled upon slander, until the fanatically hardworking O'Connor felt his mind buckle and give way. At dawn on 10 March 1902, he rode to the edge of the ocean at South Beach near Fremantle, removed his dentures, put a revolver in his mouth and blew out his brains.[15]

Less than a year later, Forrest opened the finished pipeline at Coolgardie with a quotation from Isaiah, 'They made a way in the wilderness, and rivers in the desert.' He opened a tap, and water from the coast began to gush into the desert goldfields.[16] What few noticed was the cost. The system's gargantuan steam-powered pumping stations had to be fed day and night with forests of timber—an appetite that destroyed thousands of hectares of woodlands, and set the scene for the dryland salinity that would be gnawing at the country a century later. Though the water was affordable for domestic use, and supported the lucrative gold-mining industry, extensive irrigation here would never be a commercial proposition.[17]

Water dreamers could now point to three monumental examples of how hydro-engineering promised victory over the climate: artesian water in Queensland, irrigation in Victoria, South Australia and New South Wales, and the O'Connor pipeline in the west. The new catchword for Australian patriots was 'optimism'. As the South Australian politician and water dreamer David J. Gordon put it in 1907, 'the future of Australia belongs to the optimists—to men who are prepared to back up their dreams' with investments of money. Like Deakin, he insisted that irrigation would prove that the outward appearance of Australia was an illusion. 'In those vast and silent plains of Central Australia,' he declared, 'in those hungry-looking marshes which flank our rivers, in the ranges which intersect one another throughout the continent, there are inheritances which one day will be the marvel and envy of the world.'[18]

It was an extravagant claim. The new irrigation schemes hugged the banks of the Murray River. They made no impact at all on the vast dry countries that extended beyond the horizon.

These water dreamers, or 'boosters', may have conjured a federated Australia made fertile by irrigation, but no such optimism flooded the great convention that met throughout 1897 and 1898 to hammer out an Australian constitution. Indeed delegates from New South Wales and Victoria, including Deakin, successfully argued that river water should remain a responsibility of the states. The result of these deliberations was section 100 of the Constitution, which provides that the federal government may not interfere with the 'reasonable use' of such water by the states or individuals. It was a decision that laid the ground for conflict between the states and which left the South Australians, who are downstream on the Murray from Victoria and New South Wales, with little constitutional protection. These negotiations took place at the very time the Murray River was pitifully shrivelled by the Federation Drought. When it came down to real-world negotiations, the politicians knew that they were fighting over a scarce resource. [19]

But the depletion of the Murray did not call the practicality of irrigation into question. On the contrary, drought was a great argument *for* irrigation, since irrigation, with its weirs and dams, was seen as a system of 'water conservation'. What is more, these dams would be Australia's bulwarks against Asia.

Terra nullius and the open north

If the Pont du Gard was an expression of Roman power, then the great water schemes imagined by Australians after one hundred years of colonisation were rather more expressions of anxiety. These Australians knew they had not managed to occupy the overwhelming vastness of the continent. Unlike the Romans, they had not established the patchwork of farms, mills, towns and cities that, by their own standards, the occupation of a country entailed. They thought not of a great empire but of a great emptiness. And they feared that the principle of *terra nullius* would be turned against them.

As we've seen, the idea that Aborigines never legally 'occupied' the land was deeply embedded in colonial thinking. But

Australians did not learn to use the term itself until the 1970s, when it was put on the public agenda by the *Gove Land Rights Case* (1971) in which the people of Yirrkala in Arnhem Land challenged a government decision to turn over more than 300 square kilometres of their reserve to a mining company looking for bauxite. A Northern Territory Supreme Court judge held that, although the Aborigines were unquestionably the traditional owners of Yirrkala, he was bound to follow the legal precedent that Australia was *terra nullius* (that is unoccupied) at the time of white settlement, and that, therefore, all the Aboriginal lands were the property of the Crown. This interpretation of the law was overturned in 1992 by the High Court's *Mabo* decision, which recognised the principle of enduring native title.

It is easy now to dismiss the application of *terra nullius* as a cynical and self-serving imperial fiction. Though it was certainly self-serving, it was not necessarily cynical. For the greater part of their history, most white Australians regarded the principle— whatever label they gave it—as a fundamental rule of human affairs. They expected to be judged by it, just as they believed the Aborigines had been judged. By the start of the twentieth century, white Australians knew that they had failed to occupy the centre of the continent, and they regarded the Northern Territory as perilously vacant and 'open' to the eyes of a hungry, resourceful and overpopulated Asia. The South Australian booster David J. Gordon was blunt. 'It is time we recognised,' he declared in 1907, 'that we have no right of possession unless we occupy and use.'[20] As we will see, it was a scruple that lodged itself in the Australian conscience.

The fears of an Asian deluge ran deep, and were not unique to Australia. In the late nineteenth century, much of the Anglo-Saxon world was clutched by panic that an Asian invasion was imminent. In the USA, this fear of the 'Yellow Peril' coursed through the pages of major newspapers, inflamed by such alarmist novels as *The Chinese Invasion* (1873), *Almond Eyed* (1878), and the particularly lurid *A Short and Truthful History of the Taking of California and Oregon by the Chinese in the Year AD 1899* (1882). The anxiety culminated in the *Chinese Exclusion Act* of 1882 which slashed the annual immigration of Chinese to the USA from tens of thousands to nearly zero, anticipating the White Australia Policy by almost twenty years. In Australian fiction, such fears of Asia were played out in a host of texts, typified by C. H. Kirmess's *The Australian Crisis* (1909), the tale of a Japanese army of 6000 men that secretly occupies the Northern Territory and prepares to attack the unsuspecting coastal cities from the centre. Though a squad of heroic bushmen attacks the Japanese under the banner of the 'White Guard', the yellow invader overwhelms them, and then overruns a complacent and unguarded Australia.[21]

This alarm about the 'open north' or 'the vast open spaces'— reinforced as it was by defeatist notions of emptiness, silence and the Never-Never—led to a good deal of self-examination. The all-too-evident prejudices of the White Australia Policy masked a complexity of beliefs and anxieties. By the end of the Victorian era, there were many commentators who believed that the tropics were injurious to the health of 'temperate' Europeans, and were actually more suited to the hot-blooded or 'savage' metabolism of blacks and Asians (a view still widespread in the 1940s). Others warned that Anglo-Saxons had been made soft by the fleshly indulgences of modern cities. Indeed, the US president Theodore Roosevelt warned that the white race was now facing 'race suicide' unless it stiffened its resolve, looked to its own defence and increased its birth rate.[22]

A few, like the liberal reformer Henry Bournes Higgins speaking in 1901, believed that Australians needed to preserve 'the empty north' as the white-man's buffer against Asia. An even smaller number of Australians supported the Bishop of

Capricornia Gilbert White who argued that the government should actually populate the tropics with millions of non-whites. (At least they would be *our* Asians, and not invaders.) He proposed that the tropics be separated from temperate Australia by a 'colour line'—a sort of racial rabbit-proof fence—to ensure that each race remained in its appropriate climatic zone. But most people agreed with Roosevelt when he warned Australia, 'Beware of keeping the far north empty.' Hydro-engineering promised to meet that challenge. What the explorers had failed to find, the engineers would build.[23]

The dead heart

In 1906, an English geologist named J. W. Gregory published a hefty book whose title saddled Australians with a bleak idea. It was called *The Dead Heart of Australia*. Gregory was the professor of geology at the University of Melbourne for just five extremely vigorous years from 1900. The book was based on a substantial field trip that Gregory organised for his students to the region around Lake Eyre. Here they mounted an ambitious survey of the fossils, biology and physical geography and had several encounters with local Aborigines. The publication was, however, most influential for its title. In referring to 'the dead heart' of the continent, Gregory was drawing on a traditional conceit that represents rivers as the veins and arteries of a conti-nent. Australia might be a new-born nation, he was saying, but its heart was dead.

To water dreamers of the Deakin school this was a chilling and repellent image. For them, a patriotic Australian had no choice. There was to be no more swooning over the 'death-like silence'. No more talk of a 'dead heart'. Over the next three decades, water dreamers repeatedly denounced Professor Gregory as a pessimistic Englishman who had slandered the great Australian inland.[24] If these patriots had actually read the book, they would have found that Gregory was a water dreamer himself. True, he described the region around Lake Eyre as an 'abomination of desolation'. But Gregory divined hope in the waters of the Great Artesian Basin. The soil of the region appeared rich, the atmosphere was invigorating and the climate seemed free from malaria and other subtropical diseases. 'Given but water, that country would be as fertile as a garden,' he declared. It would be 'an Eden'.[25]

In those days, Charles Summer's statue of Burke and Wills, unveiled in 1865, stood in Melbourne's Spring Street within sight of Parliament House, where McColl and Deakin had preached the gospel of irrigation. It was as if these two structures now embodied two rival codes of nationalism—as if the melancholy of necronationalism was pitted against the optimism of the hydro-engineers. Their buoyant message appealed to so many Australians precisely because the fears and uncertainties represented by Lake Eyre ran so deep. As the water dreamers knew, for most Australians in the first half of the twentieth century, the centre of Australia was Lake Eyre. The vast, sterile and uninhabitable lake really was lodged in the public imagination as 'the dead heart'. As the writer Noel Norman explained on ABC radio in 1942, it was all that remained of 'the great inland sea that once spread from Queensland nearly to Adelaide'.[26] And so Lake Eyre became the fossil of Sturt's great dream, a symbol of folly and disappointment, and a sullen threat to the future of the nation.

The pervasiveness of this bleak imagery helps to explain why the ties of empire remained strong, even though there were many reasons why Australians might have declared themselves to be a fully-fledged nation. For that majority who dwelt inside the charmed circle of citizenship, this was a modern, vigorous democracy. It had an expanding economy, an opinionated and diverse press, powerful companies, and a feisty trade union movement that was commonly accepted as a legitimate part of the social order. Through a decade of innovative government, largely under Alfred Deakin, Australia had become a 'social laboratory' for a new style of liberal capitalism, in which the state was seen not as the enemy of individual freedom (in the classic formulation of John Stuart Mill) but as the enabler of freedom. Its role was to stimulate industry, defend wage levels, and protect the weak from exploitation, illness and misfortune. At the same time, Australian women (excluding Aboriginal women) had won the right to vote in federal elections in 1902, well ahead of their sisters in the USA (1920) and Britain (1928).

This might seem a robust and distinctive base from which Australians could launch themselves free of Britain. But they did not. When an imperious English travel writer named John Foster Fraser visited in 1909, he was delighted to observe that Australians—for all their distinctive attitudes and social mores—still waved the flag of empire and called Great Britain 'home'.[27] Australia's sense of vulnerability to military attack explains the fervour of the British alliance, but it cannot explain why so many people, born and raised in Australia, still romanticised Britain as the centre of their spiritual and aesthetic lives. After all, Australia is now welded into an alliance with the USA for precisely the same reason: we hope America will spend money and lives on defending an underpopulated Australia. But Australians do not, as a consequence, mistake the USA as home.

There were myriad reasons for this dependency. Cultures forged over centuries in the northern hemisphere were not easily laid aside. The ties of trade, law, race, literature, language and family ran deep. When Christian Australians—Catholic and Protestant—went to their churches, they sang old-world hymns and celebrated the festivals of Christmas and Easter exactly as they or their parents had done at home, even though the cycle of the seasons here was absolutely reversed. Australia was the future for these settlers, but Britain and Ireland were their past. Compared to the stirring romances of England's King Arthur, or Scotland's Robert the Bruce, or the Irish hero Cúchulainn, Australia's history seemed scarcely to exist.

Nevertheless, it was now well over a century since that first convoy had cast its fishing nets on the waters of the Eora people. One key reason why these old-world bonds continued to endure after so long was *water*. Rainy Britain (or rainy Ireland for that matter) was 'a green and pleasant land'. Arid Australia was not. It was hard to belong in a land that could seem so hostile—especially for the urban majority to whom the inland was a largely unknown world.

But there was hope. As Australia embarked on the era of federation, the water dreamers declared that the droughts could be conquered and the floodwaters, particularly the wild, torrential floods of Queensland, could be dammed. The writer James Brunton Stephens had expressed this long-running hope in his famous poem 'The Dominion of Australia'. Written in 1877, it was popularised thirty years later in a landmark anthology compiled by Bertram Stevens and featured in high school textbooks into the 1930s. The poem dramatises the thirst for nationhood as a gathering flood, 'a viewless stream of Common Will'. These waters are being restrained beneath the earth, says the poem, where a 'river waits to bless...our utmost wilderness'. For, rest assured, wise men will conspire with nature, and this water will surge across the country,

> Till round our lessening wastes there glows
> A perfect zone of broadening green—
> Till all our land, Australia Felix called
> Become one Continent-Isle of Emerald.[28]

The implication of the metaphor is clear: nationhood and irrigation are welling in the national psyche as a single, redemptive force. The brown of the Australian inland will be replaced by green—the colour of life and nationhood.

These were not risible aspirations. They were the expression of a people yearning to belong. It was as if the moral worth of the country was crying out to be proved. As the visiting John Foster Fraser put it, the advocates of irrigation were declaring that 'two-thirds of the continent' were 'capable of good'.[29]

This capacity for salvation was all a question of scale. The recovery of Victoria's faltering irrigation scheme was aided by the readiness of the government to subsidise this form of agriculture by absorbing the massive cost of building and maintaining dams and weirs. It owed a great deal to the skills and idealism of an American water bureaucrat named Elwood Mead who was the foundation chairman of Victoria's Rivers and Water Supply Commission from November 1907 until 1915. Mead reorganised irrigation as a centralised system, closely administered and supervised by government and worked by farmers running independent businesses. His key achievement was to transfer water from low-yield to high-yield crops. Not only would an irrigated ten-acre allotment of orange trees bring a larger return than 300 acres of wheat or pastures of native grass, he argued, irrigation would multiply the population that could be supported on the land by 'ten to a hundred times'. It was 'a population which would live and prosper freed from the vicissitudes and losses that come with recurring years of drought'.[30]

This was all very well. But he and Deakin and the other boosters spoke as if most of the continent could be transformed by this technology, when, in reality, the irrigation schemes were confined to their own river catchments.

The Federation Drought had brought terrible suffering to settlers on the Murrumbidgee River in New South Wales,

motivating that state's government to establish the extensive
and ingenious Murrumbidgee Irrigation Area around Griffith
and Yanco. Opened in 1912, it relied on the large Burrinjuck
Dam upstream near Yass, where waters descending from the
Snowy Mountains were stored and then released during the dry
season. To the prolific children's author Ethel Turner, the
scheme's intricate network of dams and channels brought 'the
poetry of engineering' to the 'lonely stillness' of the Riverina.
'Rivers are not things that should come and go with the seasons,'
she wrote. In Australia, of all places, they should flow all year
round, filling the land 'with fatness and with beauty'. 'Here now
there rolled an inland sea,' she declared, 'a new Nile flowing
through thirsty land.' Now, at last, the river had 'a song'.[31]

Ethel Turner could not guess at the future environmental
costs of irrigation, because, like everyone else, she thought of
the river as little more than a channel of water. The new weirs
raised the level of the rivers, as they were intended to do. But
much of this water was seeping into the adjoining soil—where
deposits of salt, laid down by ancient seas, had been locked for
thousands of years. This seepage caused the level of the saline
groundwater to rise, silently accumulating the toxic salts that
would poison the soil and threaten the very life of the river a
century later. Today, this creeping menace is difficult to repel. If
engineers were to remove the weirs on the Murrumbidgee and
the Murray and restore each river to its natural levels, this would
merely increase the inflow of salty groundwater, making the
problem worse.[32] But this, and a catalogue of other problems
created by the irrigation system, lay in the future. As the new
federation took shape, the boosters' appeal to nationalist Australians was exhilarating. They were laying claim to country. They
were making it sing.

At the same time, the geography of silence was as deeply
entrenched in the Australian imagination as ever, but its

expressions were becoming more diverse. To Richard Mahony, the hero of Henry Handel Richardson's novel *Australia Felix* (1917), there was still 'something sinister in the dead stillness of the melancholy bush; in the harsh, merciless sunlight of the late afternoon'. It was a silence 'so intense that he could almost hear it'. But to the Adelaide poet and musician Nora Kyffin Thomas, the 'silence in the bush' was 'lovelier than song'. To Bishop Ernest Burgmann, recalling his boyhood near Taree in coastal New South Wales, the thick local bush was 'hushed and still', a place of silent wonder. 'You breathe slowly,' he wrote. 'Time stops…Only the soul that is stilled in its presence can hear the music of its song.'[33]

These last two spoke in solitude. They were dissenting voices—and anyway their reveries belonged to bushland close to the coast. It was the fictional Englishman Richard Mahony who expressed the anxiety felt by most Australians. For this urban majority, the remote bush of the inland was still alien and mute—a place that white Australia had failed to possess.

15

AUSTRALIA UNLIMITED

Accuse not Nature: she hath done her part;
Do thou but thine.

Milton, *Paradise Lost*

As World War I drew to its brutal and grief-stricken conclusion, the dream of transforming the bush was as vivid as ever. Even before the slaughter had ended, groups of war-sodden and disoriented ex-soldiers were becoming an unsettling presence in Australian towns and cities. One solution was to enlist these young and often disruptive servicemen in a new patriotic battle—the battle to conquer the 'vast open spaces' of Australia. The resulting Soldier Settlement Schemes turned out to be a cruel swindle. Lonely, undercapitalised men, some alongside their young wives, wrestled to clear and farm small, isolated and ill-watered properties—and watched their meagre earnings eaten up by the debts they had incurred in buying a piece of their county's gratitude.

These schemes were part of a broader determination to increase the population, especially in inland Australia—a policy known as 'closer settlement'. And, once again, it was irrigated

America that provided the hope for what Australia might one day become. The writer who did most to animate this patriotic dream during the interwar years was Edwin Brady, a handsome, doe-eyed journalist with a life-long passion for the socialist cause. Unlike his mate Henry Lawson, Brady was a genial optimist. And, unlike Lawson, he travelled enthusiastically around Australia, taking hundreds of photographs and seeing all around him the potential for agricultural development. In 1918, he published a sumptuous 1000-page tome with a defiant, American-style title: *Australia Unlimited*. It was crammed with photographs and engravings of neat fields and homesteads, sun-baked farmers, flocks of woolly merinos, orchards straining with fruit, bustling rural townships and an inexhaustible supply of water pouring out of bores, surging through irrigation channels and accumulating in mighty dams. *Australia Unlimited* was not just a compendium of achievement. It was a work of prophecy. The booster's bible.

Australians were waging a struggle against 'the last walls of nature', wrote Brady. And they would storm these sullen barricades with an 'army' of immigrants, which in a few generations could raise the population to between 100 and 500 million people—an army defending Australia against the rapacious ambitions of Asia. He preached a gospel of 'unlimited potentialities'. Look at the 'blue silent distances' of the South Australian mallee, he wrote. Thanks to 'a miracle of Australian nature' and 'a miracle of the human mind', water bores had transformed this useless country into a green patchwork of productive farms.[1]

Brady wanted to change the mind-set of Australia and to exorcise the ghosts of necronationalism. Australians, he wrote, were 'the most cheerful and prosperous population in the world', but they were in thrall to 'a brilliant band of writers and artists whose predominant note is gloom'. The explorers like Oxley and Sturt had been 'foolishly wrong'. Only Mitchell, 'an author and inventor' like Brady himself, had glimpsed the potential beneath the stark appearance of the land. Alfred Deakin had already flirted with this core premise of the argument. Now Brady spelled it out. The deserts were an illusion. They were 'a myth'. When the rains came, the 'apparent desert' was revealed for what it actually was—a garden. That was the *real* nature of Australia.[2] As for the 'dead heart', that was a life-denying concept which had to be overcome. Under a pretty photograph of white gums reflected in an outback pool, he placed the sarcastic inscription, *The 'Dead Heart' of Australia*. In reality, he insisted, the core of Australia was 'a Red Heart, destined one day to pulse with life'.[3]

By the 1920s, this profession of faith had become a patriotic truth. The press, the parliaments, the universities resounded with voices clamouring to agree with each other: Australia's five million people were too few to defend this sprawling continent. 'Australia's aim', the prime minister Stanley Melbourne Bruce proclaimed in 1923, 'is to populate her country'. Under the slogan 'Men, Money, Markets', the state and federal govern-ments embarked on a scheme costing tens of millions of pounds to bring 200,000 white European settlers across the seas to Australia by the end of the decade.[4]

But the 'weird, silent timelessness of the bush' was answering back.[5] In 1922, the English writer D. H. Lawrence visited Australia. The bush, he wrote:

> scared him…it was so deathly still. Even the few birds seemed to be swamped in silence. Waiting, waiting—they seemed to be hoarily waiting. And he could not penetrate its secret. He couldn't get at it. Nobody could get at it. What was it waiting for?[6]

Even as Lawrence was writing those words, the urge to triumph over the silence was taking on the fervour of a patriotic crusade. In magazines, the word 'desert' became taboo. As the magazine writer Noel Norman later recalled, if you were feeling particularly reckless, you might attempt to use the word 'plain'. But since that also suggested a lack of vegetation and water, the wary editor was likely to ask 'whether you were not giving a false impression'. The only really acceptable word was 'the bush'—the bush of heroic deeds, Australian pluck and hydro-engineering.[7]

But there was one influential and articulate man who rejected this boosterism as an expensive and dangerous fantasy, and who said that the emperor had no clothes. This unpopular champion was the professor of geography at Sydney University, Griffith Taylor.

Griffith Taylor

Taylor was his own man. Educated at the exclusive Sydney Grammar School, Sydney University and Cambridge, he was a tough adventurer and Antarctic explorer. He was a silvertail, a fierce defender of academic freedom and confident to the point of arrogance in the accuracy of his scientific method. His stock-in-trade was analysing climatic conditions throughout Australia and calculating the country's agricultural and population capacity. By the dramatic use of charts and graphs, he argued that Australia was divided into a number of distinct climatic regions. The productive potential of each of these could be calculated by comparing them to equivalent regions (or 'homo-climes') elsewhere in the world, where urban populations and agriculture had already established the limits imposed by climate and the physical environment. According to Taylor, this sort of analysis showed that the environment of Australia's central arid zone was the equivalent of the Sahara: it was too hot and dry, and the rainfall too erratic, to permit intensive farming or closer settlement. Brazenly defying the patriots' insistence that the deserts were simply an illusion produced by unpatriotic thinking, Taylor insisted—again and again—that the 'Empty Lands' of Australia were 'a burden to the Commonwealth rather than an asset' and that its 'vast potentialities' existed 'only in the mind of the ignorant booster'. His critics, he said, were confusing 'patriotism and rainfall'.[8]

This was seditious talk—as the government of Western Australia made clear in 1921 when it banned his pioneering text-book *A Geography of Australasia* (1914) from the state's high schools and university. The students of Western Australia would hear no talk of 'deserts'—at least not while they were in class.[9]

But Taylor was defiant. In 1923, he gave a virtuoso paper at the annual conference of the Australasian Association for the Advancement of Science, in which he laid out his principles, enunciating a position that has since become known as 'environmental determinism'. He included a map in which central Western Australia was labelled 'Almost Useless'. 'A desert by any other name is just as dry;' he declared, 'and if certain sensitive West-Australians were to call the arid centre of their state a "Garden of Eden" it would not make it easier to develop it.' As for Mr Brady's naive argument that the deserts were a myth, his data related to the 'so-called' Ninety-mile Desert near the Murray mouth. That coastal region had an average *and reliable* rainfall of some 400 millimetres per year, said Taylor, and had no bearing on our understanding of 'the true deserts of Australia'. If his critics denied the existence of Australia's deserts, then they must deny the existence of deserts anywhere in the world.[10]

In 1924, Taylor found himself at the centre of a raging debate. The editor of the *Sydney Morning Herald*, a water dreamer named Brunsdon Fletcher, provided blanket publicity for a visiting explorer of the Canadian Arctic, a darkly

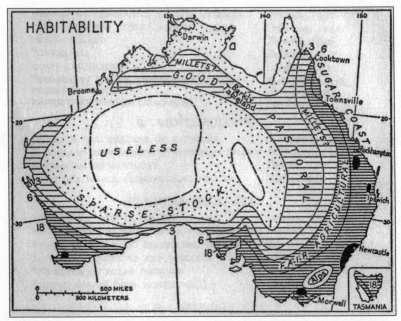

Griffith Taylor's 1923 map: 'A desert by any other name is just as dry,' he declared.

handsome American of Icelandic heritage named Vilhjalmur Stefansson. In a whirl of interviews and lectures, in venues ranging from private clubs to the Sydney Town Hall, Stefansson told enthusiastic audiences that, thanks to technology and American optimism, the American desert had 'vanished'. In fact, he said, it never really existed. It was just a question of attitude.

Brunsdon Fletcher was overjoyed. That was precisely the optimistic spirit of 'Possibilism' the *Sydney Morning Herald* wanted to promote.[11]

Griffith Taylor retorted that irrigation had left the true deserts of America untouched. It had succeeded only in river country comparable to Mildura and to the more recent irrigation schemes on the Murrumbidgee River in New South Wales. That was Taylor's enduring insight about irrigation. It would work alongside rivers. But it was a waste of water and money to pump water out of its catchment into the distant deserts. Taylor was not an opponent of closer settlement, but he insisted that it should be concentrated in the fertile country where agriculture was certain to succeed.[12]

Forget Brady's dream of several hundred million people. Using US figures linking rainfall levels to population, Taylor calculated that Australia's population would grow from the current 3 million to a sober 20 million around the year 2000, with the saturation capacity of the continent being around 60 million.[13] (His prediction for 2000 was spot on—and his 60 million now looks decidedly optimistic.) As for the threat of an invasion from the north, Asia held no fears for Professor Taylor. Today, his sweeping theories about the inherent characteristics of 'racial types' sound like the outmoded prejudices of his age (he tells us, for example, that the Aboriginal 'girl, when trained, has been found to be as useful as many of the Negro women in the USA'.) But, as it happens, he thought that Asians were sophisticated and inventive, and declared that the sooner Australians intermarried with them the better. In White Australia racial purity was a moral absolute and the tabloid press enveloped him to a righteous frenzy of ridicule: he was advocating miscegenation.[14]

The pastoral industry, however, sided with Taylor. After all, his message was that the inland should be left to the squatters, who had already tested the potential of the arid country to its limits. On the other side, Harry Nelson, a Labor member of the House of Representatives, who had led workers in industrial struggles against the cattle kings of the Northern Territory, denounced Taylor's 'alleged desert' as a lie perpetuated by the forces of privilege to keep small farmers off the land. (Taylor never forgot this attack. He noted gleefully in his autobiography that a year later Harry Nelson got himself lost in the 'alleged desert' while riding a motorbike from Alice Springs to Barrow Creek. Nelson became so thirsty that he drank motor oil. When rescuers finally found him, the honourable member was barely conscious. The oil had set in his mouth like resin, and they had to scrape it out before they could pour water down his throat.)[15]

Many of Taylor's pipe-smoking colleagues were appalled by his vulgar forays into the newspapers and magazines. Other scientists were afraid to indicate their support and left him to champion the cause alone. But to the head-kicking populists, his conclusion that two-fifths of the continent could not be settled was tantamount to treason. The equation was clear. An optimist was a patriot. A pessimist was a traitor. Taylor was libelling Australia. By 1926, it was evident that the cautious Senate of the University of Sydney (of which Brunsdon Fletcher was a member) was set to block his career. At the same time, he was being wooed by universities in the USA, where his reputation was growing. In 1928, he accepted a chair at the prestigious University of Chicago. Not for the last time, Australian popu- lists had driven out an original and provocative thinker. As far as Fletcher's *Sydney Morning Herald* was concerned, Australia was blessed to see him go.[16]

Meanwhile, Prime Minister Bruce appointed three commis- sioners to address the 'urgent problem' of Queensland's empty north. 'Only as we discharge our responsibilities as trustees of a vast and rich continent,' he warned the parliament, 'shall we be justified in the opinion of the world in retaining for it our own people.' Nothing less than 'the maintenance of the White Australia Policy' was at stake. But Taylor's warnings were begin- ning to stand up to scrutiny. When the commissioners presented their report in 1927, they warned of the deplorable 'lack of knowledge about the country and its potential', and cautioned that northern Queensland did not provide a basis for 'grandiose settlement schemes'.[17]

As Australians entered the 1930s, other scientists began to speak up. Meteorologist Henry Barkley and several others calculated that the country could support just 30 million people. The Victorian agricultural scientists H. A. Mullett and Professor S. M. Wadham fixed on a figure of 50 million.[18] Among the sceptics was the Bank of New South Wales. Being a bank, it was not motivated by patriotism or angst. It was looking for profit, and warned that the boosters' talk of 'vast empty spaces' and 'vast potentialities' were the catchphrases of the reckless optimist who claimed that places he had never seen were 'invested with mythical fertility and fabulous possibilities'. Growth was only possible in country that was already productive. The boosters simply had not done their figures.[19]

But the experts and scientists were unheeded by the popular press. The newspapers continued to publish extravagant claims about the limitless potential of the inland. *Australia Unlimited* sold throughout the 1930s, buoyed by a flood of patriotic writing about the pioneering future. Writers such as Frank Clune, Brett Hilder, Ion Idriess, Ernestine Hill and George Farwell travelled around Australia, often by car, and regularly published in the popular magazine *Walkabout* as well as producing their own books. The intrepid Ernestine Hill spoke for most of them when she declared in 1937 that 'the allegedly "dead heart of Australia" is vitally alive'. In the inland and the north, a mere ten thousand people were holding a land that would one day make room for 50 million. For her, the inland was no longer silent. It was crying out 'with all its voices for the love and faith of men'.[20]

On the other side, the objections were starting to multiply. By the 1930s, a more sophisticated appreciation of the inland was popularised by a mammal biologist named Hedley Finlayson. In the early 1930s, Finlayson travelled extensively (usually at his own expense) through the hot country of central Australia, photographing and collecting native mammals such as numbats, quolls and burrowing bettongs for the South

Australian Museum. It was a job he performed against the odds: he had lost an eye, his left hand and part of his right hand when experimenting with explosives as a chemistry student. In his bestseller, *The Red Centre: Man and Beast in the Heart of Australia* (1935), Finlayson shared his great knowledge of the animals and plants of the Simpson Desert and of the Luritdja people who were the traditional owners of that country. His message was that the whole region was facing destruction before city people had any notion of what was being lost under the hoofs of their sheep and cattle. It was, he said, a region under 'attack' in a 'campaign of settlement' waged by pastoralists, farmers and miners. This was no dead heart, he insisted. It was no desert, no lifeless void. The book was a new kind of environmental writing in Australia. It was also a plea for the rights of the Luritdja Aborigines, whom he represented as a cultured, skilful and altruistic people whose hospitality to the whites had been repaid by the sacking of their country and the ruin of their lives. Unfortunately, Finlayson's illustrations were his own grubby black and white photographs. These undermined one of his most heartfelt notions. For he was also, as Roslynn Haynes points out, the first outback writer to celebrate the brilliant colours of the inland. The soil of this country was a rich and vivid red. It was the glorious 'Red Centre'.[21]

Most of Australia's seven million people lived in a few coastal cities. Most never expected to see the great inland of the continent. But even city people knew and loved particular 'natural' locations—the fern gullies of the Dandenongs near Melbourne, the scenic Blue Mountains near Sydney, or sunny Rottnest Island off the coast near Perth. They treasured secret picnic spots, family swimming holes, winter ski slopes and the farms of country cousins, all of which, in this age of the railway and the motor car, were within range of the cities.[22]

In 1908, this deepening sense of belonging was boldly

and tenderly expressed by a young woman named Dorothea Mackellar. Feeling homesick during a trip to England, Mackellar wrote a patriotic love poem called 'Core of My Heart', which most Australians know today as 'I Love a Sunburnt Country'. The poem was published in the London *Spectator* and was soon appearing in newspapers across Australia. The joyful way in which the verses range across country and climates—from drought to flooding rains—signals a new delight in getting to know the country in its great variety. Mackellar's poem rapidly became a national favourite: it had named a sentimental pleasure in country that the settler population was starting to share. In their book *My Australia* (1939), the writers Marjorie Barnard and Flora Eldershaw revelled in this same variety, joyfully describing one country after another as if they were swooping across the continent: the choked rainforests of Cape York; the mangroves of the tropical coasts; the 'lusty' pastoral country of Queensland's Northern Rivers; 'the big dreariness of Botany Bay'; and the irrigated glories of the Riverina, a country of undulating forms like 'the notes in music'.[23]

But newspapers and magazines still insisted that the arid country was the 'real Australia', and used the term 'bush' to stand for a vast, generalised Australian landscape. In its heroic mode, the bush suggested a place of gum trees, kangaroos and sheep—a pioneering land that nurtured the tough, honest values associated with outdoor life and simple, rugged toil. For all its patriotic trappings, this idea of the bush imposed a great sameness on the country—as though the wiry tea-tree that clung to the windswept coast of southern Victoria were no different from the dripping rainforests of Kangaroo Valley in New South Wales or the eucalypts and acacias that crowned the spectacular gorges of the Kimberley coastline. This same bush could also become a place of menace: a savage, indifferent country that swallowed up lost children, that raged with mighty bushfires and that, in the searing heat of summer, was drab, lifeless and forbidding.

The bush blurred with other terms, such as 'outback', 'centre' and 'desert'. They too could be the location for pioneering stories, but they overwhelmingly suggested hot, empty country—the country 'out where the dead men lie'. Other expressions such as 'the outside country', 'the Never-Never' and 'the back o' Bourke' simply reinforced the impression that a great deal of Australia was an elusive 'middle of nowhere'. Top Enders had a keen sense of 'the tropics'—but, to people who lived elsewhere, how the tropics related to the deserts of northern Australia was all very unclear. As ever, urban Australians seemed unsure whether they should feel patriotic about the outback, amused by its folly, or simply appalled by this vast and undifferentiated 'bush'.

The patriotic optimism of the boosters was now open to debate. The *Walkabout* writer William Hatfield and the traveller Cecil Madigan each warned that the inland was too fragile or too hostile for closer settlement. By the time Madigan was appointed to a lectureship in geology at Adelaide University, at the age of thirty-three, he had been a Rhodes Scholar, explored the Antarctic with Mawson, been wounded in the Great War and worked as a geologist in the deserts of Sudan. He was not a man who could be accused of defeatism or lacking grit when he scorned proposals to flood Lake Eyre. Madigan travelled into that arid furnace by camel, and saw 'not a living thing'. As night settled, he wrote, the fossilised lake was 'enveloped by silence'. He recalled that when he was labouring through the frozen wastes of the Antarctic the silence of the ice and snow had seemed 'natural'. But here, in the lifeless heat, 'the silence could be felt', and it filled him with an uncanny sense of 'depression and fear'. To imagine that the vast deadness of Lake Eyre could be transformed into pastoral country was 'a pathetic fallacy'. Truly, this was 'the dead heart'.[24]

By the outbreak of World War II, the public conversation was awash with solutions to, and theories about, the threat of the empty spaces. In *Australia's Empty Spaces* (1938), a civil engineer named Sydney Upton condescendingly advised Australians to invest in the fertile regions and to abandon all hope of settling the arid interior. Writing in the University of British Columbia's journal *Pacific Affairs* in 1943, the Australian diplomat Howard Daniel thought that Australians had at last woken up to the folly of the 'hare-brained' schemes to populate their 'empty spaces' with the excess millions of Britain and Europe.[25]

But the boosters were not done. In 1944, Frank Clune published his popular book *The Red Heart*, reinforcing Ted Brady's claim that the 'dead heart' was actually 'the red heart, destined one day to pulsate with life'. Furthermore, Clune appropriated Finlayson's revelations that the so-called deserts were filled with life—not as an argument for ecological sensitivity, but as a sign of the region's potential for development. When the Japanese armed forces threatened Australia, the cry of 'populate or perish' seemed vindicated, and the outpouring of patriotic outrage against the notion of the 'dead heart' took on a new urgency.

Once again, it was an American example that spurred the boosters on—the titanic irrigation and hydro-electric project built by workers during the Great Depression and administered by the Tennessee Valley Authority. When it was completed in 1935, its triumphal Hoover Dam was the largest concrete structure on the planet. The great mass of water it contained was named Lake Mead, after Elwood Mead, who had returned to the USA where he had overseen construction of the dam. There was no talk of 'environmental determinism' here. This was civil engineering on a Herculean scale.

Flooding Lake Eyre

On any map of the physical geography of Australia, Lake Eyre is a tantalising feature. The vast lake is the meeting point of a great fan of rivers whose catchment covers one-fifth of the continent. If our language were better adapted to the country, we would describe the place as a *lake* only when it contains water, and discover some other name for those decades when it remains dry. But the water dreamers saw it differently. Since this *is* a lake, they said, it *ought* to contain water. To the dreamers, it was as if nature had provided a great system of waterways and storage, and was taunting us to complete the plan. Whenever the rivers of north Queensland burst their banks and flooded the surrounding countryside, the same thought recurred, and still does: this water was running to waste—if only we could save that water for later use.

In the 1930s, the water dreamer Ion Idriess began promoting this idea in his books and press articles, particularly in a series for the Sydney *Sun* in 1936. Idriess was convinced that an expansionary and militaristic Japan posed a deadly threat to an empty, under-developed Australia. He drew these concerns together in *The Great Boomerang* (1941), a book that he offered to his fellow Australians, 'not as an engineer, but merely as a dreamer with a Plan'.[26]

Idriess was a kindly man who spoke with a gentle Australian drawl. His credentials as an Australian patriot were impeccable: he was an Anzac who had been wounded at Gallipoli. It is difficult to overstate his popularity between the 1930s and the 1950s. He taught thousands of Australians their history, set out in over fifty books on such nationalistic topics as Australian battles, pearling, prospecting, Aboriginal trackers, and inland pioneers such as Sidney Kidman, Rev. John Flynn and the legendary prospector Harold Lasseter. Idriess was heir to the bush ethos of the *Bulletin*. He shared its code of masculine nationalism and its paradoxical mixture of affection and loathing for the bush, calling 'the deserts of the Kimberley', for example, 'a strange and hateful country'. His scheme to flood 'the dead heart' was all the more persuasive because he was able to synthesise two conflicting views of Australia. Unlike Brady, Idriess never denied that the inland was a desert. 'Truly', he wrote, 'the actual heart of it is dead'.[27]

Many of Idriess's books, including *The Great Boomerang*, are haunted by lonely bushmen who have died of thirst. 'The silence of the Dead Heart is an eerie silence,' he writes. 'Camped there with a silent black boy I have listened and wondered if the ghosts of the men who lie there really walk its sands again.' These, he tells us, are men who died with the words 'water is life' ringing in their ears. That was the choice. Silence or life. Death or the musical hum of water:

> When the rain comes, the river sings, hums contentedly like a purring cat, to rise in song as tributary after tributary pours in water, to roar away to majestic life. And the birds fly ahead, whistling, honking, bearing the magic news: 'The water is coming.'[28]

Idriess gave a new dimension to the project of Australia Unlimited not by proposing *a series* of irrigation projects as Brady had done, but by presenting a single monolithic scheme to re-engineer the hydrology of eastern Australia, which he called, rather grandly, 'the Plan'.

His proposal was to dam Queensland's coastal rivers and capture other runoff, particularly during floods, from channels on the seaward side of the Great Dividing Range. This water would be conveyed to the dry inland side of the Range by tunnels and released into the riverbeds that flowed toward Lake Eyre, a region to which he referred, in the US style, as 'the great lakes system'. All the water that 'ran to waste' in the wet seasons would be turned back 'into the Dead Heart'. To his eye, it was obvious that there was plenty of water to bring life to the desert, and he was dismissive of geographers who produced figures to prove otherwise.

> I leave it to your imagination. We have the majority of the rivers and the countless creeks of the Queensland coast to work upon, in the heaviest rainfall area in Australia. Every year those floods pour into the Pacific in the east, into the Gulf of Carpentaria in the north. Imagine that wealth of wasted water turned inland! Those two floods of wasted water every wet season would wash away any figures.[29]

Like his predecessors, Idriess believed that his proposals were not an artificial intervention, but that they were 'in accordance with natural laws'. The hydro-engineer had only to set the process in motion by conveying water from the eastern to the western side of the Great Dividing Range. 'Nature will attend to the rest; for she dug the channels long ago; she will carry that water right down through Queensland, then through South Australia almost to the coast.'[30]

The publication of *The Great Boomerang* coincided with the announcement of an almost identical proposal by the civil engineer John Bradfield. He too advocated turning back the Queensland rivers, notably the voluminous Tully River, but he also had plans to transform a score of depressions in the deserts and hollows in the ranges into dams—some of them, by his own assessment, 'immense'.[31]

Like Idriess, Bradfield was well credentialled as an Australian myth maker: he was the engineer who drew the original plans for the Sydney Harbour Bridge and oversaw its construction. He first proposed his hydro scheme to the Queensland premier, Forgan Smith, in 1938. Though Forgan Smith baulked at the cost, the outbreak of World War II gave Bradfield new impetus, and he launched an expanded version of his project. In October 1941, as the Menzies government was swept from power still clinging to the hope that Britain was Australia's military protector, Bradfield declared that Australia needed to stand on its own two feet. It should become independent of London and do what was necessary to 'develop, populate and defend itself'.[32] The former Queensland cricketer Frederick Timbury agreed. In *The Battle for the Inland* (1944), he declared, 'We simply must attract people to Australia'. The country was threatened by 'the teeming hordes of Asia' and could no longer be sure who its allies or its enemies might be in any future war. It was essential, he said, that Australians irrigate the inland in order to attract immigrants 'in large numbers and quickly'.[33]

The terms 'water conservation' and 'harnessing the rivers' were key. Both meant dams. 'Our coastal rivers are unharnessed,' Bradfield declared, 'and in flood time some 20 million horsepower or thereabout are lost, power that could be brought into being by hydro-electric schemes'. When rains deluged the desert, it burst into flower. That was the sign of what was possible. 'Australia's heart is not dead, heavily sandbagged maybe; it needs rejuvenating.'[34]

The Australian film director Ken G. Hall caught the mood in his film *Dad Rudd MP* (1940). This was the last in a series of broad comedies featuring the antics of the half-witted Rudd family as they struggle to make a living in rural Australia. But in this final film, Dad Rudd (played by Bert Bailey) is running for parliament. He has just one policy: to raise the height of the local dam. On election day itself, torrential rains threaten to destroy the dam wall and flood the district. But, urged on by Dad, the locals sandbag the river, defeat the flood and save their farms. In the final patriotic scene, Dad gives a speech straight to camera with the Australian flag flying in the background. This has been a story about nationhood, he tells us. About turning the tide of war. About the kind of 'faith which gives our nation strength'. This association of hydro-engineering with national salvation was not merely an exercise in war-time hyperbole. The surge of patriotism that propelled Dad from country bumpkin to noble dam-builder was a tide that had been coursing through the national psyche since 1788.

Bradfield was determined to put this passion into practice. His articles were overflowing with stupendous figures. His scheme would supply enough water to cover an area of 80 square kilometres to a depth of 20 metres. It would irrigate pasture to support three million sheep. Three million pounds worth of flax could be grown near Rockhampton on an irrigation project that would add 'scores of thousands to the population of the district'. But the most stunning figure was the cost: over £30 million. Bradfield was certain that this expenditure could be recovered in water rates. But the costs made state and federal governments blanch.[35]

When the war ended, more water dreamers joined the chorus. L. H. Luscombe, another Gallipoli veteran, published *Australia Replanned* (1945), a manifesto for enlightened social and urban planning. One of his passions was 'the Construction of an Inland Sea'. Unlike Idriess and Bradfield, he really did want to create Sturt's salt-water sea, proposing that a canal be dug from Spencer Gulf to Lake Eyre, allowing ocean liners to sail into the centre of Australia. His book included the obligatory map, in which the transformed Lake Eyre was shaped like a heart—and coloured green.

But surely, said the doubters, all this water would simply evaporate in the relentless heat. Indeed, said Bradfield and Luscombe, but evaporation was really an asset. The rising vapour would form clouds over the desert and return to the earth as rain 'over and over again'. This perpetual motion machine would transform the climate and 'redeem' the arid wastes of inland Australia. Several critics, including senior scientists at the Bureau of Meteorology, objected that this miraculous theory misunderstood the hydrological cycle. As the arid coastline of Western Australia and the desert surrounding the Dead Sea both demonstrated, evaporated water does not fall straight back to earth as rain.[36]

A government review of the Bradfield scheme by Queensland's foremost hydro-engineer William Nimmo dismissed the proposal as impractical. Bradfield had used an inappropriate German formula in his calculations, causing him to overstate the yield of the rivers by a massive 250 per cent. Nimmo also showed that some of Bradfield's key diversions would not flow by gravity as he had claimed. Furthermore, there was a fundamental principle at stake. Nimmo endorsed the Taylor principle: water should be used to maximise agricultural output in its own catchment. It should not be squandered in the deserts. Though the Bradfield–Idriess scheme attracted patriotic headlines, there was never any danger of it being built.[37]

Meanwhile, other writers were raising the cry: 'develop the north'. From the 1920s, Raphael Cilento, an extreme right-winger who was a prominent army doctor specialising in tropical medicine, had been urging white Australians to assert their supremacy over far north Queensland. Like many medical specialists, he scoffed at the traditional view that the tropics threatened the health of white men and sapped the fertility of their wives. In the 1940s, Cilento and his supporters dreamed of the north thronging with white families, building an economy based on tea, coffee, rubber and a host of other tropical crops.[38]

Today, it is easy to satirise these projects as bombastic and indifferent to economic or environmental costs and to the rights of Aborigines. But in the aftermath of the war and with a communist revolution sweeping through China, Australians had good reason to want to populate the 'empty north'. More than ever, those 'vast open spaces' seemed to be unguarded against the armies of Asia. But, as the agricultural chemist Geoffrey Leeper argued, such fears were scarcely rational. Irrigation would make the land *more* tempting to an invader, not less. Far from being an inducement, the forests of the north and the sprawling deserts of the interior presented formidable barriers to any would-be enemy. Until the Chinese turned the Great Gobi Desert into paradise, there was no chance they would invade inland Australia.[39]

Even in the face of such compelling arguments, the water dreamers would not be silenced. Australians would not own their country until they had occupied it. And that meant taking control of its water.[40]

The Snowy

In 1968, as a new Asian war raged in Vietnam, I travelled by bus along with other boys from my school to the Snowy Mountains Scheme in the high country of southern New South Wales. When we arrived, we discovered that the scheme was buzzing with schoolchildren, all equipped with charts, pamphlets and books prepared by the Snowy Mountains Authority. In the age of the astronauts, we young Australians were confronted by modern technology on a monumental scale. The dam wall of Lake Eucumbene, the largest of the scheme's sixteen major reservoirs, cradled an ocean of icy water high in the mountains. From these heights, pipelines plunged down rocky slopes, forcing torrents of water into shiny hydro-electric stations, most of them deep below the ground. In subterranean chambers, turbines stood humming in rows like the components of a giant space station. Compared to the wheezing coal-powered stations of Victoria's La Trobe Valley, which we had visited and sketched the previous year, these sleek generators were purring with the promise of a clean, electric future. When the water had done its work here, we were told, it was piped inland to supplement irrigation on the Murrumbidgee and the Murray Rivers. In the centre of the scheme huddled the alpine town of Cooma. Here, in a concreted civic square, a forest of flagpoles clattered with the flags of over thirty nations, a tribute to the 70,000 migrants who had worked on the project since 1949. Frankly, the scale and audacity of the scheme were thrilling.[41]

As it was being built, the Snowy Scheme had its critics. It would be too costly. It would never work. It would trample on the constitutional powers of the states. But the chorus of support was overwhelming. For the left-leaning architects of Postwar Reconstruction, the scheme was integral to their sweeping plan for security, prosperity and an end to the division of society into winners and losers. As the Labor prime minister Ben Chifley put it, the Snowy Scheme was 'a plan for the nation'. But this was a scheme that transcended ideologies: to Chifley's successor, the Liberal Robert Menzies, the scheme was a victory over parochialism. It taught 'everybody in Australia to think in a big way, to be thankful for big things, to be proud of big enterprises'.[42]

At the same time, water dreamers in north-western Australia were promoting the idea of a hydro-electric and irrigation scheme on the Ord River, a mammoth project that was completed in 1971. One prominent advocate of the scheme was the well-connected journalist Henrietta Drake-Brockman, who drew on the most enduring trope of Australian colonisation when she longed for the day when 'man' had at last broken 'the silence of a country that seems—to those who know it—as ancient as time itself!'[43]

The historian Wayne Reynolds argues that despite the rhetoric the real motivation for the Snowy Mountains Scheme lay in a covert government strategy to acquire the expertise and the

power-generation capacity to develop the atomic bomb. As
Reynolds shows, secret Department of Defence files leave no
doubt that there was a nuclear dimension to the scheme.[44] He
may well be right: without this grimmer purpose, the great
Snowy Mountains Scheme may never have won support in
Canberra. But its popularity in the wider community had
nothing to do with bombs. The Snowy Mountains Scheme
satisfied Australians' long-held desire to redeem the country
with engineering. It was the realisation of more than a century
of water dreaming. True, the Snowy Mountains Scheme did not
aim to bring life to the dead heart. It did not make the deserts
bloom. But this heroic project was the biggest public works
project Australians had ever undertaken—and one of the
grandest hydro schemes in the world.

Today, the benefits of the Snowy are in doubt. In a study of
water diversion schemes around the world, the environmental
scientists Fereidoun Ghassemi and Ian White concede that the
scheme has contributed to economic and social development. But
they calculate that the scheme cost a heart-stopping $9 billion at
current values: supplying farmers with massively subsidised water.
The system's contribution to the electricity grid is marginal. It
has exacerbated salinity in the irrigated regions. And it has
decimated the Snowy River.[45] These environmental misgivings
are now widely shared. Few Victorians oppose government plans
to increase flows in the Snowy River, which, until recently,
surrendered 99 per cent of its headwaters to scheme. But in the
1940s, the project was a source of swelling pride and reassurance.
It was proof that white Australia had triumphed over the raw
wilfulness of nature. If there was ever a scheme that would make
the country hum with industry, this was it.

The Snowy was also a sign that Australia was gradually
transferring its dependency from England to the United States.
Based on the great Tennessee Valley Authority (TVA), the

scheme was American in both its modernity and its size. These links were tangible: the project's first engineers were trained by the TVA, which was itself becoming a symbol of progress in Australia. Indeed, an image of the TVA's Great Boulder Dam even appeared in advertisements for Feltex carpets: a emblem of how science was contributing to 'the convenience and comfort of everyday life'.[46] As a popular song about the scheme put it, 'We'll blow down a mountain and build you a dam, Bigger and better than Old Uncle Sam.'[47]

By the 1960s, many Australians had abandoned the idea that irrigation was a deterrent to Asian aggression.[48] If Asia, or Asian communism, was a threat, then Australia would rely on the military power of the USA for its defence, not on market gardens in the desert. In any case, as the bitter political struggles over the Vietnam War indicated, Australians were now divided over whether the country was vulnerable to Asian military ambitions.

Whatever their views on this question, few Australians now spoke of the centre as if it was a menace. There was a fundamental sign that this was so. Australians had stopped referring to Lake Eyre as the centre or dead heart of Australia. In 1962, the lake enjoyed a new kind of exposure in the newspapers and newsreels. That year, the British driver Donald Campbell brought his futuristic, finned car the Bluebird to Lake Eyre, where he intended to break the land speed record. Ironically, his attempt was foiled by torrential rains. But in 1964, he returned and succeeded in his quest. After that, Lake Eyre ceased to be a subject of public passion or dismay. The centre of Australia had shifted—to Ayers Rock.

Inventing Uluru

Today, people across the world have an image of the Rock as a huge red dome that has stood in the centre of Australia since the beginning of time, radiating an aura of Aboriginal spiritual power. But this idea of the Rock only began to take shape in the 1960s. At the end of World War II, it had no significance in non-Aboriginal Australia at all. It was simply an oddity in the distant desert, which most people knew, if they knew it at all, from black-and-white photographs in magazines. The standard tourist guide of the period, *The Australian Blue Book* (1942), did not even mention it.

But it had begun to flicker in the pages of the popular *Walkabout* magazine. In 1941, the bush writer Frank Clune published an account of a gruelling eight-day camel trip to 'the mysterious monolith in mid-Australia, which is named by the Aborigines *Oolera* and by the Whites "Ayers Rock"'. Clune described the Rock in alienating terms. 'It crouches in the plain like a giant turtle,' he wrote. 'The nearer we came to it the bigger it looked until it half-blocked the sky...The larger it gets the smaller you feel.' For Clune, it was an embodiment of the timelessness, of the primordial quality of central Australia. 'Its shadow across the sands relentlessly marks the passage of the days. The years. The centuries.' Situated in an official Aboriginal reserve, it was 'one of the last remaining sanctuaries where, unmolested by civilisation, the Aboriginal tribes may live and hunt in the fashion of their forefathers since the Dawn of Time.' Descriptions of the Rock as alien and menacing were commonplace. According to *Walkabout* in 1946, the 'monolith' crouched on the plain 'like some prehistoric monster'. Even in the 1960s, a popular tourist guide by Bill Beatty was still describing it as 'an incredible monster asleep on the lonely plain' which, if it awakened, 'would resent the intrusion of white people'.[49]

But Frank Clune's article struck a chord that was new. He placed Ayers Rock 'in the heart of the continent'. It was the 'Red Heart of the Country'. It was, he said, in 'our Centre'. Critical to this centrality was its Aboriginal provenance. Clune wrote of the Rock as if it were Australia's Stonehenge—a spiritual focus of Aborigines in 'ancient times'.

In 1948, an Alice Springs truck driver named Len Tuitt graded a rough track from Alice to the Rock and began to take a few plucky tourists there in a rugged military vehicle called a Blitz Buggy, and later in a Volkswagen Kombi. In the mid-1950s, he sank a bore and erected two large water tanks. These were the first 'tourist facilities' at the Rock, controlled not by the local Aborigines but by the white entrepreneurs. Tuitt, more than anyone else, reinvented Ayers Rock as a white man's tourist attraction.[50] Gradually, the accounts that reached urban Australia began to paint the Rock in the golds, reds and purples of sunset.

For Australians were now learning to see central Australia in colour, thanks largely to the painter Albert Namatjira, a Western Arrernte man living at Hermannsburg mission. During the 1940s and 1950s, his watercolours, mainly of the MacDonnell Ranges, introduced whites to an inland in which pink and purple cliffs rose above brilliant red plains, in which sensuous white gum trees writhed against a vivid blue sky. Reproductions of his paintings became so common in suburban living rooms across Australia, that they were the subject of satire as well as objects of beauty. At the same time, colour photographs in such magazines as *Walkabout* showed urban Australians that these colours were really out there.

During the same period, Bill Harney, the first ranger at the Rock, became close to the local Aboriginal groups—in fact he married an Aboriginal woman—and reached a mass audience with his homespun guide book *To Ayers Rock and Beyond* (1963). This represented the Rock as an Aboriginal spiritual site, and portrayed the owners as dignified people with a living culture. Two years later, the Cambridge-trained anthropologist

C. P. Mountford published the results of two decades of research among the local people in his popular *Ayers Rock, Its People, Their Beliefs and Their Art* (1965)—a book that likewise dramatised Uluru as an Aboriginal place, alive with *tjukurpa* (stories of the law, or dreamtime). In recent times, Harney and Mountford have been criticised by both Aborigines and whites: Harney for his paternalism and his disregard for the provenance of stories, and Mountford for appropriating secret Aboriginal cultural material.[51] But their writings did feed sympathetic interest in Aborigines that was swelling in the brick-veneers of postwar Australia. It was an age, too, of Aboriginal activism, when indigenous leaders like the Gurindji man Vincent Lingiari, the veteran activist Pearl Gibbs, the charismatic intellectual Charles Perkins and the untiring Faith Bandler from the Federal Council for Aboriginals and Torres Strait Islanders impressed the injustices suffered by Aborigines on to the consciences of white people of goodwill. The result was that, in 1967, 90 per cent of white Australians supported a landmark referendum to acknowledge Aborigines as full citizens. By then, the domestic airline TAA (Trans Australia Airlines) was encouraging tourists to fly to Alice Springs. Its advertisements declared Ayers Rock to be the 'Centre of Attraction'.[52]

By 1985, Uluru was one of three internationally recognised icons of Australia—along with the Sydney Harbour Bridge and the Sydney Opera House. By then, the ideology of assimilation had given way to a new politics that valued cultural diversity and which recognised that Aboriginality was not about to erased. The new wisdom was that Aboriginal land rights would begin to undo the great wrong that had been done to Aborigines under the cloak of *terra nullius*. That year, following a protracted legal battle, the federal government handed ownership of Uluru to a community of Yankunytjatjara and Pitjantjatjara speakers who lived near the Rock and referred to themselves as Anangu. The land grant arose from a belief within the federal Labor government, and among liberal-minded Australians generally, that land rights were the key to restoring dignity and purpose to the broken Aboriginal communities of inland Australia.

The healing of wounded Aboriginal cultures was not so easily achieved. The pain and the injustice endure. But the shift of the centre from Lake Eyre to Uluru is a key symptom of a newfound empathy among settler Australians. Lake Eyre, 'the dead heart', had been a symbol of disappointment, alienation and rejection. But Uluru spoke of reconciliation. Where Lake Eyre cried out for the inland to be changed, Australians venerated Uluru as a place where nature, spirituality and the diverse human cultures of the country converged. It was a place of hope.

16

NEW BEGINNINGS

The banks of a river may belong to one man or one industry or one State, but the waters which flow between the banks should belong to all the people.

LYNDON B. JOHNSON, ON SIGNING THE US *CLEAN WATER ACT*

Human nature

High in the forests of Bali, a cascade of rivers and streams begins its descent to the sea. For a thousand years, the people of the island have maintained an intricate network of tunnels, canals and pipes that directs this water on its downward journey from one terraced field to the next. Each year, Bali's 1500 community groups, the *subaks*, meet to consult the gods and to discuss how this bounty will be shared as it murmurs through their green farms and gardens. This is Bali's 'water temple system'—a unity of nature, spirituality and engineering that binds the people to the rhythms of their beautiful island.[1]

In its own way, Bali's ingenious irrigation system prefigures Major Mitchell's notion of nature brought to fruition by the art of engineering. The same is true of the great eel traps and swamp drainage systems that Aborigines constructed in the Western District of Victoria, consisting of thousands of metres of channels and earthworks. Equally striking is the great fishery on the Barwon River, near the head of the Darling at Brewarrina. This magical structure, Australia's Stonehenge, has fallen into disrepair. Old photographs show that the fishery, the cultural birthright of the Ngemba people, was once a swirling maze of graceful stone walls that snaked its way through the water over a distance of five hundred metres. It was the largest network of stone fish traps in Australia, and is a triumph of human creativity.[2]

By contrast, the ailing rivers of Australia betray a failure to develop the sense of stewardship, understanding and responsibility for country that is the sign of belonging. Where these older, indigenous systems interacted with the natural environment for centuries, the heroic irrigation works of modern Australia—notably in the Murray–Darling Basin—have alienated themselves from the very rivers on which they rely. The vision was grand, and the intentions were often idealistic. But we have flogged those rivers to the edge of extinction in just four generations.

These failures are not, of course, the entire story. While Australians were forging and challenging mythologies in the desert, they omitted to write some of their most successful water engineering projects into the nationalist legend. The most notable of these is the water supply for Melbourne, which originates in the forested hillside catchments to the north of the sprawling city. For 150 years, these leafy woodlands have been fenced off and entirely devoted to collecting cool, clean water. The system is a model of how a publicly owned catchment can be managed for long-term sustainability and social good. By contrast, thirsty Adelaide—a city cursed by insufficient and sub-standard drinking water—has denied its own proximity to the highest rainfall zone in arid South Australia. The Mount Lofty Ranges are the city's natural catchment—but rather than collecting the rains that fall so generously on these hillsides, Adelaide's law-makers have allowed that land to be bought by private speculators for urban development.[3]

Silent auction

The water dreamers, for all their grandeur of vision, failed to learn the lessons of the Tank Stream and of Busby's Bore. They failed to understand we cannot strip water from its environment or pipe it around the country at will. Water, whether it supplies a city, farms or industry, is sustainable only when it is part of a healthy, living system. There is a lesson here for some environmentalists as well. A farm, factory or a town is not an alien place. Each needs to be embraced as an integral part of the catchment in which it lies. As Landcare groups, and a score of other community organisations around the country, are now acknowledging, the river, the farm, the factory, the wetland and the town are all working parts of the one dynamic environment. Until all users of the river overcome the imagined division between the 'natural' environment and 'artificial' human activity—until they deeply feel the interconnectedness of humanity and the natural world—Australians will continue to damage the lands and waters that sustain them.

The struggle to reconcile the economy and the environment made headlines on the shores of Tasmania's Lake Pedder in 1967. That year, the Tasmanian government dissolved the national park that protected the lake and the surrounding forests, opening the way for the state's powerful Hydro-Electric Commission to dam the valley. While the Snowy Mountains Scheme was being hailed as a triumph, it was at Lake Pedder that the engineers first sensed that a tide of anger was rising against them. The man who did most to turn the current was the photographer Olegas Truchanas. His images of the region were artful photographs that showed a pristine lake lapping a pink quartz beach cradled in a stark, glacial valley. They were visions of an unpeopled paradise. Despite a broad protest campaign, the engineers triumphed, flooding the lake and its enchanted pink beach in the interests of hydro-electricity. For those who grieved, it was if a place of silent wonder and spiritual purity had been drowned beneath a hydro scheme that nobody needed.

By now, the conservation movement was swelling across Australia. Far from being a child of the political left, environmentalism disregarded old political distinctions. Indeed, when the government-funded Australian Conservation Foundation was established in 1965, its president was Sir Garfield Barwick, the formidable chief justice of the High Court—a man every bit as conservative as his born-to-rule name suggests.

A decade later, environmentalism was defining itself as a vigorous force in political debate, challenging the development-at-any-cost agenda shared by many capitalists, engineers and blue-collar unions. In the late 1970s, Tasmania's Hydro-Electric Commission was pushing ahead with more schemes. It now proposed to dam the Franklin, a river flowing through the tall timber forests of Tasmania's lonely western coast. Most local residents wanted the jobs that the project promised to their isolated region. They were contemptuous of the 'tree-hugging greenies' who streamed into the district and whose values and alternative lifestyles were so at odds with their own culture of tough, rural pragmatism. But the Tasmanian Wilderness Society, led by the steely calm activist Bob Brown, spoke for the Franklin. With memories of the drowned Lake Pedder still raw, the Wilderness Society's campaign to save the 'wild river' was soon winning support across the island state and on the mainland. Early in 1983, with a federal election approaching, the Liberal prime minister Malcolm Fraser was championing the economic benefits of the dam. But the opposition Labor Party, led by the genial Bob Hawke, risked the ire of the construction unions by embracing the river. On 2 March 1983, the Wilderness Society ran a full-page advertisement in both the Melbourne *Age* and the *Sydney Morning Herald*. Readers were confronted by 'Rock Island Bend', an arresting photo taken by Peter Dombrovskis, a protégé of Truchanas. It showed the Franklin River swirling through a wooded canyon swathed in a dreamy haze of water and mist—as if Dombrovskis's camera had revealed a world hidden from the naked eye: a world of forest dreams and river magic. The caption read, 'Could you vote for a party that would destroy this?' This story-book landscape became the defining image of 'Tasmanian wilderness' and helped carry Labor to victory in what became known as the 'No Dams' election. The anthem of the campaign was a protest song written by the singer Shane Howard and performed by members of the bands Goanna and Redgum. Its message was simple. 'O, wilderness,' it said, 'Your silence sings to me.'

As we've heard, the talk of 'pristine forests' as sanctuaries of silence had precedents in colonial Australia. There were always a few souls who regretted the noise of the axe and who—like Lieutenant Tuckey on the Aboriginal shores of Port Phillip, or William Westgarth strolling across the Yarra wetlands— discovered peace in the solitude. Indeed, it was in the green forests of coastal New South Wales in the 1860s that the colonists established Australia's first national parks. Today, the environmental movement has built this reverence for 'unspoilt wilderness' to a major quality of Australian life—a serene challenge to the hubbub of commercial exploitation.

These values are so ubiquitous that photographs of unpeopled, natural landscapes adorn the website and publications of Tourism Australia, while ecotourism companies invite you to canoe down Tasmania's Gordon River and 'immerse yourself in the smells and silence of the wilderness'. The idea is equally popular in Canada, where a tourist lodge on the icy Atlantic coast offers its patrons 'the profound silence' of a 'pristine wilderness'.[4] In its way, this newfound veneration of the wild fulfils the ideal that Marcus Clarke sought in his notion of weird melancholy, but never quite attained. In the silence of untrammelled nature, say the champions of wilderness, people commune with the deeper meanings of their country and confront the secret truths of their own private selves.

There is an obvious contradiction here. Ecotourism threatens to rupture the very solitude that it extols. As the Australian artist Marie-Louise Anderson complains, the noise of the tourist operators' trucks and helicopters is itself a kind of assault. It 'breaks the silence inherent in wilderness', she writes, so that the wilderness 'no longer seems like a wilderness' at all.[5]

Talk of 'unspoilt' or 'pristine' wilderness also sits uncomfortably with Aboriginal claims on country. As the anthropologist Deborah Bird Rose points out, wilderness erases the way Aborigines have shaped and nurtured the country. Likewise, the Aboriginal intellectual Marcia Langton dismisses the idealised wilderness as a self-serving European fantasy—just one more version of the lie of *terra nullius*.[6] Making the same point, though with a quite different ideological intent, is the free-market historian Geoffrey Blainey. The environmentalists who valorise South America's Amazon as 'a silent majestic river', he points out, are actually silencing the 5000-year human history of the rainforests—a history of economic development which, Blainey insists, is the stuff of human progress.[7]

These are persuasive arguments. They remind us that wilderness, on its own, does not provide a blueprint for developing and using the resources of the earth in ways that are creative, productive and sustainable. Certainly, there is good reason to set aside sanctuaries where natural systems and species are left to spin their web of life. And there is no doubt that the wilderness movement has awakened many Australians to a more spiritual relationship to country. But the idea of wilderness, with its emphasis on isolation and protection, does not serve Aboriginal rights. Nor does it directly advance the design of sustainable farms, cities and industries. The need for such designs is now urgent.

The crisis

Like the rivers, groundwater, too, is under stress. In the wheat belt of Western Australia's south-west corner, rising groundwater, caused by the almost total deforestation of the region, has scarred the landscape with pink and white tumours of salt. In the absence of a unified strategy to deal with this problem, individual wheat farmers have bulldozed drains along the lowest contours of their properties to carry saline runoff into neighbouring lands, where the same primitive technology funnels the toxic water further down the line.

By the 1990s, salinity in the Murray–Darling Basin was also out of control. Wasteful irrigation had raised the groundwater table, conveying ancient salts to the surface, poisoning productive country and leaching into the river. In recent years, salt levels in some of the drought-depleted wetlands of the catchment have reached three times the concentration of sea water, killing plants and animals. At the same time, the combined effects of drought and excessive irrigation have been bleeding the river dry.

Attitudes along the river have been changing. For the past century, most irrigators throughout the Murray–Darling Basin thought of the local river as little more than an open channel supplying them with water. However, that fallacy was unmasked in the summer of 1991, when the Darling River became clotted with a toxic mass of blue-green algae one thousand kilometres long—the largest such bloom ever recorded anywhere in the world. The algae, which are an endemic plant, had become bloated on a cocktail of sewage, animal waste and fertiliser. Vivid television images of the afflicted river alarmed the general population and galvanised the politicians. Normally sceptical irrigators now acknowledged that the environmental crisis on the river was systemic and that their own oversized industry was a principal cause.[8]

The irrigators cooperated by fixing the 'Murray–Darling Cap' in June 1995—an agreement that set a maximum water use for the Basin at a level slightly below the prevailing rate of exploitation. The purpose was to allow a little more water for the river, known to the irrigators (you can hear the lingering resentment) as 'duck water'.

The Cap did not fix the problem. As everyone now agrees, too many people held entitlements to pump water from the river. It was 'over-allocated'. In 2002, a group of prominent scientists, including the zoologist Tim Flannery and the water scientist Peter Cullen, entered the debate as the Wentworth Group. In a series of statements including their *Blueprint for a Living Continent*, they identified the disaster and called on governments to halve the volume of water being pumped from the river. With policy makers, scientists and opinion leaders acknowledging the crisis, the Howard government instituted a national water policy which was reinforced by the Rudd government after it came to power in December 2007. By then, Australia's largest river had not flowed at its mouth, without the assistance of dredging, for a decade. The waters in the adjoining Coorong wetlands were so diminished, and so toxic with salt and acid, that environmental scientists were declaring that only a mass-transfusion of water would save that idyllic region from annihilation.[9]

Water trading

The chief instrument of these reforms is a mechanism generally referred to as 'water trading'. In the world of water management, it seems that almost everyone—farmers, banks, water corporations, agribusinesses and environmentalists—is in favour of it.

The policy abandoned Alfred Deakin's fundamental principle that irrigators should not hold property rights in water. Under Deakin's scheme, the water, in effect, belonged to the river—and the irrigators had an entitlement to use an allocated amount on their farms, for which they paid a small annual fee. By the 1980s, irrigation had earned a reputation as a wasteful and cavalier industry. Some producers practised flood irrigation, simply allowing water to slosh across their properties. Others grew pasture—an activity that would be unprofitable if they were required to buy water at a realistic market price. In any case, the devices used to meter water flowing on to the farm were unreliable and easy to circumvent. During the 1990s, I met three irrigators who confessed to jamming their meters or to secretly pumping directly from the river in the dead of night. Though such acts of theft were policed by official bailiffs, the penalties were inconsequential. As one of the irrigators told me, 'It was all good sport.' This major industry was crying out for reform.

Water trading was introduced by various states in the 1990s to expose irrigators to 'the discipline of the market'. Its purpose was to drive up the cost until water found its 'true value'. If water was expensive, said the system's advocates, then irrigators would use it more efficiently, reducing waste, lowering the groundwater table and helping to reduce salinity.

Under the new arrangement, the irrigator's right to use water was converted into a form of tradable property called a 'water access entitlement', commonly referred to as a licence. This licence enables him to sell his water allocation. It works like this. Farmer Brown might decide to sell his entire allocation for the next six months to Farmer Green. This deal (or 'transfer') is generally managed by a water brokerage company such as Waterfind. There are several reasons why Brown might decide to sell. In a drought, he might prefer a guaranteed income over the gamble of planting a crop. In a wet year, Brown might have access to more water than he needs. Or he might be a speculator who has acquired hundreds of licences simply so that he can sell water.

The cost of water and licences rises and falls with the seasons. But over the past two decades, water has increased in price by an order of magnitude. In 2008/2009, the mean price of Murray water reached $1060 a megalitre.[10] By then, it was clear that some water-intensive crops, such as almond growing, were becoming unsustainable. Time will show how this process transforms the industry. Trading may eventually close small dairy farms and move the water to large-scale rice or cotton stations. Or it may favour the profitable fruit and vegetable market.

Water trading provides the irrigator with a second, more radical option. He can sell his water licence, once and for all. This effectively strips his irrigation block of its water. A farmer might do this for one of several reasons. He could be planning to retire—and regard the sale of his licence as a golden hand-shake. He might be a borrower under pressure from the bank. Or he might decide to cash in and buy his water from year to year, or to take advantage of schemes that allow him to lease back his water for a fixed period.

Buyers must themselves be accredited: a buyer could be another grower, a large agribusiness or a town council, or even one of the global corporations that are acquiring control over water across the planet. In the words of Tom Rooney, the chief executive of Waterfind, the Australian water market has transformed river water into a 'commodity'—and just as open to speculation as oil or steel. This is a world-wide trend. As the global business magazine *Fortune* told its readers in May 2000, water has become 'one of the world's great business opportunities'.[11]

All this buying and selling does not, of itself, advantage the environment. On the contrary, the new water market ensures that every litre in an already 'over-allocated system' is horded on-farm, sold or put to immediate use. Even water that once ran, unused, past the farm gate, will now be sold out of the river. Unless the government intervenes.

This is precisely what has happened. In 2008, the federal government announced that it would enter the market on behalf of the environment, spending over $3 billion to 'buy back' water and water licences. Most stakeholders, including the Australian Conservation Foundation, believe that as long as the government buys from 'willing sellers' then this multi-billion-dollar commitment to the environment is justified. However, there are a few dissenters.

The critics

The Canadian water campaigner Maude Barlow condemns this new water market as part of a global capture of water—and of the public commons in general—by corporate interests. Barlow maintains that plans to drive up the cost of water, thereby making recycled and desalinated water competitive, merely serve the interests of the water corporations. The market, she says, has a vested interest in neglecting clean, free rivers, and in ignoring the rights of the poor, because the big profits are to be made in providing expensive, processed water to those who can pay.[12]

Barlow sounds a valid warning. The extensive discussions that preceded the Australian reforms assumed that the market would be orderly and rational. The reformers talked of irrigators trading water up and down the river as if they were so many shopkeepers swapping goods along the high street. But water is becoming big business. As the world is now learning, the market is not the perfect, self-regulating mechanism that the ideologues have been spruiking for the past thirty years. People who believe that their sole responsibility is to themselves or their shareholders are not worthy guardians of the planet. There is reason to be alarmed that we are already seeing some Australian companies accumulating millions of dollars worth of licences with the clear intention of becoming traders and specu- lators in water. Some properties, especially some of the large cotton growers in Queensland, already have on-farm dams that dwarf Sydney Harbour. These growers are in position to hoard water and manipulate the costs and supplies of downstream users. Now there is talk that global corporations are also starting to acquire licences: early in 2009, for example, water broker Gil Sibley reported that 'an important overseas interest' was bidding for a major package of licences that had just gone on sale.[13] As many countries have found in the aftermath of privatising their water supplies, the short-term profit of global water corpora- tions do not always serve the long-term needs or rights of local citizens.[14]

There is other potential for harm. As I have explained, the sale of a licence can take an irrigation farm out of production regardless of its long-term viability. There is no doubt that the irrigation industry must reduce in size. But random property sales of this kind are no substitute for systematic planning. It would have been more effective to identify those regions where irrigation is sustainable—and to close it down in those regions where the ecological impact is severe or the infrastructure is too antiquated. Politically, of course, this is difficult, because farmers maintain the fiction that their moral rights to their property outstrip the rights of shopkeepers or urban house owners, whose properties can be compulsorily acquired in the public interest (in order, say, to build a freeway).

In any case, this 'property right' is nothing more than a gift from their fellow tax-payers, who, having handed over the property, are now required to 'buy it back' on behalf of the environment. Taxpayers have good reason to ask why a few individuals have been the beneficiaries of such largesse, why irrigators stand to receive billions of dollars of public money for an asset that, until recently, they did not even own. All this, because the river is now required to pay for its own water.

I don't want to be misunderstood. Now that we have a water market, the government's sweeping commitment to the environment is vital. It signifies a massive and welcome change of heart. But we need to question the logic that brought us to this point. The idea of buying water so that it can run down a river is bizarre.

Even so, it is too late to turn back. This market must now be made to work in the interests of rural communities, efficient food production and sustainable rivers. Just as we are, at last, realising that the global money markets require regulation, rigorous government supervision will be essential if this water auction is to produce a sustainable irrigation industry. The risk is great. The commodification of our rivers replicates white Australia's oldest folly: it treats water as if it can be separated from the environment, as if it can be trucked around the country regardless of the logic of the land. It treats 'the market' as more natural than nature itself.

The point is that a healthy river is not only a utility. Whether we are talking about the Rhine, the Nile, the Amazon or the Murray, the health of the river and the life that it sustains are essential to the spiritual wellbeing of its people. If we truly belong to the land in which we live, then our rivers are part of who we are.

Hope

In thousands of suburban gardens, there is evidence that Australians are not hard-wired to act as the selfish, acquisitive beings on whom market theories are premised. Fully installed, an average domestic rainwater tank costs around $4000—which makes tanks one of the most expensive ways of obtaining household water. Yet thousands of city dwellers buy them, simply because they feel they should. Somehow, a plastic tank on the side of their house connects them and their gardens to the rhythms and logic of the wider environment. In this driest of continents, a plastic tank is a way of belonging. I suspect that Major Mitchell would be delighted.

All culture—all understanding—is generated at the sites of contradiction. The meanings of silence slip and mutate around us. At Uluru, the silence itself is up for sale. Guests at the nearby Yulara resort are invited to enjoy a dinner of 'bush tucker' served on candle-lit tables under the stars, against the background of the Rock. Here, say the advertisements, you eat and drink 'in the stillness, broken only by the strains of a lone didgeridoo, and the gentle murmur of an appreciative audience'. The name of this event is 'the Sounds of Silence'.[15] It would be easy to be cynical about this 'tourist experience'. But in its way, this too is a symptom of change. This veneration of the silence carries with it a new hope of reconciliation. Between settlers and the indigenous peoples. And between settlers and the land itself.

Yes, there is hope. The First Fleeters were wet-country people. But today's settler Australians are changing. They are learning to hear their country and to speak about it differently. They have new words, new aspirations and a new respect for silence. They are learning too, that theirs is not 'a new country'. They are starting to imagine that they share an Australian story that stretches back over 40,000 years. They are starting to belong.

NOTES

Introduction

1   A. G. L. Shaw, *The Economic Development of Australia* (1944), pp.7, 12.
     Eleanor Dark in George Farwell and Frank Johnston (eds), *This Land
     of Ours: Australia* (1949), p.11.

2   Comparative average rainfall: Claus Schonfeldt, 'Future Water
     Resources for South Australia', *ATSE Focus*, no.111, March/April
     2000. Water per head: B. L. Finlayson and T. A. McMahon, 'Global
     Runoff' in William A. Nierenberg (ed.), *Encyclopedia of Earth System
     Science*, vol.2, 1992, pp.409–22. My remarks ignore Antarctica, which
     is often described as the 'driest continent' because it has almost no
     rainfall. This is a rather peculiar use of language, since Antarctica
     consists almost entirely of fresh-water ice.

3   Key works by Australian writers are Griffiths, *Forests of Ash* (2001);
     Bonyhady, *The Colonial Earth* (2000); Seddon, *Landprints* (1997) and
     The Old Country: Australian Landscapes, Plants and People (2005);
     Lines, *Taming the Great South Land* (1991); Flannery, *The Future
     Eaters* (1994); Bolton, *Spoils and Spoilers* (1992).

4   Simon Schama, *Landscape and Memory* (1995), p.61.

5   Mark Smith's essay appears in Joan E. Cashin (ed.), *The War Was You
     and Me: Civilians in the American Civil War* (2002). See also his
     Listening to Nineteenth Century America (2001). Clearly, such ideas are
     reverberating. While I was finalising my own research, the Sydney
     historian Diane Collins published 'Acoustic Journeys: Exploration
     and the Search for an Aural History of Australia', *Australian Histor-
     ical Studies*, vol.37 issue 128, October 2006. On the principles of aural
     history see Peter A. Coates, 'The Strange Stillness of the Past:
     Toward an Environmental History of Sound and Noise', *Environ-
     mental History*, vol.10, no.4, October 2005.

6   Mark M. Smith, 'Echoes in Print: Method and Causation in Aural History', *The Journal of the Historical Society*, vol.2, issue 3–4, 2002, p.333.

7   The quotation comes from the novel *The Boy and the Bush* (2002), p.94, which D. H. Lawrence produced by rewriting a manuscript (now lost) by Mollie Skinner, a Quaker writer who owned the guest house where he stayed in Perth. He expressed similar ideas in his autobiographical Sydney novel *Kangaroo* (1963), p.352.

8   G. L. Wood, 'The Metes and Bounds of Australian Development', *Walkabout*, 1 September 1949, pp.14–15.

Chapter 1: The Cadigal Stream

1   These places were home to convicts James Brown, John Allen, William Brough, John 'Black' Caesar, Michael Denison, William Dring, William Edmund and James Heading, transported on the *Alexander*, from *First Fleet Online*, http://firstfleet.uow.edu.au.

2   Record of Robert Abel from *First Fleet Online*.

3   John Hunter, *An Historical Journal of Events at Sydney and at Sea* (1968), p.300.

4   Watkin Tench, *1788* (1996), p.40. This popular edition contains Tench's *A Narrative of the Expedition to Botany Bay* and its sequel *A Complete Account of the Settlement at Port Jackson*, both written during the first years of the settlement.

5   Tench, *1788*, pp.40–41.

6   Arthur Phillip, *The Voyage of Governor Phillip to Botany Bay* (1879), entry for 18 January 1788. The book was compiled in London from Phillip's own dispatches and journals, and is written in the third person.

7   George P. Worgan, *Journal of a First Fleet Surgeon* (1978), para.4.

8   Worgan, *Journal*, paras.4–5.

9   Tench, *1788*, p.40.

10 David Collins observed that 'the swampy ground every where around threatened us with unhealthy situations' in *An Account of the English Colony in New South Wales* (1789), vol.1, p.4. Phillip complained of 'the swamps rendering the most eligible situation unhealthy', Phillip to Sydney, 15 May 1788, *Historical Records of New South Wales* (hereafter

HRNSW), 1.2.121–2; Hippocrates, *On Airs, Waters and Places*, 1849, §7.

11   J. F. Campbell, 'The Valley of the Tank Stream', *Royal Australian Historical Society Journal*, vol.10, no.2, Sydney, 1924, pp.63–103.

12   Diana Plater, *Other Boundaries: Inner-city Aboriginal Stories* (1994), p.25. Information about the Cadigal (or Gadigal) clan is largely derived from the writings of the colonists, so there is some doubt about what the cove was actually called. Some sources contend that 'Warran' simply meant 'over there'.

13   *HRNSW*, 1.2.122.

14   Collins, *An Account*, vol.1, ch.1.

15   Collins, *An Account*, vol.1, ch.1.

16   The writings of Milton were almost sacred or prophetic texts in eighteenth-century England. Watkin Tench briefly takes on the voice of Satan from *Paradise Lost* (Book 2:917) during his exploration of the Blue Mountains (*1788*, p.111).

17   Simon Schama, *Landscape and Memory* (1995), part 1.

18   Virgil, *The Aeneid*, Book 6, line 179 ff.; Dante, *The Inferno*, Canto 1, lines 1–3; George Martin, 'Change on the Ottawa', in William Lighthall (ed.), *Songs of the Great Dominion* (1889), p.39; Gaston Bachelard, *The Poetics of Space* (1969), p.188 quoted in Roslynn Haynes, *Seeking the Centre* (1998), p.1.

19   Phillip to Sydney, 9 July 1788, *Historical Records of Australia* (hereafter *HRA*), 1.1.20.

20   See for example Thomas Watling, *Letters from an Exile at Botany Bay* (1794), letter 13 December 1791, which includes the observation 'Often amid these coveted solitudes do I wander by the silent moon, along the margin of some nameless stream'.

21   George Barrington, *The History of New South Wales* (1802), p.48.

22   James Tucker, *Ralph Rashleigh* (1952), p.68.

23   *Journal of Lieutenant William Bradley* quoted in Baiba Berzins, *The Coming of the Strangers* (1988), p.21. The nature of the trespass is described by Philip Jones, *Ochre and Rust: Artefacts and Encounters on Australian Frontiers* (2007), p.26.

24 Edward Eyre, *Journals of Expeditions of Discovery*, p.247; F. S. Colliver, 'The Australian Aboriginal and his Water Supply,' *Archaeology Papers*, vol.5, 1974; Henry Reynolds, *With the White People* (1990), pp.29, 35.

25 T. L. Mitchell, *Three Expeditions into the Interior of Eastern Australia* (1839), vol.1, 'Modes of drinking au naturel'.

26 Charles Sturt, *Journal of the Central Australian Expedition* (1984), p.25.

27 H. Lourandos, 'Swamp Managers of Southwestern Victoria', in D. J. Mulvaney and J. P. White (eds), *Australians to 1788* (1987).

28 Jeannette Hope and Gary Vines, *Brewarrina Aboriginal Fisheries Conservation Plan* (1994); Mary Gilmore, *Old Days, Old Ways* (1986), pp.161–2; R. H. Mathews, 'The Aboriginal Fisheries at Brewarrina,' *Journal of the Royal Society of NSW*, vol.37, 1903; Peter Dargin, *Aboriginal Fisheries of the Darling–Barwon Rivers* (1976).

29 Marcia Langton, 'Earth, Wind, Fire and Water: the Social and Spiritual Construction of Water in Aboriginal Societies' in B. David, B. Barker, I. J. Niven (eds), *The Social Archaeology of Australian Indigenous Societies* (2006), pp.148–9.

30 Most of these massacre sites are well known. Hospital Creek is near Brewarrina in NSW. See Dargin, *Aboriginal Fisheries*, p.51; 'Our Inland Towns—Brewarrina', *Dubbo Dispatch*, 19 March 1869; G. M. Smith, 'Pioneers of the West: The Massacre at Hospital Creek', *Sydney Mail*, 12 September 1928, p.55.

Chapter 2: The Valley of the Tank Stream

1 John White, *Journal of a Voyage to New South Wales* (1962), p.133.

2 Hunter, *An Historical Journal*, opening of ch.3. I am struck by the power of this incident thanks to Inga Clendinnen's *Dancing with Strangers* (2003).

3 White, *Journal of a Voyage*, p.111; William Bradley, *A Voyage to New South Wales* (1969), entry for 29 January 1788; Tench, *1788*, p.45; Ralph Clark, *The Journal and Letters of Lt. Ralph Clark* (1981) entry for 11 February 1788.

4 Tench, *1788*, pp.45, 91; Collins, *An Account of the English Colony*, entry for February 1788. The historian James Kohen suggests that La Pérouse triggered conflict by violating a sacred site, in *The Darug and their Neighbours* (1993), p.49.

5   Map of 'Sydney Cove Port Jackson' by Lieut. William Bradley, drawn March 1788, reproduced in Tim Flannery (ed.), *The Birth of Sydney* (1999), facing p.196; 'Sketch of Settlement at Sydney Cove,' by Lieut. William Dawes, July 1788, reproduced in Campbell, 'The Valley of the Tank Stream,' p.68.

6   Clark, *Journal and Letters*, entry for 27 February 1788, p.102.

7   White, *Journal of a Voyage*, 2 February 1988; Clark, *Journal and Letters*, 28 February 1788, p.102; see also Clark's letter to Kempster, 10 July 1788, p.262.

8   Bradley's map, 'Sydney Cove Port Jackson' in Flannery, *Birth of Sydney*, p.196; Phillip, *The Voyage*, ch.13.

9   Rainfall figures from the websites of the Bureau of Meteorology, BBC weather and Météo France.

10 Governor Phillip to Lord Sydney, dispatch 15 May 1788, *HRA*, 1.1.23. I am indebted to Dr Ian Thomas, a palaeobotanist at the University of Melbourne for identifying 'samphose' as 'a variant or perhaps plural of samphire, an old English staple'.

11 Daniel Southwell, 'Journal', printed in *HRNSW*, 1.2.667; Ross to Under Secretary Nepean, 16 November 1788, *HRNSW*, 1.2.200.

12 Tench, *1788*, p.65; Phillip, *The Voyage*, 15 April 1788.

13 Clark, *Journal and Letters*, 19 February 1788, p.100.

14 Governor Phillip to Lord Sydney, 15 May 1788, *HRA*, 1.1.23.

15 White, *Journal of a Voyage*, pp.118–20; Collins, *English Colony in New South Wales*, vol.1, pp.30–1; Bradley, *A Voyage to New South Wales* quoted in John Cobley, *Sydney Cove* (1986), p.145; records of Okey and Davis in *First Fleet Online*; death toll calculated by Josephine Flood, *The Original Australians* (2006), p.37.

16 Tench, *1788*, p.91; Collins, *An Account*, entries for February and May 1788; Phillip to Sydney, 10 July 1788, *HRNSW*, 1.2.179–80. See also White, *Journal of a Voyage*, pp.118–20, 30 April 1788; Kohen, *The Darug and their Neighbours*, p.49.

17 White, *Journal of a Voyage*, pp.136–7; Collins, *An Account*, entry for June 1788.

18 Phillip to Sydney, 15 May 1788, *HRNSW*, 1.2.133; Terry Kass et al., *Parramatta* (1996), p.12; Kohen, *The Darug and their Neighbours*, ch.1. George Rose is named in Russel Ward, *Finding Australia* (1987), p.199.

19 Judy Campbell, *Smallpox and Other Diseases in Aboriginal Australia 1780-1880* (2002). Campbell uses modern epidemiological techniques to challenge the influential claim made by Noel Butlin in *Our Original Aggression* (1983) that smallpox was introduced, perhaps deliberately, by the colonists. The suffering of the Aborigines provoked such palpable dismay among the British officers that any idea that this was a case of germ warfare is fanciful: see Collins, *An Account of the English Colony*, vol.1, ch.7; Tench, *1788*, pp.102–3; Hunter, *An Historical Journal*, entry for June–July 1790.

20 Tench, *1788*, p.111, entry for 26 June 1789.

21 George Forbes, *History of Sydney* (1926), p.29; Collins, *An Account*, vol.1, ch.2.

22 Campbell, 'The Valley of the Tank Stream', p.91.

23 *Australian National Dictionary* (1988), p.663.

24 Record of Robert Abel from *First Fleet Online*. Description based on whipping of Paddy Galvin aged twenty, at about the same time, in Joseph Holt, *Memoirs of Joseph Holt* (1838), pp.121–2.

25 Campbell, 'The Valley of the Tank Stream', p.69.

26 A. Phillip to W. W. Grenville, 4 March 1791, *HRA*, 1.1.247.

27 Sydney Water, *Tank Stream: Sydney's First Water Supply*, 2-page pamphlet, www.sydneywater.com.au/WhoWeAre/OurHeritage Assets/brochures.cfm; *ADB*: Grose.

28 Kass, *Parramatta*, pp.39–41.

29 Collins, *An Account*, vol.1, pp.138–9; Cobley, *Sydney Cove*, pp.11, 141, 276.

30 Collins, *An Account*, vol.1, ch.11 and vol.2, final page of ch.3; *ADB*: Pemulwuy; Kass, *Parramatta*, pp.48–9.

31 *Sydney Gazette*, 18 December 1803. This restated an order issued on 14 October 1802.

32 Government & General Orders, 4 Oct 1803, *HRA*, 1.5.67. See also 'Proclamation re the Preservation of Timber', 21 June 1803, *HRA*, 1.2.363.

33 *HRA*, 3.1.2192.

34 Anderson: *Sydney Gazette*, 12 June 1808, p.1; regulations: *Sydney Gazette*, 23 April 1809, p.1.

35 Alan Atkinson, *The Europeans in Australia* (1997), vol.1, pp.197–8; Berzins, *The Coming of the Strangers*, pp.45–6.

36 Marsden, 'A few General Observations upon the Barter of Spirits in the Colony of New South Wales', MSS 18, Mitchell Library, in Crowley, *A Documentary History of Australia* (1980), vol.1, p.152.

37 *Sydney Gazette*, 11 February 1810, p.2.

38 G. Johnston to Earl of Liverpool, 16 Nov. 1810 in Macarthur Papers, vol.2, A2898, Mitchell Library, Sydney. For the demolitions as a cause of rebellion see Bonyhady, *The Colonial Earth*, ch.2 and Michael Duffy, *Man of Honour: John Macarthur* (2003), pp.261–6.

39 *Sydney Gazette*, 23 April 1809, p.1.

40 *Sydney Gazette*, 15 September 1810.

41 Leaching groundwater: Campbell, 'The Valley of the Tank Stream', pp.65, 71. Infectious filth: *Sydney Gazette*, 11 February 1810.

42 See James Taylor's *Panoramic views of Port Jackson* at the State Library of NSW website (image no. a928605). For Lycett paintings see John McPhee, *Joseph Lycett: Convict Artist* (2006).

43 Charles Sturt, *Two Expeditions into the Interior of Southern Australia* (1833), vol.1, pp.1–2; John Busby's report to Sir Thomas Brisbane, 28 June 1825, *HRA*, 1.11.682. Also, Margo Beasley, *The Sweat of their Brows: 100 Years of the Sydney Water Board* (1988), p.3.

44 Sturt, *Two Expeditions*, vol.1, pp.xviii–xix, 1–2. He arrived in 1827.

45 Grand Jury reports in *Sydney Gazette*, 23 April 1827, p.3; Kelly's slaughterhouse and bad behaviour reported on 19 October 1927, pp.2, 3, and 21 January 1828, p.2.

46 *The Times*, 20 August 1827 quoted in Bill Luckin, *Pollution and Control: A Social History of the Thames in the Nineteenth Century* (1986), p.12.

47 John Busby's report to Sir Thomas Brisbane, 28 June 1825, *HRA*, 1.11.683.

48 *Sydney Gazette*, 21 January 1828, p.2f; 23 January 1828, p.2c.

49 Grand Jury report in *Sydney Gazette*, 23 July 1828. See David Clark, '"Worse than Physic": Sydney's Water Supply 1788–1888', in Max Kelly (ed.), *Nineteenth-Century Sydney: Essays in Urban History* (1978), p.5.

50 *Australian*, 9 December 1826, p.2.

Chapter 3: Mr Busby's Bore

1 Under Sec. Horton to Sir Thomas Brisbane, 19 August 1823, *HRA*, 1.11.107.

2 Description based on Paul Ashton and Kate Blackmore, *Centennial Park: A History* (1988), pp.11–15.

3 Ashton, *Centennial Park*, pp.11–23, including quote about timber in the 1820s from evidence to a Commission to Inquire into the Supply of Water to Sydney and Suburbs, *NSWLCV&P*, 1869, pp.93–4.

4 Busby's report to Sir Thomas Brisbane, 28 June 1825, *HRA*, 1.11.682; M. J. Dale and P. J. Burgess, 'Busby's Bore—Sydney's Second Water Supply', *Australian Geomechanics*, no.15, June 1988, p.13.

5 Earl Bathurst to Governor Darling, dispatch 8 January 1926, *HRA*, 1.12.141–3.

6 J. Busby to Governor Darling, letter 19 January 1826, *HRA*, 1.13.364–5.

7 *Sydney Gazette*, 20 February 1828, p.2d.

8 John Hirst, *Convict Society and Its Enemies* (1983), p.66–8. On the noxious state of the prison drains see 'Grand Jury', *Sydney Gazette*, 23 April 1827, p.3.

9 I calculated this by allowing for roughly 300 construction days per year for 10 years. The total length is 3.4 km.

10 Gov. Bourke to E. G. Stanley, 16 May 1834, *HRA*, 1.27.439. The 1903 quote is from W. V. Aird (ed.), *The Water Supply, Sewerage and Drainage of Sydney* (1961), p.7. Also, Jeffcoat, *More Precious than Gold*, p.32; Hirst, *Convict Society*, pp.66–8; Sydney Water, *Busby's Bore*, c.2000, www.sydneywater.com.au/WhoWeAre/OurHeritageAssets/brochures.cfm; Dale and Burgess, 'Busby's Bore'; *ADB*: John Busby.

11 *Currency Lad*, 15 September, 1832, p.2.

12 Bourke docked Busby's salary on grounds of incompetence, triggering a protracted dispute that Busby eventually won. The mass of paperwork can be traced through *HRA*, 1, vols 17, 19, 26.

13 Dale and Burgess, 'Busby's Bore', p.13.

14 Michel Wuttmann et al., 'The Qanats of 'Ayn-Manâwîr, Kharga Oasis, Egypt', *Journal of Achaemenid Studies and Researches*, no.1, 2001, www.achement.com; James Wellard, *Lost Worlds of Africa* (1967), pp.63–4.

15   Dimensions from Dale, 'Busby's Bore' which also quotes the water engineer J. Warner, 'Detailed Survey of the Water Tunnel and Shafts between Lachlan Swamps and Hyde Park, 1854'.

16   Aird, *The Water Supply*, p.6; gushing water: *Sydney Herald*, 1 May 1837.

17   Clark, 'Worse than Physic', pp.55–6; Dale and Burgess, 'Busby's Bore', p.13; Aird, *The Water Supply*, p.6.

18   Evidence of Thomas Woore in John Smith, *Sydney Water Supply: Report* (1869) cited in Ashton, *Centennial Park*, p.23.

19   *SMH*, 7 March 1851, p.2.

20   *Report from the Board Appointed to Enquire into the Best Means of Affording a Supply of Pure Water to the City of Sydney, NSWLCV&P* (1852) cited in Clark, 'Worse than Physic', p.57.

21   Aird, *The Water Supply*, pp.xiv–xvi.

22   Smith, *Sydney Water Supply*, p.18.

23   Smith, *Sydney Water Supply*, pp.18, 22, 24 and Minutes of Evidence, p.1; *SMH*, 24 June 1867.

Chapter 4: The Silent Continent

1   H. R. Mill, *The Record of the Royal Geographical Society* (1930), p.1.

2   Recent works in this tradition are D. Gregory, *Geographical Imaginations* (1995); Jane M. Jacobs, *The Edge of Empire* (1996); H. J. de Blij and Alexander B. Murphy, *Human Geography: Culture, Society, and Space* (2006).

3   Patrick Brantlinger, 'Victorians and Africans: The Genealogy of the Myth of the Dark Continent', *Critical Inquiry*, vol.12, no.1, 1985, pp.166–203, also in his *Rule of Darkness: British Literature and Imperialism* (1988); Sir Samuel Baker, *The Albert N'Yanza* (1866), p.xxii quoted by D. Hammond and A. Jablow, *The Africa That Never Was* (1977), p.51.

4   T. W. Freeman, 'The Royal Geographical Society and the Development of Geography', in E. H. Brown (ed.), *Geography Yesterday and Tomorrow* (1980), p.46.

5   Quoted in Richard Flanagan, *A Terrible Beauty: History of the Gordon River Country* (1985), p.67.

6   Geoffrey Blainey, *A Land Half Won* (1983), pp.54–5.

7   Joseph Hawdon, *The Journal of a Journey from New South Wales to Adelaide (the Capital of South Australia) performed in 1838* (1952), entry for 12 March 1838.

8   Recently, Blainey has criticised the image of a silent and pristine nature which he rejects as a romantic fiction peddled by the environmental movement (*A Short History of the World* (2000), pp.35–6).

9   Mitchell, *Three Expeditions*, vol.2, entry for 20 August 1836; Tench, *1788*, p.111.

10   That is not to say that the colonists were unaware of the legal dimensions of *terra nullius*. Writing in 1845, the Aboriginal sympathiser and explorer Edward Eyre declared, 'Without laying claim to this country by right of conquest, without pleading even the mockery of cession, or the cheatery of sale we have unhesitatingly entered upon, occupied, and disposed of its lands, spreading forth a new population over its surface, and driving before us the original inhabitants. To sanction this aggression, we have not, in the abstract, the slightest shadow of either right or justice—we have not even the extenuation of endeavouring to compensate those we have injured, or the merit of attempting to mitigate the sufferings our presence inflicts.' (Eyre, *Journals*, vol.2, 'Manners and Customs of the Aborigines of Australia', ch.1.) The statement anticipated the High Court's *Mabo* decision by 147 years.

11   Mitchell, *Three Expeditions*, vol.1, ch.2, p.36.

12   Graeme Davison, *The Unforgiving Minute: How Australians Learned to Tell the Time* (1993), p.7ff.

13   Harry Lourandos, *Continent of Hunter-Gatherers* (1997), pp.8–9. Sturt stumbled on this different sense of historical time in 1844. As he travelled from Lake Victoria up the Darling, he became alarmed when Aborigines started warning him that he was heading into territory where there had recently been a massacre. A week later, he realised that the stories related to a deadly confrontation between Aborigines and Major Mitchell several years earlier (*Journal of the Central Australian Expedition*, pp.31–41).

14   George Farwell, *Riders to an Unknown Sea. The Story of Charles Sturt: Explorer* (1963), p.4.

15   W. C. Wentworth, *Statistical, Historical, and Political Description of the Colony of New South Wales* (1819), Part One; W. C. Wentworth,

Australasia: A Poem Written for the Chancellor's Medal at the Cambridge Commencement, July 1823 (1823).

16 Martin Thomas, *The Artificial Horizon: Imagining the Blue Mountains* (2003), p.43–50. His population figures: Commonwealth Bureau of Census and Statistics, *Demography Bulletin*, no.65, 1947, p.153. Ecological impact: Tom Perry, *Australia's First Frontier* (1965), p.27. Blaxland's account is his *Journal of a Tour of Discovery Across The Blue Mountains* (1913), 'Dedication' (which takes the form of a letter to Oxley).

17 Andy Macqueen, *Blue Mountains to Bridgetown* (1993), ch.7; C. Cunningham, *The Blue Mountains Rediscovered* (1996), pp.74–84, 127–39; and see *ADB* entries for Francis Barrallier and for the convict bushman John Wilson who seems to have reached there in 1798.

18 Blaxland, *Journal*, entry for 3 June.

19 Blaxland, *Journal*, entries for 12, 13 May; birds in Alec Chisholm, 'Flora and Fauna of the Blue Mountains' in Patricia Rolfe (ed.), *The Blue Mountains* (1964), pp.139–45.

20 J. D. Lang, *A Sermon Preached on Sunday, June 15, 1823, to the Congregation of Scots Presbyterians, in Sydney, New South Wales* (1823), pp.5–6 in F. Crowley, *A Documentary History of Australia* (1980), vol.1, p.301.

21 Sturt, *Two Expeditions* (1833), vol.1, p.xv.

22 Mark M. Smith, 'Listening to the Heard Worlds of Antebellum America', *Journal of the Historical Society*, vol.1, June 2000, p.67.

23 Philip Jones, *Ochre and Rust: Artefacts and Encounters on Australian Frontiers* (2007), pp.28–9, 123–4; Mitchell, *Three Expeditions*, vol.1, pp.34, 304–5.

24 George French Angas, *Savage Life and Scenes in Australia and New Zealand* (1847), vol.1, p.44.

25 W. Howitt, *Land, Labour and Gold* (1972), pp.252, 188. Howitt was a Quaker who loved gum trees.

26 The writings of Mr Bennett quoted with approval by Angas, *Savage Life*, vol.1, p.222.

27 From the opening paragraph of John Filson, *The Adventures of Col. Daniel Boon [sic]: Formerly a Hunter* (1784).

28 Allan Nevins and Henry Steele Commager, *America: The Story of a Free People* (1966), p.v.

29 Henry Thoreau, *Walden* (1854), 'Spring', par.34. See also Tom Lynch, 'The "Domestic Air" of Wilderness: Henry Thoreau and Joe Polis in the Maine Woods', *Weber Studies*, Fall 1997, vol.14, no.3.

30 Wallace Stegner, 'Coda: Wilderness Letter' in his *The Sound of Mountain Water* (1969).

31 Edmund Burke, *A Philosophical Inquiry into the Origin of Our Ideas of the Sublime and Beautiful* (1756), part 2.6.

32 Ernest Giles, *Australia Twice Traversed* (1889), vol.2, pp.227–8; Oxley quoted in A. E. Lawrence, *Taming the Wilderness* (1985), p.2; David W. Carnegie, *Spinifex and Sand* (1898), pp.249, 251; Henry Thoreau, *The Maine Woods* (1864), p.140; Henry Lawson, 'Hungerford' in *While the Billy Boils* (1896). Today, Australians are just as likely to associate the term 'wilderness' with the notion of 'pristine country' championed by the environmental movement.

33 Henry Kingsley, *The Recollections of Geoffry Hamlyn* (1952), p.219; Cotton quoted in Andrew Brown-May, *Melbourne Street Life* (1998), p.18.

Chapter 5: Sounds of Water

1 *Bulluk* is the word for *swamp* in the language shared by the Bunurong and Woiworung: Meyer Eidelson, *The Melbourne Dreaming* (1997), pp.152, 155.

2 Kristin Otto ('Secrets of the Yarra', *The Source*, Melbourne Water, Issue 35, October 2005) lists the former billabong in Melbourne's Botanic Gardens, the Merri Creek confluence, Bolin Bolin Billabong (in what is now Bulleen), Pound Bend and Yering Station as important ceremonial sites. The indigenous use of the country is described in Susan Priestley, *South Melbourne* (1995), ch.1 and in Gary Presland, *Aboriginal Melbourne* (1994). These are key sources for this chapter.

3 E. L. Montefiore's etching 'Melbourne from the Falls' (1837) shows Bunurong people in shelters and canoeing by the falls (Priestley, p.9). The children's 'wondrous feats in swimming and diving' are described in Edmund Finn, *The Chronicles of Early Melbourne* (1976), p.517.

4 Bunjil stories told by Kulin elders Joy Murphy-Wandin and Carolyn Briggs on the website *Yarra Healing* www.yarrahealing.melb.catholic.edu.au/kulin/b_story.html, and in A. Massola, *Bunjil's Cave* (1968).

5 James Fleming, 'The Voyage of His Majesty's Colonial Schooner *Cumberland* from Sydney to King Island and Port Phillip in 1802–3',

see entries for 1, 2 February for the lagoons, birds, heat, storm and return to boat; 4, 7, 8 February, for sightings of Aborigines.

6   Most details from the introduction to Currey's edition of Fleming's journal; also *ADB*: Grimes. For Grimes' refusal to share his map, see Fleming's comment preceding his entry for 27 February.

7   Fleming, 'Voyage', 4–8 February. The Falls were near the current Queens Bridge (originally called Falls Bridge), which intersects with the diagonal Sandridge Bridge on the southern bank. We get an idea of the extent of the reef from Frederick McCubbin's oil painting *Falls Bridge, Melbourne, 1882* (NGV), which shows a stretch of shadowy rocks in the river. The surveyor William Lonsdale estimated the drop at 3½ feet at low tide and 1ft at high tide (Lonsdale to Col. Sec., 30 May 1838 in *Historical Records of Victoria*, vol.3, p.230). This collection also contains several illustrations of the falls, some showing a much higher tide.

8   Comments following Fleming's entry for 26 February. Fleming's negative assessments of the soil as 'swampy' or 'stony' are written onto Grimes' map (see Currey's edition).

9   J. H. Tuckey, *An Account of a Voyage to Establish a Colony at Port Philip* (1805), quoted in Ross Gibson, *South of the West* (1992), p.67.

10 *Colonial Times* (Hobart), 1 December 1826.

11 John Dunmore Lang, 'D'Entrecasteaux' Channel, Van Diemen's Land', written May 1823, published 1872, in John Leonard (ed.), *Australian Verse: An Oxford Anthology* (1998), p.388.

12 Boyce, *Van Diemen's Land* (2008), ch.14. For stories told by descendants of these Aborigines see SBS documentary *First Australians*, episode 2, directed by Rachel Perkins (2008). Batman wrote about the shooting to Anstey, 7 September 1829, Archives Office of Tasmania, CSO1/320/7578 quoted by Boyce, p.201. Other quotes from *ADB*: Batman.

13 *First Australians*, episode 2.

14 John Batman, *The Settlement of John Batman in Port Phillip: From his Own Journal* (1856), entry for 31 May 1835.

15 Batman, *Settlement*, 13 May, 1 June 1835.

16 Edward Stone, Assistant Protector of the Aborigines, quoted in Craig Robertson, *Buckley's Hope* (1980), Preface.

17 Paul Carter, *Living in a New Country* (1992), pp.125–8.

18   Edward M. Curr, *Recollections of Squatting in Victoria* (1965), p.1.

19   Westgarth quoted in Charles Daley, *The History of South Melbourne* (1940), p.8.

Chapter 6: Ruins of Hope

1   John Oxley, *Journals of Two Expeditions into the Interior of New South Wales* (1820), entries for 23 April, 11 June, 8 September 1818.

2   Elizabeth Macarthur to Bridget Kingdon, 1795, in Flannery, *Birth of Sydney*, p.138; Bowen quoted in Bonyhady, *Colonial Earth*, p.7; Stirling quoted in William J. Lines, *An All Consuming Passion* (1994), p.49; Mrs Gawler reporting her husband's words in letter 7 December 1838 in Louise Brown (ed.), *A Book of South Australia: Women in the First Hundred Years* (1936).

3   Batman, *Settlement*, 29 May 1835; Angas, *Savage Life and Scenes*, vol.1, p.215.

4   Rhys Jones, 'Fire-stick Farming', *Australian Natural History*, vol.16, no.7, 1969, pp.224–8. The pollen evidence is reviewed by A. Peter Kershaw et al., 'A History of Fire in Australia' in Ross A. Bradstock et al. (eds), *Flammable Australia* (2002), pp.3–20. See supporting analysis in Jamie Kirkpatrick and Kerry Bridle (eds), *People, Sheep and Nature Conservation: The Tasmanian Experience* (2007), chs.4, 5. David Horton, *The Pure State of Nature* (2000) argues that naturally occurring fires and environmental variability account for the existence of the parks. As an environmentalist, he is determined to defend the concepts of 'nature' and 'pristine wilderness' against claims that Aborigines were the architects of the natural environment.

5   Hunter, *An Historical Journal of Events at Sydney*, ch.3, para.21; T. L. Mitchell, *Journal of an Expedition into the Interior of Tropical Australia* (1848), p.412–4.

6   Southwell, 'Journal', entry 27 May 1788.

7   The first scholar to draw attention to this trope was Bernard Smith, *European Vision and the South Pacific* (1985), p.279. These four examples are quoted by Simon Ryan, *The Cartographic Eye* (1996), pp.78–9; they are Eyre, *Journals*, vol.1, p.327; Stuart, *Journals*, p.151; Sturt, *Two Expeditions*, vol.2, p.163; Mitchell, *Journal*, p.237.

8   Giles, *Australia Twice Traversed*, ch.2.3.

9   Ryan, *The Cartographic Eye*, p.79; see also pp.123–7.

10 Mitchell, *Journal of an Expedition*, p.65; Edward Eyre, 'An account of the Manners and Customs of the Aborigines and the State of Their Relations with Europeans' ch.2 in his *Journals*, vol. 2; Report of the Select Committee on Aborigines, *Great Britain, Parliamentary Papers*, 1837, vol.7, no.425, pp.10–11.

Chapter 7: The Myth of the Inland Sea

1   'Under the Outback', *Science*, vol.288, no.5471, 2 June 2000, p.1581, www.sciencemag.org.

2   Walter Raleigh, *The Discovery of the Large, Rich, and Beautiful Empire of Guiana* (1848), p.liii; Bayard Taylor, *Eldorado* (1850) quoted in Ray Allen Billington, *The Westward Movement in the United States* (1959), p.150; Robert Kelly, *Battling the Inland Sea* (1989), pp.5–6. John R. Sellers, 'Mapping the American Revolution and Its Era', in *The American Revolution and Its Era*, Library of Congress, USA, 2000, http://memory.loc.gov/ammem/gmdhtml/armhtml/armessay.html; Rev. James Erhardt, 'On an Inland Sea in Central Africa', *Proceedings of Royal Geographical Society*, vol.1, 1855, p.8 and Oliver Ransford, *Livingstone's Lake: The Drama of Africa's Inland Sea* (1966); Philip Ball, *H$_2$O: A Biography of Water* (1999), p.49.

3   R. Bourke to Lord Glenelg, 14 June 1837, *HRA*, 1.18.780.

4   Alan Moorehead, *Cooper's Creek* (1963), p.10; Farwell, *Riders to an Unknown Sea*, Foreword; Frank Flynn, *The Living Heart* (1964), pp.12–13; Marcia McEwan, *Great Australian Explorers* (1979), p.217; Derek Parker, *Outback* (2007), p.8 (the incredulous italics are mine).

5   For examples, see Russel Ward, *Concise History of Australia* (1992), p.93; J. Macdonald Holmes, *The Murray Valley* (1948), p.6; A. K. Macdougall, *The Big Treasury of Australian Folklore* (1990), p.195; Haynes, *Seeking the Centre*, p.38. A web search shows that the term 'fabled inland sea' is still in general use.

6   A. C. Gregory, *Journals of Australian Explorations* (1884), entry for 31 July 1858.

7   Sturt, *Narrative of an Expedition into Central Australia* (2001), ch.1, ch.2.4; quotation from Ernest Scott, *The Life of Captain Matthew Flinders* (1914), ebook, p.38, which gives the source as 'Abridged narrative, Flinders Papers'.

8   Matthew Flinders, *A Voyage to Terra Australis* (1814), vol.1, pp.132–3 and entry for 20 February 1802.

9   Rev. Julian Tenison-Woods, *A History of the Discovery and Exploration of Australia* (1865), vol.1, p.341; Ernest Favenc, *The History of Australian Exploration* (1888), Introduction, part 1.

10 www.riverland.net.au/~heinz/riddles.htm.

11 Sir Joseph Banks to Under Secretary King, Soho Square, 15 May 1789, *HRA*, 1.2.231.

12 Haynes, *Seeking the Centre*, p.41. The term *inland sea* appears in her index; *great river* does not.

13 Daniel Brock, *To the Desert with Sturt* (1975), p.165.

14 Gibson, *South of the West*, pp.9–10.

15 Sir Joseph Banks to Under Secretary King, 15 May 1798, *HRA*, 1.2.231; Proposal by Mr James Ballantine, enclosed in Under Secretary Horton to Governor Darling, 20 October 1827, *HRA*, 1.5.556; *Argus*, 7 March 1854, p.4; Tenison-Woods, *Discovery and Exploration*, p.191.

16 Parker, *Outback*, p.8.

17 Melbourne University Press media release dated November 2001.

18 Michael Cannon, *Exploration of Australia* (1999), p.69.

19 Macquarie to Lord Bathurst, 5 September 1817, *HRA*, 1.9.356; *ADB*: John Oxley.

20 Bernard de Voto (ed.), *The Journals of Lewis and Clark* (1953), p.xxxvii.

21 Macquarie to Lord Bathurst, 5 September 1817, *HRA*, 1.9.356.

22 He wrote these lines in a poem, 'Lines by J. O. on quitting the Lachlan Swamps', SZ 7, p.317a, Colonial Secretary's Papers (1788–1825), State Records NSW, quoted in Richard Johnson, *Search for the Inland Sea* (2001), p.76.

23 Oxley, *Journals*, entries 20 May, 30 June 1817.

24 Oxley, *Journals*, entry 7 July 1817, and Appendix III (letter 30 August 1817).

25 Macquarie to Bathurst, 5 September 1817, *HRA*, 1.9.478.

26 Wentworth, *Statistical, Historical, and Political Description*, 'Country West of Blue Mountains'.

27 Oxley, *Journals*, Appendix no.V (letter by J. T. Campbell).

28 Oxley, *Journals*, Appendix no.V (letter to Macquarie, 1 November 1818).

29 Oxley, *Journals*, 3 July.

30 Oxley, *Journals*, 18 July, 11 August 1818; E. E. Morris, *Austral English* (1898), p.298.

31 Oxley, *Journals*, 17, 18, 19 August 1818.

32 Oxley, *Journals*, 23 September 1818.

33 Quote in Tenison-Woods, *Discovery and Exploration*, vol.1, p.204.

34 Catalogue of Oxley's library (Mitchell Library MS, A5322) and the genre are discussed in Paul Genoni, *Subverting the Empire* (2004), pp.32–40; Mitchell, *Three Expeditions*, vol.1, p.5.

35 Oxley, *Journals*, 20 May, 16 July 1818.

36 Oxley, *Journals*, appendix, part 3, no.5.

37 Giles, *Australia Twice Traversed*, p.xxiii. By contrast he denigrated Sturt precisely because his assessment of inland Australia was so pessimistic.

Chapter 8: River of Dreams

1 Phillip Parker King, *Narrative of a Survey of the Intertropical and Western Coasts of Australia* (1827), vol.1, quotes from introduction and 20 February 1818. Other details based on illustrations and maps in this vol. and on personal visit.

2 T. J. Maslen, *The Friend of Australia: Or a Plan for Exploring the Interior and Carrying on a Survey of the Whole Continent of Australia* (1830), pp.136–7.

3 Maslen, *The Friend of Australia*, pp.136–7. Speculation that Maslen was not the author has been dispelled by Karen S. Cook, a map specialist at the University of Kansas. She has been generous with her detailed research and alerted me to the two versions of the famous map ('Thomas John Maslen and "The Great River or Desired Blessing" on His Map of Australia', *The Globe*, no.61, 2008, pp.11–2). For Maslen's other enthusiasms see Hilary Arnold, 'T. J. Maslen's account of York in 1843 and his suggestions for the redevelopment of the city', *York Historian*, no.19, 2002, pp.48–59.

4 Maslen, *The Friend of Australia*, p.62.

5   Maslen, *The Friend of Australia*, pp.vii, 377–9. He read the story in the *Australian*, 22 August 1828. It also appeared as 'Lake in the Interior', *Asiatic Intelligence*, January 1830, section 2, p.22.

6   Maslen, *The Friend of Australia* (1836), pp. 374, 377.

7   http://www.sl.nsw.gov.au/discover_collections/history_nation/exploration/maslen/maslen.html

8   The letter is enclosed in Under Secretary Horton to Governor Darling, Downing Street, 20 October 1827, *HRA*, 1.13.556.

9   W. K. Hancock, *Australia* (1945), pp.13–14.

10   Charles Sturt, *Two Expeditions*, vol.1, opening of ch.1.

11   Allan Cunningham, 'Brief View of the Progress of Interior Discovery in New South Wales' reprinted in Kathleen Fitzpatrick (ed.), *Australian Explorers: A Selection of their Writings* (1957), pp.80–83.

12   Allan Cunningham, 'Draft of a report for the Australia Agricultural Company', Mitchell Library MS A570, quoted in W. G. McMinn, *Allan Cunningham* (1970), p.83.

13   McMinn, *Allan Cunningham*, pp.86–7. McMinn's source for the quotation is Darling to Goderich, 12 November 1827, Governor's Despatches, Mitchell Library A1267/4.

14   Fitzpatrick, *Australian Explorers*, p.16.

15   Speech to the Adelaide Mechanics' Institute, *South Australian Register*, 30 May 1840, p.4; McMinn, *Allan Cunningham*, pp.86–7.

16   Sturt, *Two Expeditions*, vol.1, pp.67, 71.

17   Sturt, *Two Expeditions*, vol.1, p.73.

18   Sturt, *Two Expeditions*, vol.1, p.66.

19   Sturt, *Two Expeditions*, vol.1, p.86.

20   Sturt, *Two Expeditions*, vol.1, pp.93–6, 105.

21   Sturt, *Two Expeditions*, vol.1, pp.99, 100, 104.

22   Sturt, *Two Expeditions*, vol.1, p.108.

23   Sturt, *Two Expeditions*, vol.1, appendix, p.216.

24   Farwell, *Riders to an Unknown Sea*, p.28.

25   Gov. Darling to Viscount Goderich, 14 April 1931, *HRA*, 1.16.242.

26   Sturt, *Two Expeditions*, vol.2, pp.1–2.

27   Mitchell, *Three Expeditions*, vol.1 is his account of the expedition.

28 Mitchell, *Journal of an Expedition into the Interior of Australia*, 1 October 1846.

29 Mitchell in *Journal of the Royal Geographical Society of London*, vol.7, 1837, pp.280–1; see Paul Carter, *The Road to Botany Bay* (1987), pp.111–13.

30 Mitchell, *Three Expeditions*, vol.2, p.170; vol.1, p.7.

31 L. B. Gardiner, *Thomas Mitchell* (1962), p.30. The extent of Mitchell's misrepresentation is demonstrated by Brian Finlayson, 'Sir Thomas Mitchell and Lake Salvator: An Essay in Ecological History', *Historical Studies*, 1981, vol.21, no.8, pp.212–28. Carter debates Finlayson and explores the wider issues in *Road to Botany Bay*, pp.107–13, 132–5 (quotes on pp.113, 108).

32 Mitchell, *Three Expeditions*, vol.1, pp.12, 41, 27.

33 Mitchell, *Journal of an Expedition*, p.65 and see pp.412–4.

34 Mitchell, *Three Expeditions*, vol.1, ch.1, p.192–4.

35 Gipps to Lord John Russell, 28 Sept, 1840. *HRA*, 1.20.839.

36 John William, 'News from an exiled contributor' (dated Melbourne, 1 July 1843), *Blackwood's Edinburgh Magazine*, February 1844, p.188.

37 George Gipps to Lord John Russell, 28 September 1840, *HRA*, 1.20.838–9.

38 Four outstanding examples are C. C. Petrie, *Tom Petrie's Reminiscences of Early Queensland* (1904); Gordon Buchanan, *Packhorse and Waterhole: With the First Overlanders to the Kimberleys* (1933); Mary Durack, *Kings in Grass Castles* (1959) and Mary Gilmore, *Old Days: Old Ways* (1934). One fine exception is E. M. Curr's *Recollections of Squatting in Victoria* (1883), written by a second-generation squatter who pioneered northern Victoria. All these books show a deep sympathy for the suffering inflicted on Aborigines by the squatters and their stock.

Chapter 9: Silence Victorious

1 John Lort Stokes, *Discoveries in Australia...the Voyage of H.M.S. Beagle* (1846), vol.2, entries for 21 October, 8, 9, 10, 14 November.

2 J. Hayter, *The Landsman's Log-book*, (1842), p.121; *South Australian Register*, 30 May 1840, p.5.

3 Eyre, *Journals*, vol.2, pp.128, 133.

4　'Exploratory Expedition to the Northward', *South Australian Register*, 30 May 1840, pp.4–5.

5　'Exploratory Expedition to the Centre of New Holland', *South Australian Register*, 20 June 1840, p.5.

6　*South Australian Register*, 23 May 1840; Malcolm Uren and Robert Stephens, *Waterless Horizons: The Extraordinary Life-story of Edward John Eyre* (1941), p.109; Eyre reports Sturt's views and his own in *Journals*, vol.1, chs.1, 2.

7　Sturt to Campbell, 3 July 1840, in 'B. M. S., Copies of Letters from Charles Sturt to Charles Campbell Esque, 1840 to 1845', MS Austral., s.4, folios 341–60, Sturt Papers, Rhodes House, Oxford.

8　Jill Waterhouse, 'Introduction' to Sturt, *Journal of the Central Australian Expedition*, pp.4–5; Sturt, *The Central Australian Expedition 1844–1846* (2002), pp.xxvii, 5, 37–8. Sturt later expressed his desire to be governor in Sturt to Shaw, 23 August 1860, RGS Correspondence 1851–60.

9　Sturt to Sir Ralph Darling, 5 March 1844, Charles Sturt Papers, Mss Australia, s.5, folio 23; Sturt to Lady Darling, 1 May 1844, *loc. cit.*, folio 39.

10　Sturt, *Narrative of an Expedition*, ch.1, p.21.

11　Sturt to Campbell, 18 June 1845, Charles Sturt Papers, Australia S.4, folios 341–360 in 'B.M.S. Copies of Letters from Charles Sturt to Charles Campbell'.

12　George Gipps to Lord John Russell, Sydney, 28 September 1840, *HRA*, 1.20.844; Sturt to Darling, 25 January 1843 (folio 9); Darling to Stanley, 7 September 1843 (folio 18); Sturt to Darling, 5 March 1844 (folio 23), Charles Sturt Papers, Mss Australia, s.5.

13　'Grey's letter of Instructions to Sturt' in Langley, *Sturt of the Murray*, Appendix D.

14　As Sydney's Governor George Gipps put it, 'The expectation of finding a large River, or an Inland Sea sufficiently near to be of any use to our settlers has altogether vanished.' (George Gipps to Lord John Russell, Sydney, 28 September 1840, *HRA*, 1.20.844.)

15　Cf. Paul Carter, 'About Paradise Parrots and Other Australian Legends of Place and Identity', *Haiku Review*, no.3, 2007.

16　Sturt to George Macleay, 27 April 1844, Charles Sturt Papers, Mss Australia, s.5, folio 28–31.

17 Sturt to Lady Darling, 1 May 1844, Charles Sturt Papers, Mss Australia, s.5, folio 39.

18 Sturt to Lady Darling, 1 May 1844, Roland Boer, *Last Stop before Antarctica: The Bible and Postcolonialism in Australia* (2001), p.65.

19 Sturt, 'Charlotte Diary', pp.78–9, 'Charlotte Diary' is my title for a bound set of letters Sturt wrote to his wife Charlotte, Bodleian Library of Commonwealth and African Studies, Rhodes House, Oxford (Charles Sturt Papers, Mss Australia s.4.); Langley, *Sturt of the Murray*, p.215; Sturt to Sir Ralph Darling, 5 March 1844, Charles Sturt Papers, Mss Australia, s.5, folio 23; and see Sturt to Lady Darling, 1 May 1844, *loc. cit.*, folio 39.

20 S. T. Gill, 'The Departure of Captain Sturt on his Expedition into the Interior', lithograph in George French Angas, *South Australia Illustrated* (1846) reproduced in Ann Millar (ed.), *I See No End to Travelling* (1986), p.135.

21 Sturt, *Narrative*, ch.2, pp.27–32. For more on the Aboriginal guides see Brock, *To the Desert*, pp.8, 9, 63, 95, 110, 150; 'Charlotte Diary', pp.23, 36.

22 The 'Charlotte Diary' was published as Jill Waterhouse (ed.), *Journal of the Central Australian Expedition* (1984). My page numbers refer to this edition. Quotations are from p.22; 'silence of the grave' from Sturt, *Two Expeditions*, vol.2, p.59. Sturt's several accounts of this journey are identified by Richard C. Davis in *The Central Australian Expedition*, pp.lvi–lxiii.

23 Brock, *To the Desert*, pp.11, 16, 120, 113, 141, 160–61, 182, 196, 199, 205. Brock, however, was wary of Sturt's Anglican 'Papistry' (p.179). Sturt, meanwhile, looked to the squatter to take on the social role of the 'English country gentleman' ('Charlotte Diary', p.248). Browne (quoted in Michael Langley, *Sturt of the Murray* (1969), p.203) went on to wonder why Sturt had selected a team of men who were either brutes, or too old. Given Sturt's excitable mental state it may not be too much to suggest that Messrs Poole and Flood were chosen for their names—as if these were some kind of sign.

24 Tenison-Woods, *Discovery and Exploration*, vol.1, p.342.

25 See Kay Schaffer, *Women and the Bush* (1988); Ryan, *The Cartographic Eye, passim*.

26 Brock, *To the Desert*, curse to Aborigines: p.18; cruelty: pp.11–12; toilers: pp.34–5, 167–72. Sturt originally ordered that two men keep watch (*Narrative*, p.30), but often only one man was on duty.

27 Sturt, *Narrative*, vol.2, ch.1.

28 Sturt, 'Charlotte Diary', p.34.

29 Figures obtained by doing a word-search on ebook editions. A decade earlier, he had written how, on his journey down the Murray, he had 'unhesitatingly plunged into the Morass, & traversed gloomy wilds' ('Copy of M.S. Fragment by Charles Sturt', Charles Sturt Papers, Rhodes House, MS Australia, s.4, fol.317, MS B1, p.318).

30 Sturt, *Narrative*, p.355. Sturt drew maps illustrating this (Journal MSS. Sturt, 1847, Folder h. in despatches from Sturt to Lord Stanley, Principal Sec. of State for the Colonies. RGS, London).

31 A MS draft of Sturt's journal, entry for 4 November 1844, Journal Mss Australia 1847, Sturt c.1, Royal Geographical Society, London. Another version appears in Sturt, *The Central Australian Expedition*, p.82.

32 See Richard C. Davis's introduction to Sturt, *The Central Australian Expedition*, p.xlii.

33 Brock, *To the Desert*, p.49.

34 Sturt, *Central Australian Expedition*, p.92 (10 November 1844).

35 Sturt, *Narrative*, p.114.

36 Simon Ryan discusses this sea imagery in detail, concluding that, by representing everything as ocean, Sturt was imposing a 'blank' on the landscape in order to make it available for possession (*Cartographic Eye*, p.120). This really does overstate the power of 'projection' in the imperial cause.

37 Brock, *To the Desert*, p.67.

38 Brock, *To the Desert*, p.106.

39 Sturt, 'Charlotte Diary', p.44; Brock, *To the Desert*, p.115; long quote from Langley, *Sturt of the Murray*, p.203.

40 Schaffer, *Women and the Bush*, p.60. I am not contesting the overall argument of Schaffer's provocative book, but I fundamentally reject her reading of the explorers. Annette Kolodny, *The Lay of the Land* (1975), p.9 and (quoting Wolcott) *The Land Before Her* (1984), pp.3–5.

41 Gibson, *South of the West*, p.89; Falkiner, *The Writers' Landscape: Wilderness* (1992), p.118; Catriona Elder, *Being Australian* (2007), p.71. For other versions see Ryan, 'The Bosom of Unknown Lands' in *Cartographic Eye*; Haynes, *Seeking the Centre*, pp.50–2; Jill Cowley, 'Sisters Across the Ocean', *CRM*, vol.22, no.9, 1999, p.59; Kathleen McPhillips, 'Response', *Journal of Feminist Studies in Religion*, vol.21, no.1, 2005, p.149.

42 Gibson, *South of the West*, pp.88–9; Schaffer, *Women and the Bush*, p.60.

43 Education Department Victoria, *The Victorian Reading-Books: Eighth Book* (1928), p.4; Mitchell, *Three Expeditions*, vol.2, p.170 (my italics). This citation appears in Gibson's footnotes, but his quotation does not match the source. I am not denying that later writers used the image of Australia as a ravished woman or, for that matter, as a withered crone. Its insertion in the textbook indicates just how acceptable this trope later became. It occurs, for example, in the writings of Manning Clark, A. D. Hope and in the exploration histories of Ernest Scott. In the original Mitchell passage, however, the category of power is not gender, but race.

44 Schaffer, *Women and the Bush*, p.60; Ryan, *Cartographic Eye*, p.196; Gibson, *South of the West*, p.88–9. Haynes, *Seeking the Centre*, p.51. See Greg Dening's gentle critique of Ryan's fixation with the explorers' phallocentrism in 'The Randy and Imperial Eye', *Readings/Writings* (1998), pp.76–80.

45 J. D. Hennessey, *An Australian Bush Track* (1896), p.163; Sturt, *Narrative*, p.308. See also Allan Cunningham, 'Journal, 31 April 1818', in Ida Lee (ed.), *Early Explorers in Australia* (1825), ch.10. For Moses wearing a veil see Exodus 34:33.

46 Sturt, *Narrative*, p.271; Ryan, *Cartographic Eye*, p.196. It is the sole example of 'the veil' actually quoted by Gibson (p.127) and by Schaffer (p.60).

47 Sturt quoted in Eyre, *Journal*, p.9; Eyre in *A Dinner for Mr Eyre in Adelaide August 1841*, [no author], a reprint of a report in *South Australian Register*, 28 August 1841, p.12; Brock, *To the Desert*, p.1 (my italics); and see colonial historian Samuel Bennett's description of the Blue Mountains as 'a great blue curtain...which hid the western interior' in his *History of Australian Discovery* (1865), vol.1, pp.157–8. For the Biblical veil see Numbers 18:7.

48 Boer, *Last Stop before Antarctica*, p.86; Samuel Prout Hill, 'Australia' in William Henry Wells, *A Geographical Dictionary of the Australian Colonies* (1848), p.ix.

49 Patrick White, *Voss: A Novel* (1957), p.44.

50 John McDouall Stuart, *Explorations Across the Continent of Australia* (1863), p.30.

51 Sturt, *Narrative*, opening of ch.6, ch.7, entry for 10 June.

52 Sturt, 'Charlotte Diary', pp.45–9; Sturt to Campbell, 18 June 1845, Charles Sturt Papers, Australia S.4. folios 341–60.

53 Ernest Favenc, *The Explorers of Australia* (1908), pp.160–1.

54 Brock, *To the Desert*, p.165; Sturt, 'Charlotte Diary', p.55.

55 Sturt to Campbell, 18 June 1845.

56 Sturt, 'Charlotte Diary', pp.84, 86; Brock, *To the Desert*, p.208.

57 Sturt, *Two Expeditions*, vol.2, p.59.

58 Sturt to Dr Shaw and the Council of the Royal Geographical Society, London, 12 February 1854, RGS Correspondence, 1851–60, Royal Geographical Society, London.

59 Sturt, report of 19 January 1858, Public Record Office, London: C.O. 201/507 Misc. 1858 Aust.855.2128 NSW 5158 cited in J. H. L. Cumpston, *Augustus Gregory and the Inland Sea* (1972), pp.64–5.

Chapter 10: Mapping the Silence

1 The literary historian G. A. Wilkes observes that the landscape of colonial writing changed from green to brown, as dreams of British Arcadia gave way to the dun-brown bush, in introduction to A. J. Boyd, *Old Colonials* (1974), p.5.

2 F. W. L. Leichhardt, *Journal of an Overland Expedition* (1847), 24 May 1845; Mitchell, *Journal of an Expedition*, 13 February 1845, pp.57–9; Stuart, *Explorations*, 10 May 1862, p.23.

3 White, *Voss*, p.67.

4 *ADB*: George Goyder; D. W. Meinig, *On the Margins of the Good Earth* (1962); Daniel Connell, *Water Politics in the Murray-Darling Basin* (2007), p.2.

5 Richard Hengist Horne, *The South Sea Sisters* (1866) in Richard Fotheringham (ed.), *Australian Plays for the Colonial Stage* (2006), p.210.

6   Arthur Bayldon, 'Plains: Near Hay, New South Wales' in his *The Western Track and Other Verses* (1905).

7   Thomas Heney, 'The Boundary Rider' in Walter Murdoch (ed.), *The Oxford Book of Australasian Verse* (1918), no.48.

8   Roderic Quinn, 'Noon on the Barrier Ranges,' *Poems* (1920).

9   Boyd, *Old Colonials*, pp.201–2.

Chapter 11: Necronationalism

1   Ludwig Leichhardt to Schmalfuss Leichhardt, 27 September 1841 quoted in Colin Roderick, *Leichhardt: The Dauntless Explorer* (1988), p.155.

2   The common view that Leichhardt (like Voss) was crazy implies a kinship with the forces that killed him. In fact, historians disagree. In 1941, Alec Chisholm represented him as a deluded incompetent, but a finer man emerges in major studies by E. M. Webster, Colin Roderick and Dan Sprod.

3   In 1855, the North Australian Expedition found artefacts that suggested Aborigines had attacked the party (Royal Geographical Society, *Proceedings*, London, 1855, p.19). The swashbuckling Cecil Madigan reported his own search for Leichhardt in the 1930s in *Crossing the Dead Heart* (1974). See 'Banjo' Paterson's mockery of those 'Rash men that know not what they seek' in his poem 'The Lost Leichhardt' in L. Kramer (ed.), *My Country* (1985), vol.1, p.286.

4   Randolph Stow, 'The Singing Bones' in *Selected Poems: A Counterfeit Silence* (1969).

5   Tim Bonyhady, *Burke and Wills: From Melbourne to Myth* (1991), pp.198, 201–2, 293; Sarah Murgatroyd, *The Dig Tree* (2002), pp.245, 333–4; cost of Sturt's expedition in Glen McLaren, *Beyond Leichhardt* (1996), p.188.

6   Moorehead, *Cooper's Creek*, p.209; Clark, *A History of Australia*, vol.3, p.158.

7   Murgatroyd, *The Dig Tree*, p.352 and see p.341. It is now official policy to omit apostrophes from place names—either by deleting the 's' (transforming *Cooper's Creek* into *Cooper Creek*) or by adopting the German possessive form (*Halls Gap, Wilsons Promontory, Aireys Inlet*). This 'consistency' is apparently some sort of virtue.

8　Murgatroyd, *The Dig Tree*, p.341. Manning Clark makes the same point in *A History of Australia*, vol.3, pp.154–5.

9　From Clarke's famous preface to Adam Lindsay Gordon's poems, *Sea Spray and Smoke Drift* (1876).

10　G. P. Marsh, *Man and Nature* (1864), p.36.

11　Charles Tompson, 'Retrospect' in his *Wild Notes from the Lyre of a Native Minstrel* (1826); Von Mueller quoted in Lines, *Taming the Great South Land*, p.116.

12　C. M. Hall, *Wasteland to World Heritage* (1992), pp.88–92.

13　David Hennessey, *The Bush Track: A Story of the Australian Bush* (1913), pp.177–8.

14　Ernest Favenc, *Voices of the Desert* (1905), preface.

15　A. G. Stephens, 'Says and Hearsays', *Bookfellow*, no.4, 29 April 1899, p.1.

16　Definition of 'Never-Never' in *Australian National Dictionary*; F. Cooper, *Wild Adventures in Australia* (1857), p.68; Boake's poem was published in the *Bulletin* and in his posthumous *Where the Dead Men Lie and Other Poems* (1897).

17　Marcus Clarke, 'Pretty Dick', *Holiday Peak and Other Tales* (1873). See Peter Pierce, *The Country of Lost Children: An Australian Anxiety* (1999) and Kim Torney, *Babes in the Bush: The Making of an Australian Image* (2005).

18　White, *Voss*, p.475.

19　Joan Lindsay, *Picnic at Hanging Rock* (1970), pp.39–40.

20　Vance Palmer, *The Legend of the Nineties* (1954), p.144.

21　Arthur Bayldon, 'The Creek', in *The Western Track*; H. E. Boote, 'The Creek' in Mary E. Wilkinson (ed.), *Nature Poems* (1919); Miles Franklin quoted in *Straight Left* (1982), p.230; Mitchell, *Three Expeditions*, vol.2, 16 July 1836; Furnley Maurice, 'A Drinking Lullaby', *Melbourne Odes* (1934), p.39; Andrew Garran (ed.), *Picturesque Atlas of Australia* (1888), p.200.

22　Roderic Quinn, 'Noon on the Barrier Ranges' in *Poems*.

Chapter 12: The Great Artesian Basin

1　Aborigines and groundwater: research by Brad Moggridge reported in Judy Skatssoon, 'Aboriginal people built water tunnels', *ABC*

Science Online, 15 March 2006, www.abc.net.au/science/news/stories/ s1590192.htm; wells in Simpson Desert: Department of Environment and Heritage (SA), *Simpson Desert*, 'Aboriginal Culture and History' www.parks.sa.gov.au/simpson_cp/about/index.htm#aboriginal; Murgin dreaming: W. Lloyd Warner, 'Spiritual conception in Murgin thought' (1937), in Max Charlesworth et al. (eds), *Religion in Aboriginal Australia* (1984), pp.125–134.

2   John Mather, 'British Hydrology—a brief history', *The UK Ground-water Forum*, c.2004 www.groundwateruk.org/html/depth1.htm; 'Response to John Seaward, "An account of wells and borings by John Seaward"' (OC 43), Institution of Civil Engineers Original Communications 1829–32, nos 44–80.

3   *Australian*, 15 November, 9 December, 1826, p.2. (Wentworth no longer owned the paper he co-founded, but it kept faith with his core ideas.)

4   Letters and editorials in *South Australian Register*, 19, 24, 26, 31 January 1860 (final quote, 19 January); State Library of South Australia, *Essay on the River Torrens*, www.slsa.sa.gov.au/manning/ pn/t/torrens.htm.

5   Walter Gibbons Cox, *Artesian Wells as a Means of Water Supply* (1895), pp.13–14; Mather, 'British Hydrology'; H. C. Russell, 'The River Darling—The Water which should Pass through it', *Journal and Proceedings of the Royal Society of New South Wales*, vol.13, 1879, p.169.

6   R. Tate, 'Geology in Its Relation to Mining and Subterranean Water Supply in South Australia,' *Transactions and Proceedings of the Royal Society of South Australia*, vol.16, 1883, p.156; mound spring ecology: Matthew Chambers et al., *Salt Pipewort Recovery Plan* (2002). On the fascinating debates around the origins of groundwater see A. E. Faggion, 'The Australian Groundwater Controversy, 1870–1910', *Historical Records of Australian Science*, vol.10, no.4, 1995.

7   For the dissenting view that this is 'plutonic water' see articles by L. A. Endersbee on the website of the Academy of Technological Sciences and Engineering.

8   C. S. Wilkinson, 'Notes on the Occurrence of Artesian wells in the Albert District, NSW', *Proceedings of the Linnean Society of NSW*, vol.6, part 1, 1882, pp.155–7; Sturt, *Two Expeditions*, vol.1, p.108.

9   John Wright, *Water Conservation etc., paper read before the Engineering Association of New South Wales on March 23, 1882*, pp.6–7.

10 Simon Fraser, *The True Story of the Beginning of the Artesian Water Supply of Australia* (1914); Christina Burr, 'Some Adventures of the Boys: Enniskillen Township's "Foreign Drillers," Imperialism, and Colonial Discourse, 1873–1923', *Labour/Le Travail*, Spring 2003, §12–14.

11 Fraser citing government statistics, p.14.

12 A. B. Paterson, 'The Man from Snowy River', in *The Man from Snowy River and Other Verses* (1895).

13 Henry Lawson, 'The Men Who Made Australia' in *When I Was King* (1906); and 'The Bush Undertaker' first published in *The Antipodean*, 1892.

14 George Essex Evans, 'An Australian Symphony: Written in an Australian Solitude', *The Secret Key and Other Verses* (1906). In a more necronationalist vein, see Victor James Daley's poem 'The Muses of Australia' in which the greatest muse, the muse of tragedy, walks the deserts 'in silence dread'.

15 Barcroft Boake, 'A Vision Out West', in his *Where the Dead Men Lie*, ebook, p.18.

16 Letter (29 December 1888) quoted by A. G. Stephens in the afterword to Boake, *Where the Dead Men Lie*, pp.109, 126. For Quatermain's suicidal disillusionment with 'civilisation', see H. Rider Haggard, *Allan Quatermain* (1887), Introduction.

17 William Gay, 'Australia Infelix' in J. J. Stable, *The High Road of Australian Verse* (1929), p.78.

18 William Mark Adams and Martin Mulligan, *Decolonizing Nature* (2003), pp.23–4.

19 A. B. Paterson, 'Song of the Artesian Water', *Rio Grande and Other Verses* (1917), first published *Bulletin*, 1896.

20 Clarice G. Crosbie, 'A Vision of Fountains' in Mary Wilkinson (ed.), *Nature Poems*.

21 Lawson wrote several irrigation poems. This is from 'My Land and I' in *When I Was King* (1905). In his poem 'Bourke', Lawson altered his fateful years on the Darling to 'ninety-one and ninety-two', with hypnotic effect.

Chapter 13: Dick Hardwicke to the Rescue

1   The term 'Lemurian novel' was popularised by John Docker in *The Nervous Nineties* (1991); J. J. Healy identified the Theosophical influence in 'The Lemurian Nineties', *Australian Literary Studies*, vol.8, no.3, 1978. See also David Hatcher Childress, *Lost Cities of Ancient Lemuria and the Pacific* (1988) and 'The Lost Continent of Lemuria', *Virtual Library of Sri Lanka*, website. The name was proposed by the English zoologist Philip Sclater in 'The Mammals of Madagascar', *Quarterly Journal of Science*, 1864. The lemur is unique to Madagascar, but resembles small mammals found in India, including the loris.

2   Al Gabay, *The Mystic Life of Alfred Deakin* (1992), p.24.

3   H. P. Blavatsky, *The Secret Doctrine* (1925), vol.2, pp.141, 189, 193–7 (long quote, p.197, her italics).

4   Hennessey, *An Australian Bush Track* was republished as *The Bush Track: A Story of the Australian Bush* (1913). References are to this edition.

5   Mrs Campbell [Rosa] Praed, *My Australian Girlhood* (1902), p.10 quoted in Healy, 'The Lemurian Nineties', p.309.

6   Tim Dolan surveyed library borrowing records and found that in 1901 Rider Haggard was in Australian readers' top ten authors (Tim Dolan, 'The Secret Reading Life of Us' in Brian Matthews (ed.), *Readers, Writers and Publishers: Essays and Poems* (2004), pp.115–133).

7   Convicts in Tench, *1788*, p.208; Flinders, *Voyage*, vol.1, pp.132–3; *Argus*, 7 March 1854, p.4.

8   Carlton Dawe, *The Golden Lake, or, The Marvellous History of a Journey through the Great Lone Land of Australia* (1891), ebook p.60, http://purl.library.usyd.edu.au/setis/id/dawgold.

9   Hennessey, *The Bush Track*, p.187.

10 Ernest Favenc, *The Secret of the Australian Desert* (1896), p.213. Favenc ended *The History of Australian Exploration* declaring that the 'apparently unlimited artesian supply' would place Australia 'among the recognised powers of the world'.

11 Dawe, *The Golden Lake*, p.89.

12 Healy, 'The Lemurian Nineties', p.311.

13 Rosa Praed, *Fugitive Anne*, ebook pp.72, 151, 125; Dawe, *The Golden Lake*, p.150.

14 Dawe, *The Golden Lake*, p.152.

15 Dawe, *The Golden Lake*, p.33.

16 Hennessey, *The Bush Track*, pp.185, 314.

17 Dawe, *The Golden Lake*, pp.90, 92.

18 In *Fugitive Anne*, we are told, with a sense of wonder and paradox, that the desert was once a sea on pp.33, 104, 142, 153, 171, 204, 305 (three times), and an 'inland sea' on pp.71, 104 and 135.

19 Dawe, *The Golden Lake*, p.50.

20 Dawe, *The Golden Lake*, p.62.

21 Praed, *Fugitive Anne*, pp.187–8.

22 G. Firth Scott, *The Last Lemurian*, pp.55–9.

23 Melissa Bellanta, 'Fabulating the Australian Desert: Australia's Lost Race Romances, 1890–1908', *Philament*, no.3, April 2004 www.arts. usyd.edu.au/publications/philament/issue3_Critique_Bellanta.htm. For further discussion of the novels along the same lines see Lindy Stiebel and Norman Etherington, 'Fantasy Maps' in N. Etherington (ed.), *Mapping Colonial Conquest* (2007), particularly p.64.

24 Dawe, *The Golden Lake*, p.116. And see *The Last Lemurian* in which Dick Halwood's kiss revives a long-dead white girl, whose body has been preserved in a cave in the heart of the lost tribe's country. As that degenerate race melts away, the girl embraces Dick, recognising that the time has come for a 'new and grander race' to fulfil the destiny of Australia.

25 On the meaning of 'dispersal' see Jonathon Richards, *The Secret War: A True History of Queensland's Native Police* (2008), pp.77–8, 94.

26 W. H. Corfield, *Reminiscences of Queensland* (1921), p.10.

27 Ray Evans, 'The Aboriginal Crisis', in *Proceedings of the 7th Conference of the Samuel Griffith Society*, Adelaide, 1996.

28 W. H. Willshire, *Land of the Dawning* (1896), pp.40–1.

29 Long quotation from Simpson Newland, *Paving the Way* (1893), p.143. For the historical implications of the novel see Robert Foster et. al., *Fatal Collisions: The South Australian Frontier* (2001), ch.2. Newland's complex personality is discussed in *ADB*.

30 H. Bloxham, *Fringe of the Never-Never* (1909), pp.4, 63–4, 80.

31 Ann McGrath, *'Born in the Cattle': Aborigines in Cattle Country* (1987), p.6. I borrowed the phrase 'the battle for the waterholes' from McGrath.

32 Dawe, *Golden Lake*, p.73.

33 Scott, *Last Lemurian*, pp.31–3.

34 Praed's father told her about these events when she was an adult (McCann, 'Unknown Australia: Rosa Praed's Vanished Race', *Australian Literary Studies*, vol.22, no.1, May 2005, pp.37–50). The number killed is discussed in Patricia Clarke, *Rosa! Rosa! A Life of Rosa Praed* (1999), p.18.

35 McCann, 'Unknown Australia', pp. 37–50; Clarke, *Rosa! Rosa!*, p.18; Windschuttle, 'The truth about our Aboriginal history,' Address to the National Press Club, Canberra, 19 April, 2001, www.sydneyline. com/National%20Press%20Club%20debate.htm. Gordon Buchanan, in his biography of his pioneering father, concludes that these revenge parties punished 'guilty and innocent' Aborigines alike and inflamed violence on the frontier in *Packhorse and Waterhole* (1933), pp.21–2.

36 Praed, *Fugitive Anne*, p.64. Anne says Aborigines killed a squatter who had murdered their relations with poisoned Christmas puddings. I suspect that this is Praed's moral equivalent for a crime that she is not prepared to name: generally Aborigines were exacting revenge for rape (see McCann, p.38).

37 Hudson Fysh, *Taming the North* (1950), p.25.

Chapter 14: Change of Heart

1 Mitchell, *Three Expeditions*, vol.2, 3 November 1836, 'The Murray', and his *Journal of an Expedition*, 1 September 1848; C. H. Gregory, 'Address of the President', *Institution of Civil Engineers, Minutes of Proceedings*, vol.27, January 1868, pp.181–2.

2 Favenc, *History of Australian Exploration*, final page. *Bulletin*, 5 December 1896, p.6 is dismayed to note the popularity of this sentiment.

3 Stuart Macintyre, *A Colonial Liberalism* (1991), pp.122, 125; B. R. Davidson, *Australia Wet or Dry?* (1969), p.53; *ADB*: James Moorhouse.

4   *ADB*: Hugh McColl; Ian Tyrrell, *True Gardens of the Gods: Californian–Australian Environmental Reform* (1999), pp.13, 103–20.

5   J. M. Powell, *An Historical Geography of Modern Australia* (1988), p.24.

6   Alfred Deakin, *Irrigation in Western America* (1884), pp.7–8; Davidson, *Australia Wet or Dry?*, pp.53–4.

7   Deakin, *Irrigation in Western America*, pp.73–4; Connell, *Water Politics*, pp.48–56, 75; J. M. Powell, *Watering the Garden State* (1989), pp.12–17. On California see William L. Kahrl, *Water and Power* (1982); and Marc Reisner's powerful critique of the USA's 'hydraulic society', *Cadillac Desert* (1993).

8   Connell, *Water Politics*, p.75.

9   Sturt, *Two Expeditions*, vol.2, ch.4, para.27; Walter Murdoch, *Alfred Deakin* (1923), pp.93–4.

10 Powell, *Watering the Garden State*, pp.117–27; 'gang of swindlers' in *Clarion*, 10 May 1909, p.15; 'idea which had failed' in Deakin's private notes 'The Medley', 31 January 1903, Deakin Papers National Library of Australia, quoted by John La Nauze, *Alfred Deakin* (1965), vol.2, p.84.

11 *West Australian Parliamentary Debates (WAPD)*, 1896, vol.9, pp.130–51.

12 A. G. Evans, *C. Y. O'Connor* (2001), p.147–8.

13 F. W. Robins, *The Story of Water Supply* (1946), p.199.

14 Fred Alexander et al., *The Origins of the Eastern Goldfields Water Scheme* (1954); *WAPD*, 1898, vol.12, George Leake: p.650, Forrest: p.686.

15 *Sunday Times*, 9 February 1902; Evans, *C. Y. O'Connor*, pp.191–2, 219, 225.

16 The speech is quoted on a plaque at the Coolgardie end of the pipeline.

17 Samuel Wadham, *Land Utilization in Australia* (1939), p.237.

18 David J. Gordon, *Conquering the Desert: Conservation–Reclamation–Irrigation. A National Policy for a Progressive People* (1907), pp.5, 10.

19 Connell, *Water Politics*, pp.56–69.

20 Gordon, *Conquering the Desert*, p.37.

21 C. H. Kirmess, *The Australian Crisis* (1909), serialised in *Lone Hand* the previous year. This anxiety is explored in David Walker, *Anxious Nation: Australia and the Rise of Asia* (1999), pp.98–112. For US parallels see Stanford M. Lyman, *Roads to Dystopia* (2001), p.72.

22 Warwick Anderson, *The Cultivation of Whiteness* (2002), pp.73–86. On the 1940s see Gerald Mussen, *Australia's Tomorrow* (1944), p.80. For Roosevelt and the global debate see Marilyn Lake and Henry Reynolds, *Drawing the Global Colour Line* (2008), ch.4.

23 Higgins: *Commonwealth Parliamentary Debates*, vol.4 (6 Sept. 1901), p.4659 cited by Anderson, *Cultivation of Whiteness*, p.91; Gilbert White, *Thirty Years in Tropical Australia* (1918), pp.100–1; Roosevelt quoted in Walker, *Anxious Nation*, p.114. This argument was still current in the 1930s: see Edward Masey, 'Vast Open Spaces: A Study of the Population Problem,' *The Publicist*, August 1936, pp.8–11.

24 e.g. Frank Clune, *The Red Heart* (1944), pp.1–2.

25 J. W. Gregory, *The Dead Heart of Australia* (1906), ch.18.

26 Noel Norman, 'The Dead Heart', ABC radio 2FC, 8 November 1942, Australian Archives, NSW Series SP 300/1, Box 9.

27 John Foster Fraser, *Australia: The Making of a Nation* (1910), p.11.

28 James Brunton Stephens, 'The Dominion of Australia (A Forecast, 1877)' popularised in Bertram Stevens (ed.), *An Anthology of Australian Verse* (1906).

29 Fraser, *Australia*, pp.81–2.

30 Elwood Mead, 'Irrigation in Victoria' in A. M. Laughton, T. S. Hall (eds), *Handbook to Victoria* (1914), p.259.

31 Ethel Turner, *Captain Cub* (1917), pp.159–62.

32 Ticky Fullerton, *Watershed: Deciding Our Water Future* (2001), p.98.

33 H. H. Richardson, *Australia Felix* (1971), p.189; Nora Kyffin Thomas, 'Silence in the Bush' in Wilkinson (ed.), *Gleanings*; E. H. Burgmann, 'The Education of an Australian' extracted in Alec Chisholm, *Land of Wonder* (1979), p.36.

Chapter 15: Australia Unlimited

1 Edwin Brady, *Australia Unlimited* (1918), pp.447, 633, 690.

2 Brady, *Australia Unlimited*, pp.639, 628.

3 Brady, *Australia Unlimited*, pp.628–31.

4   Stuart Macintyre, *The Succeeding Age* (1986), pp.200, 209.

5   Lawrence and Skinner, *The Boy and the Bush*, p.94.

6   Lawrence, *Kangaroo*, p.8.

7   Noel Norman, 'The Dead Heart', ABC radio 2FC, 8 November 1942, Australian Archives, NSW Series SP 300/1, Box 9.

8   Griffith Taylor, 'Geography and Australian National Problems', *Australasian Association for the Advancement of Science*, 1924, pp.433–87; 'ignorant booster' in Griffith Taylor, *Environment, Race and Migration* (1937), p.410. Key sources for this section are Marie Sanderson, *Griffith Taylor* (1988); Griffith Taylor, *Journeyman Taylor* (1958); Powell, *An Historical Geography*, pp.129–49.

9   Sanderson, *Griffith Taylor*, p.109.

10   Taylor, 'Geography and Australian National Problems', pp.466–74.

11   *SMH* ran a heroic profile of Stefansson on 24 May 1924, p.5, followed by coverage on 27, 28, 29, 30 May, 2 June, a detailed report of his ideas on 7 June 1924, supported by the 'possibilism' editorial on 9 June.

12   Taylor's ideas in 'Geography and ... Problems', p.486, *Argus*, 2 April 1921, and *Journeyman Taylor*, p.182. Fletcher contrasted their positions in *Water Magic* (1945). Stefansson visited outback South Australia and sent dispatches to *SMH* and the *Argus* including 'Central Australia: Neglected Asset', *Argus*, 8 August 1924, p.9; 'Into the "Dead Heart"', *Argus*, 21 July, p.11; 'Key to the Interior', *Argus*, 5 August, p.11. The *SMH* published key letters on the debate on 24, 31 May, 7, 28 June (all on p.13), and 23 June, p.5.

13   Taylor, 'Geography and Australian National Problems', p.451.

14   Taylor, *Australia*, p.459; Powell, *An Historical Geography*, pp.133–5.

15   Nelson reported in 'The Territory: A Rich Land', *SMH*, 24 May 1924, p.6; Taylor's recollection in *Journeyman Taylor*, pp.180–81.

16   *SMH* declared pessimism unpatriotic in 'Libelling Australia', 31 May 1924 p.10; see also *Commonwealth Parliamentary Debates*, 1924, 107, 2592–2593; Fletcher, *Water Magic*, p.54; *Journeyman Taylor*, p.182–4; Sanderson, *Griffith Taylor*, pp.121–2; 'Australia was blessed to see him go': *SMH*, 3 August 1928.

17   Bruce in House of Representatives, *Parliamentary Debates*, 10 February 1926; report in Bank of NSW, 'Australia's Vast Empty Spaces', *Circular*, 31 August 1936, p.8.

18 Edward Masey, 'Vast Open Spaces', pp.8–11.

19 Bank of NSW, 'Australia's Vast Empty Spaces'.

20 Ernestine Hill, *The Great Australian Loneliness* (1937), p.340.

21 H. H. Finlayson, *The Red Centre: Man and Beast in the Heart of Australia* (1935), pp.1–2, 34, 12, 73–5; Haynes, *Seeking the Centre*, p.148 and in the documentary *Wilderness Explored: Australia's Red Heart*, dir. Jeremy Bristow, BBC (2008).

22 See Tom Griffiths, *Hunters and Collectors* (1996), pp.141–9, and Tim Bonyhady's masterly essay on the colonial love of ferns in *The Colonial Earth*, ch.4.

23 They wrote under the pseudonym M. Barnard Eldershaw, *My Australia* (1939), pp.130–3, 149.

24 W. Hatfield, *Australia Through the Windscreen* (1936); C. T. Madigan, 'Central Australia: The One Good Year in Ten', *SMH*, 13 March 1937. Madigan's account of a trip through the Simpson Desert is published as *Crossing the Dead Heart* (1946).

25 Howard Daniel, Review of *Australia's Empty Spaces* in *Pacific Affairs*, March 1943, pp.3, 119–20.

26 Ion Idriess, *The Great Boomerang* (1941), p.229; on the Japanese threat see Idriess, *Forty Fathoms Deep* (1937), pp.342–3 and Idriess, *Must Australia Fight?* (1939).

27 On the Kimberley: *Walkabout*, November 1934, p.23; Idriess, *Great Boomerang*, p.8.

28 Idriess, *The Great Boomerang*, pp.32, 100. The line 'water is life' echoes through the entire book.

29 Idriess, *The Great Boomerang*, p.218.

30 Idriess, *The Great Boomerang*, pp.212, 217.

31 J. J. C. Bradfield, 'Rejuvenating the Sand Bagged Heart of Australia', *Queensland Geographical Journal*, vol.47, 1941–2, p.85. Bradfield's schemes and theories are summarised in *The Australian Encyclopaedia*, 1958, vol.9 under 'Water Diversion Schemes'.

32 J. J. C. Bradfield, 'Watering Inland Australia', *Ridge's*, 1 October 1941, p.606; see also his 'Rejuvenating Inland Australia', *Walkabout*, July 1941, pp.7–15, and his article in *Australian Quarterly*, vol.14, no.1, 1942. See J. M. Powell, *Plains of Promise, Rivers of Destiny* (1991), pp.156–62.

33   F. R. V. Timbury, *The Battle for the Inland* (1944), p.73.

34   Bradfield, 'Watering Inland Australia', pp.586, 606.

35   Bradfield, 'Rejuvenating the Sand Bagged Heart of Australia', p.85; 'Watering Inland Australia', p.588; Richard Raxworthy, *The Unreasonable Man: The Life and Work of J. J. C. Bradfield* (1989), p.137.

36   Bradfield 'Watering Inland Australia', pp.586, 588, 606; L. Luscombe, *Australia Replanned* (1945), p.91. The critics included Adelaide geographer Ann Marshall, 'Climate Aspects of the Bradfield Scheme', *JAIAS*, vol.10, no.4, 1944, pp.165–8 and the Bureau of Meteorology in 'Bradfield Scheme for "Watering the Inland": Meteorological Aspects', *Bulletin*, no.34, 1945, p.25. In support of his climate-change theory, Bradfield was able to cite one renegade meteorologist: E. T. Quayle.

37   W. H. R. Nimmo, 'The Bradfield Scheme', *Queensland Parliamentary Papers*, 1947–8, vol.2, p.640; J. D. Lang, 'Australia's Water Resources', *Walkabout*, 1 January 1947, pp.13–14, 18. In a recent study, two ANU scientists concluded that the scheme was too costly and risky to be viable: Ghassemi and White, *Inter-Basin Water Transfer* (2007), ch.6.

38   Anderson, *The Cultivation of Whiteness*, ch.5; Mussen, *Australia's Tomorrow*, p.80.

39   G. W. Leeper reviewing Idriess and Timbury's *Onward Australia* in *Meanjin*, vol.4, no.1, 1945, pp.89–90 quoted by Margriet Bonnin, 'A Study of Australian Descriptive and Travel Writing', p.146.

40   The schemes continued. In 1950, for example, the socialist Michael Sawtell revived the idea of digging a channel to flood Lake Eyre with sea water. See 'Filling Lake Eyre', *SMH*, 25 May 1950, p.2, and letters on 29 May, p.2 and 31 July 1950, p.2.

41   William Lines recalls that in Perth in the 1960s, schoolchildren and visitors to the state were taken to view that city's dams as if they were 'icons to a rational and technical order under construction in Australia' (*Taming the Great South Land*, p.xx).

42   H. C. Coombs, *Trial Balance* (1981), pp.66–8; Lionel Wigmore, *Struggle for the Snowy* (1968), p.viii; Chifley and Menzies in Brad Collis, *Snowy: The Making of Modern Australia* (1990), pp.38, 45.

43   H. Drake-Brockman, 'Water Means Wealth', *Walkabout*, 1 October 1944, p.5.

44   Wayne Reynolds, *Australia's Bid for the Atomic Bomb* (2000), p.54.

45 Ghassemi and White, *Inter-Basin Water Transfer*, ch.4, particularly p.105.

46 Ad for Feltex carpets. *Walkabout*, 1 May 1947. Also H. Drake-Brockman, 'Water Means Wealth'.

47 Bill Lovelock (words and music), *Snowy River, Roll!* (1953).

48 The Snowy Mountains Authority's glossy 44-page promotional book, *The Snowy Mountains Story* (c.1965) tells visitors that the scheme serves two needs—food and power (pp.6–8). It contains no mention of defence.

49 Frank Clune, 'Ayers Rock', *Walkabout*, 1 October 1941, pp.11–15; 'Dawn of Time': *Walkabout*, 1 December 1946; p.24; Bill Beatty, *Unique to Australia* (1962), p.154. The gradual banishment of the Aborigines from the Uluru story can be traced. They are present in the accounts of the early explorers but gradually become both 'ancient' and 'absent' in accounts during the 1950s and 1960s (see, for example, Ruth Ross, 'Learning Australia by Air', *Walkabout*, November 1968).

50 Barry Hill, *The Rock: Travelling to Uluru* (1994), pp.84–5.

51 Hill, *The Rock*, has a great deal to say about the shortcomings of Mountford and Harney (e.g. pp.1, 105, 122). For further discussion of these two see Ken Gelder and Jane M. Jacobs, *Uncanny Australia* (1998), ch.6, especially pp.113–15.

52 Advertisement, *Walkabout*, May 1968, p.40.

Chapter 16: New Beginnings

1 The key study is J. S. Lansing, 'Balinese "Water Temples" and the Management of Irrigation', *American Anthropologist*, 1987, vol.89, no.2, pp.326–41.

2 Dargin, *Aboriginal Fisheries of the Darling–Barwon Rivers*.

3 Peter Schwerdtfeger, 'Water Resources in South Australia: Down the Drain after 170 Years', 2006, www.airborneresearch.com.au/peter_schwerdtfeger.htm.

4 www.rifflinhitchlodge.com.

5 Marie-Louise Anderson, 'Feeling Connected', Monash University, www.utas.edu.au/arts/imaging/anderson.pdf

6   Deborah Bird Rose, *Nourishing Terrains: Australian Aboriginal Views of Landscape and Wilderness* (1996); Marcia Langton, 'The European Construction of Wilderness', *Wilderness News*, Wilderness Society, Summer 1995–96.

7   Blainey, *Short History of the World*, pp.35–6.

8   Jason Alexandra and David Eyre, 'Water and Environment', in Michael Johnson and Stephen Rix (eds), *Water in Australia* (1993), pp.98, 115–18; CSIRO, 'Toxic Algal Blooms', *Ecos*, no.72, 1992; John Whittington, 'Blue-Green Algae: A Preventable Emergency?', *Australian Journal of Emergency Management*, Spring 1999, pp.20–22.

9   Wentworth Group, *Submission to Senate Inquiry into the Urgent Provision of Water to the Coorong and Lower Lakes* (2008), www. wentworthgroup.org/category/articles/.

10   Asa Wahlquist, 'Murray River Entitlements up for Sale', *Australian*, 19 March 2009.

11   Quote in David Stevenson, 'Can water trading prevent droughts?', *Money Week*, 1 August 2008.

12   Maude Barlow, *Blue Covenant* (2007); *Fortune* quoted in John Louma, 'Water Thieves', *The Ecologist*, March 2004.

13   Asa Wahlquist, 'Murray River Entitlements up for Sale'.

14   See Louma, 'Water Thieves'; Barlow, *Blue Covenant*; Marq de Villiers, *Water* (1999).

15   Cheryl Fitzell, 'Listening to the Sounds of Silence', *Travel Australia*, 27 June 2006.

ACKNOWLEDGMENTS

Thanks to the corps of librarians who have so diligently assisted my research. I was extremely lucky in my choice of supervisors for the doctoral thesis which produced this book. Associate Professor Brian Finlayson inducted me into the ways of geographers—and took me on several road trips, including visits to Longreach in central Queensland and drought-stricken West Wyalong in New South Wales. His expertise in hydrology kept me anchored in the real world. Professor Stuart Macintyre was a rigorous, wise and generous supervisor in history.

My colleagues Sara Wills and Graham Willett provided gracious feedback. Since I began this project, I have received open-hearted encouragement from the filmmaker Michael Cordell, with whom I travelled the length of the O'Connor pipeline where I learned invaluable lessons in the art of documentary making. Thanks to Ian Thomas who took me on my second trip to Lake Eyre and to my friend Professor Kate Darian-Smith, who generously read and commented on several drafts.

Writers need a place to write—and I would not have completed this book without the kindness of Paul Cox, Kate Parkin and Bill Hamilton. Preparing this book for publication has been a joy thanks to the diligence and enthusiasm of my editor Jane Pearson and the team at Text. I owe the deepest debts to Jo Goodie with whom I first stood on the shores of Lake Eyre, to Jane Warren who took me punting in Oxford and to my wife Hannie Rayson whose love is my inland sea.

ILLUSTRATIONS

COLOUR PLATES

1. Major James Taylor, 'View of Port Jackson' (c.1821), engraved by R. Havell & Sons, Mitchell Library, State Library of New South Wales

2. John Black Henderson, 'The Tank Stream Sydney, 1852', Mitchell Library, State Library of New South Wales

3. T. J. Maslen, map of 'The Great River or the Desired Blessing' in *The Friend of Australia* (1830), Mitchell Library, State Library of New South Wales

4. Thomas Mitchell, 'Salvator River', National Library of Australia, nla.pic-an5356969

5. Charles Sturt, 'The Depot Glen, 1844', National Library of Australia, nla.pic-an5263644

6. Public funeral of the Australian explorers Burke and Wills 1863, National Library of Australia, nla.pic-an8960207

7. Sidney Nolan, 'Burke and Wills Expedition', 1948, enamel on board, 91.3x122.2cm, Nolan Gallery, Cultural Facilities Corporation, ACT, gift of the artist 1975 © Nolan Gallery, Cultural Facilities

8. Illustration from *The Secret of the Australian Desert*, Blackie, London, 1896

9. Louis Buderus, Early artesian bore struck in Ash Street, Barcaldine, Queensland, 1893, State Library of Queensland, image no. 46711

10. Ion Idriess, 'The Plan', from Idriess *The Great Boomerang*, Angus and Robertson, Sydney, 1941

11. L. H. Luscombe, 'Proposed Inland Sea and River System' (detail) from Luscombe, *Australia Replanned*, Ruskin Press, Melbourne, 1945

BLACK AND WHITE ILLUSTRATIONS

'Opening Up The Continent', chart from *The Australian Encyclopaedia*, Oxford University Press, Melbourne, 1958, vol.3

Griffith Taylor, 'Future settlement of Australia as determined by the environment' (detail), from *Australia: A Study of Warm Environments and their Effect on*

British Settlement, Methuen, London, 1947

All other maps by Tony Fankhauser.

BIBLIOGRAPHY

THESES

Bonnin, Margriet, 'A Study of Australian Descriptive and Travel Writing, 1929–1945, Ph.D. Thesis, University of Queensland, 1980

Cathcart, Michael and Martin, Susan K, 'Seaing the Inland: Fiction and Hydro-Engineering in Nineteenth Century Australia'. Unpublished paper presented at The Australian Centre, University of Melbourne, 11 June 1991

Clement, Cathie, 'Australia's North-West: A Study of Exploration, Land Policy and Land Acquisition, 1644–1884', Ph.D. Thesis, Murdoch University, 1991

Thompson, Christina, 'The Paradigm Journey to the Paradigm Elsewhere: Studies in South Pacific Romance', Ph.D. Thesis, University of Melbourne, 1990

NEWSPAPERS & JOURNALS

Argus (Melbourne), 1854–1900, 1924: *Australian* (Sydney), 1826–28; *Bell's Life in Victoria and Sporting Chronicle*, 1857–1862: *Blackwood's Edinburgh Magazine*, 1848; *Brisbane Courier*, 1888; *Bulletin*, 1880–1900; *Clarion*, 1907–1909; *Colonial Times* (Hobart), 1826; *Currency Lad*, 1832; *Hobart Town Courier*, 1836; *Journal of the Royal Geographical Society of London*, 1837–1900; *South Australian Register*, 1836–1860; *Sydney Gazette*, 1808–1828; *Sydney Morning Herald* (SMH), 1840–1890; *Walkabout*, 1934–1974.

MANUSCRIPTS

Bradfield Papers, Mitchell Library, Q631.1/B

Brady, E. J., Papers, La Trobe Library, Melbourne, MSS 12249 and 8625

Clune, Frank, Correspondence, Mitchell Library, MS 605

Institution of Civil Engineers, London, extensive holdings of letters, documents and books relating to water supply in Australia

Nathan, Sir Matthew, Papers, Ms Nathan 655–656, Bodleian Library of Commonwealth and African Studies at Rhodes House, Oxford, UK

Norman, Noel, 'The Dead Heart' by 'Offsider', script for talk on ABC radio station 2FC, 8 November 1942, Australian Archives, NSW Series SP 300/1

Northern Australian Expedition, Journal Mss Australia, 1837, Royal Geographical Society, London

Phillips, J. R., Letterbook, Mss. Austr.s.1. Bodleian Library of Commonwealth and African Studies at Rhodes House, Oxford, UK. Phillips was protector of Aborigines in WA

Royal Geographical Society Correspondence, 1851–60, An extensive collection which includes letters by Sturt, Eyre, Mitchell, Grey, Gawler and letters about the Northern Australia Expedition, Library of the Royal Geographical Society, London

Royal Geographical Society Journal, Mss Australia, 1838–1844, Articles and correspondence to the RGS journal relating to Australia—organised by years, includes a Ms draft of Sturt's 1844 journal (Sturt c.1), Library of the Royal Geographical Society, London

Seaward, John, 'An account of wells and borings by John Seaward' (OC 43) Institution of Civil Engineers Original Communications 1829–1832, Nos 44–80, Institution of Civil Engineers, Archives Register, London

Sturt Papers, MSS Australia s.4 and s.5—a major collection of letters and MSS by Sturt including the 'Charlotte Diary', Bodleian Library of Commonwealth and African Studies at Rhodes House, Oxford, UK

BOOKS

Adams, William Mark and Mulligan, Martin, *Decolonizing Nature: Strategies for Conservation in a Post-Colonial Era*, Earthscan, London, 2003

Aird, W. V. (ed.), *The Water Supply, Sewerage and Drainage of Sydney*, Metropolitan Water Sewerage and Drainage Board, Sydney, 1961

Alexander, Fred, Crowley, F. K., and Legge, J. D., *The Origins of the Eastern Goldfields Water Scheme in Western Australia: An exercise in the interpretation of historical evidence*, University of Western Australia Press, Perth, 1954

Anderson, Warwick, *The Cultivation of Whiteness: Science, Health and Racial Destiny in Australia*, Melbourne University Press, Melbourne, 2002

Angas, George French, *Savage Life and Scenes in Australia and New Zealand: Being an Artist's Impressions of Countries and People at the Antipodes*, 2 vols., Smith Elder, London, 1847

Angas, George French, *South Australia Illustrated*, Thomas McLean, London, 1846

Ashton, Paul and Blackmore, Kate, *Centennial Park: A History*, University of New South Wales Press, Sydney, 1988

Atkinson, Alan, *The Europeans in Australia*, Oxford University Press, Melbourne, 1997

Australian Dictionary of Biography, www.adb.online.anu.edu.au. I have cited entries thus, *ADB*: Charles Sturt

Australian Encyclopaedia, The, 10 vols, Angus & Robertson, Sydney, 1958

Baker, D. W. A., *The Civilised Surveyor: Thomas Mitchell and the Australian Aborigines*, Melbourne University Press, Melbourne, 1997

Ball, Philip, *H₂O: A Biography of Water*, Weidenfeld & Nicolson, London, 1999

Barlow, Maude, *Blue Covenant: The Global Water Crisis and the Coming Battle for the Right to Water*, Black Inc., Melbourne, 2007

Barrington, George, *The History of New South Wales, Including Botany Bay, Port Jackson, Parramatta, Sydney, and all its Dependencies*, M. Jones, London, 1802

Batman, John, *The Settlement of John Batman in Port Phillip: From his own Journal*, Melbourne [1856], facsimile edition, Quest, Melbourne, 1985

Bayldon, Arthur, *The Western Track and Other Verses*, H. T. Dunn, Sydney, 1905

Beale, Edgar, *Sturt, the Chipped Idol: A Study of Charles Sturt Explorer*, Sydney University Press, Sydney, 1979

Beasley, Margo, *The Sweat of their Brows: 100 Years of the Sydney Water Board 1888–1988*, Water Board, Sydney, 1988

Beatty, Bill, *Unique to Australia*, Ure Smith, Sydney, 1952. Revised editions 1962, 1975

Bennett, Samuel, *The History of Australian Discovery and Colonisation*, 2 vols, Hanson & Bennett, Sydney, 1865

Berzins, Baiba, *The Coming of the Strangers: Life in Australia 1788–1822*, Collins/State Library of New South Wales, Sydney, 1988

Billington, Ray Allen, *The Westward Movement in the United States*, D. Van Nostrand Co, Princeton, 1959

Blainey, Geoffrey, *A Land Half Won*, Sun Books, Melbourne, 1983

Blainey, Geoffrey, *A Short History of the World*, Viking, Melbourne, 2000

Blainey, Geoffrey, *The Tyranny of Distance: How Distance Shaped Australia's History*, Sun Books, Melbourne, 1966

Blavatsky, H. P., *The Secret Doctrine: The Synthesis of Science, Religion, and Philosophy*, [1888], 2 vols, Aryan Theosophical Press, California, 1925

Blaxland, Gregory, *Journal of a Tour of Discovery Across The Blue Mountains, New South Wales, in the Year 1813*, Australian Historical Society, Sydney, 1913

Bloxham, H. K., *On the Fringe of the Never-Never*, NSW Bookstall Co., Sydney, 1909

Blue Book, The, Blue Star, Sydney, 1942

Boake, Barcroft, *Where the Dead Men Lie and Other Poems*, Angus & Robertson, Sydney, 1897

Boer, Roland, *Last Stop before Antarctica: The Bible and Postcolonialism in Australia*, Sheffield Academic Press, Sheffield UK, 2001

Bolton, Geoffrey, *Spoils and Spoilers: A History of Australians Shaping their Environment*, Allen & Unwin, Sydney, 1992

Bonyhady, Tim, and Tom Griffiths (eds), *Words for Country: Landscape and Language in Australia*, University of New South Wales Press, Sydney, 2002

Bonyhady, Tim, *Burke and Wills: From Melbourne to Myth*, David Ell Press, Sydney, 1991

Bonyhady, Tim, *The Colonial Earth*, Miegunyah Press, Melbourne, 2000

Bourke Historical Society, *History of Bourke*, a multi-volume local history published over many years

Boyce, James, *Van Diemen's Land*, Black Inc., Melbourne, 2008

Boyd, A. J., *Old Colonials* [1882], edited by G. A. Wilkes, Sydney University Press, Sydney, 1974

Bradfield, J. J. C., *Queensland—The Conservation and Utilization of Her Water Resources: A Report*, Sydney, 1938

Bradley, William, *A Voyage to New South Wales*, Trustees of the Public Library of NSW with Ure Smith, Sydney, 1969

Brady, Edwin. J., *Australia Unlimited*, George Robertson, Melbourne, 1918

Brock, Daniel George, *To the Desert with Sturt: A Diary of the 1844 Expedition*, Kenneth Peake-Jones (ed.), Royal Geographical Society of Australasia, Adelaide 1975.

Brown, E. H. (ed.), *Geography Yesterday and Tomorrow*, Oxford University Press, Oxford, 1980

Brown, Louise, et al. (eds), *A Book of South Australia: Women in the First Hundred Years*, Rigby, for the Women's Centenary Council of S.A., Adelaide, 1936

Brown-May, Andrew, *Melbourne Street Life: The Itinerary of Our Days*, Australian Scholarly Publishing, Melbourne, 1998

Buchanan, Gordon, *Packhorse and Waterhole: With the First Overlanders to the Kimberleys*, Angus & Robertson, Sydney, 1933

Burke, Edmund, *A Philosophical Inquiry into the Origin of Our Ideas of the Sublime and the Beautiful* [1756], Part 2.6, Harvard Classics, vol.22, part 2, 2001

Butlin, Noel, *Economics and the Dreamtime: A Hypothetical History*, Cambridge University Press, New York, 1993

Campbell, Judy, *Smallpox and Other Diseases in Aboriginal Australia 1780–1880*, Melbourne University Press, Melbourne, 2002

Cannon, Michael, *The Exploration of Australia*, Reader's Digest, Sydney, 1999

Carnegie, David W., *Spinifex and Sand: A Narrative of Five Years' Pioneering and Exploration in Western Australia*, C. Arthur Pearson, London, 1898 (facsimile edition, Penguin, 1973)

Carter, Paul, *Living in a New Country: History, Travelling and Language*, Faber & Faber, London, 1992

Carter, Paul, *The Road to Botany Bay: An Essay in Spatial History*, Faber & Faber, London, 1987

Carter, Paul, *The Sound in Between*, New South Wales University Press, Sydney, 1992

Charlesworth, Max, et al. (eds), *Religion in Aboriginal Australia: An Anthology*, University of Queensland Press, Brisbane, 1984

Childress, David Hatcher, *Lost Cities of Ancient Lemuria and the Pacific*, Adventurers Unlimited Press, Illinois, 1988

Chisholm, Alec, *Land of Wonder: The Best Australian Nature Writing*, Allen & Unwin, Sydney, 1979

Chisholm, Alec, *Strange New World: The Adventures of John Gilbert and Ludwig Leichhardt*, Angus & Robertson, Sydney, 1941

Clark, C. M. H., *A History of Australia*, 6 vols, Melbourne University Press, Melbourne, 1961–87

Clark, Ralph, *The Journal and Letters of Lt. Ralph Clark, 1787–1792*, Australian Documents Library/ Library of Australian History, Sydney, 1981.

Clarke, Marcus, *Holiday Peak and Other Tales*, G. Robertson, Melbourne, 1873

Clarke, Marcus, Preface to *Poems of the late Adam Lindsay Gordon* [1887], Samuel Mullen, London, 1887

Clarke, Patricia, *Rosa! Rosa! A Life of Rosa Praed, Novelist and Spiritualist*, Melbourne University Press, Melbourne, 1999

Clendinnen, Inga, *Dancing with Strangers*, Text, Melbourne, 2003

Clune, Frank, *The Red Heart: Sagas of Centralia*, Hawthorne Press, Melbourne, 1944

Cobley, John (ed.), *Sydney Cove: 1795–1800*, Angus & Robertson, Sydney, 1986

Collins, David, *An Account of the English Colony in New South Wales*, Cadell and Davies, London, 2 vols, 1798, 1802

Collis, Brad, *Snowy: The Making of Modern Australia*, Hodder & Stoughton, Sydney, 1990

Connell, Daniel, *Water Politics in the Murray–Darling Basin*, Federation, Sydney, 2007

Coombs, H. C., *Trial Balance: Issues of My Working Life*, Macmillan, Sydney, 1981

Cooper, Frederic, *Wild Adventures in Australia and New South Wales*, James Blackwood, London, 1857

Corfield, W. H., *Reminiscences of Queensland, 1862–1899*, A. H. Frater, Brisbane, 1921

Cox, W. Gibbons, *Artesian Wells as a Means of Water Supply*, Sapsford, Brisbane, 1895

Crowley, Frank, *A Documentary History of Australia*, Nelson, Melbourne, 5 vols., 1980

Cumpston, J. H. L., *Augustus Gregory and the Inland Sea*, Roebuck, Sydney, 1972

Cumpston, J. H. L., *Charles Sturt: His Life and Journeys of Exploration*, Georgian House, Melbourne, 1951

Cumpston, J. H. L., *The Inland Sea and the Great River: The Story of Australian Exploration*, Angus & Robertson, Sydney, 1964

Cunningham, Chris, *The Blue Mountains Rediscovered: Beyond the Myths of Early Australian Exploration*, Kangaroo Press, Sydney, 1996

Curr, E. M., *Recollections of Squatting in Victoria* [1883], Melbourne University Press, Melbourne, 1965

Daley, Charles, *The History of South Melbourne: From the Foundation of Settlement at Port Phillip to the Year 1938*, Robertson & Mullens, Melbourne, 1940

Dargin, Peter, *Aboriginal Fisheries of the Darling–Barwon Rivers*, Brewarrina Historical Society, Brewarrina, 1976

David, B., B. Barker, I. J. Niven (eds), *The Social Archaeology of Australian Indigenous Societies*, Aboriginal Studies Press, Canberra, 2006

Davidson, B. R., *Australia Wet or Dry?*, Melbourne University Press, Melbourne, 1969

Davison, Graeme, *The Unforgiving Minute: How Australians Learned to Tell the Time*, Oxford University Press, Melbourne, 1993

Deakin, Alfred, *Irrigation in Western America*, Royal Commission on Water Supply, Government Printer, Melbourne, 1884

Dening, Greg, *Readings/Writings*, Melbourne University Press, Melbourne, 1998

Dermody, Docker and Modjeska (eds), *Nellie Melba, Ginger Meggs and Friends: Essays in Australian Cultural History*, Kibble Books, Malmsbury, Vic., 1982

De Villiers, Marq, *Water: The Fate of Our Most Precious Resource*, Stoddart, Toronto, 1999

de Voto, Bernard (ed.), *The Journals of Lewis and Clark*, Houghton Mifflin, Boston, 1953

Dixon, Robert, *Writing the Colonial Adventure: Race, Gender and Nation in Anglo-Australian Popular Fiction 1875–1914*, Cambridge University Press, Cambridge, 1995.

Docker, John, *The Nervous Nineties: Australian Cultural Life in the 1890s*, Oxford University Press, Melbourne, 1991

Duffy, Michael, *Man of Honour: John Macarthur—Duellist, Rebel, Founding Father*, Macmillan, Sydney, 2003

Durack, Mary, *Kings in Grass Castles*, Constable and Co., London, 1959

Education Department Victoria, *The Victorian Reading-Books: Eighth Book*, H. J. Green, Government Printer, Melbourne, 1928

Eidelson, Meyer, *The Melbourne Dreaming: A Guide to the Aboriginal Places of Melbourne*, Aboriginal Studies Press, Canberra, 1997

Elder, Catriona, *Being Australian: Narratives of National Identity*, Allen & Unwin, Sydney, 2007

Eldershaw, M. Barnard (pseud.), *My Australia*, Jarrolds, London, 1939

Etherington, Norman (ed.), *Mapping Colonial Conquest Australia and Southern Africa*, University of Western Australia Press, Perth, 2007

Evans, A. G., *C. Y. O'Connor: His Life and Legacy*, University of WA Press, Perth, 2001

Evans, George Essex, *The Secret Key and Other Verses*, Angus & Robertson, Sydney, 1906

Eyre, Edward, *Journals Of Expeditions Of Discovery into Central Australia And Overland From Adelaide To King George's Sound In The Years 1840–1*, 2 vols, T & W. Boone, London, 1845

Eyre, Edward, *Reports and Letters to Governor Grey from E. J. Eyre at Moorundie*, Sullivan's Cove, Adelaide, 1985

Falkiner, Suzanne, *The Writers' Landscape: Wilderness*, Simon & Schuster, Sydney, 1992

Farwell, George, and Frank H. Johnston (eds.), *This Land of Ours: Australia*, Angus & Robertson, Sydney, 1949

Farwell, George, *Riders to an Unknown Sea. The Story of Charles Sturt: Explorer*, Macmillan, Melbourne, 1963

Favenc, Ernest, *The Explorers of Australia and Their Life-Work*, Whitcombe & Tombs, Melbourne, 1908

Favenc, Ernest, *The History of Australian Exploration*, Turner & Henderson, Sydney, 1888

Favenc, Ernest, *The Secret of the Australian Desert*, Blackie, London, 1896

Favenc, Ernest, *Voices of the Desert*, Elliot Stock, London, 1905

Filson, John, *The Adventures of Col. Daniel Boon* [sic]; *Containing a Narrative of the Wars of Kentucke* [1784], www.earlyamerica.com/lives/boone

Finlayson, H. H., *The Red Centre: Man and Beast in the Heart of Australia*, Angus & Robertson, Sydney, 1935

Finn, Edmund, *The Chronicles of Early Melbourne, 1835 to 1852: Historical, Anecdotal and Personal, by 'Garryowen'*, [1888], Melbourne Heritage Publications, Melbourne, 1976

Fitzpatrick, Kathleen (ed.), *Australian Explorers: A Selection of their Writings*, Oxford University Press, London, 1958

Flanagan, Richard, *A Terrible Beauty: History of the Gordon River Country*, Greenhouse, Melbourne, 1985

Flannery, Tim (ed.), *The Birth of Sydney*, Text, Melbourne, 1999

Flannery, Tim, *The Future Eaters: An Ecological History of the Australasian Lands and People*, Reed Books, Sydney, 1994

Fleming, James, *The Voyage of His Majesty's Colonial Schooner 'Cumberland' from Sydney to King Island and Port Phillip in 1802–3*. There are three editions. (1) John J. Shillinglaw (ed.), *Historical Records of Port Phillip: The First Annals of the Colony of Victoria*, Melbourne, 1879. (2) The same republished with introduction and notes by C. E. Sayers, Melbourne: Heinemann, 1972, pp.12–39. (3) John Currey (ed.) *A Journal of Grimes' Survey: The Cumberland in Port Phillip January–February 1803*, Banks Society, Melbourne, 2002

Fletcher, C. Brunsdon, *Water Magic: Australia and the Future*, John Sands, Sydney, 1945

Flinders, Matthew, *A Voyage to Terra Australis…Prosecuted in the Years 1801–3*, 2 vols., G & W Nichol, London, 1814

Flood, Josephine, *The Original Australians*, Allen & Unwin, Sydney, 2006

Flynn, Frank, *The Living Heart*, F. P. Lemard, Sydney, 1964

Forbes, George, *History of Sydney: From the Foundation of the City in 1788 up to the present time, 1926, Compiled from Authentic Sources*, William Brooks & Co., Sydney, 1926

Foster, Robert, Hosking, Rick and Nettelbeck, Amanda, *Fatal Collisions: The South Australian Frontier and the Violence of Memory*, Wakefield Press, Adelaide, 2001

Fotheringham, Richard (ed.), *Australian Plays for the Colonial Stage*, University of Queensland Press, Brisbane, 2006

Fraser, John Foster, *Australia: The Making of a Nation*, Cassell, London, 1910

Fraser, Simon, *The True Story of the Beginning of the Artesian Water Supply of Australia*, George Robertson, Melbourne, 1914

Fullerton, Ticky, *Watershed: Deciding Our Water Future*, ABC Books, Sydney, 2001

Furphy, Joseph, *Such Is Life*, Angus & Robertson, Sydney, 1945

Fysh, Hudson, *Taming the North*, Angus & Robertson, Sydney, [1933], 1950

Gabay, Al, *The Mystic Life of Alfred Deakin*, Cambridge University Press, Cambridge, 1992

Gardiner, L. B., *Thomas Mitchell*, Oxford University Press, Melbourne, 1962

Garran, Andrew (ed.), *Picturesque Atlas of Australia* [1888]. Facsimile edition, Ure Smith, Sydney, 1974

Gelder, Ken and Jane M. Jacobs, *Uncanny Australia: Sacredness and Identity in a Postcolonial Nation*, Melbourne University Press, Melbourne, 1998

Genoni, Paul, *Subverting the Empire: Explorers and Exploration in Australian Fiction*, Common Ground Publishing, Melbourne, 2004

Ghassemi, Fereidoun and White, Ian, *Inter-Basin Water Transfer: Case Studies from Australia, United States, Cananda, China and India*, International Hydrology Series, Cambridge University Press, Cambridge, 2007

Gibson, Ross, *South of the West: Postcolonialism and the Narrative Construction of Australia*, Indiana University Press, Bloomington, 1992

Gibson, Ross, *The Diminishing Paradise: Changing Literary Perceptions of Australia*, Sirius, Sydney, 1984

Giles, Ernest, *Australia Twice Traversed: The Romance of Exploration*, S. Low, Marston, Searle & Rivington, London, 1889

Gilmore, Mary, *Old Days: Old Ways* [1934], Angus & Robertson, Sydney, 1986

Gordon, Adam Lindsay, *Sea Spray and Smoke Drift*, Clarson, Messina, Melbourne, 1876

Gordon, David J., *Conquering the Desert: Conservation—Reclamation—Irrigation. A National Policy for a Progressive People*, Government Printer, Adelaide, 1907

Greenblatt, Stephen, *Marvelous Possessions: The Wonder of the New World*, Oxford University Press, Oxford, 1991

Gregory, A. C. and F. T. Gregory, *Journals of Australian Explorations*, Government Printer, Brisbane, 1884

Gregory, J. W., *The Dead Heart of Australia: A Journey Around Lake Eyre in the Summer of 1901–1902*, John Murray, London, 1906

Griffiths, Tom, *Forests of Ash: An Environmental History*, Cambridge University Press, Melbourne, 2001

Griffiths, Tom, *Hunters and Collectors: The Antiquarian Imagination in Australia*, Cambridge University Press, Cambridge, 1996

Gunn, Mrs. Aeneas, *We of the Never Never*, Hutchinson & Co., London, 1907

Haggard, H. Rider, *King Solomon's Mines* [1885], *She* [1887], *Allan Quatermain* [1887], Octopus, London, 1979

Hall, Colin Michael, *Wasteland to World Heritage: Preserving Australia's Wilderness*, Melbourne University Press, Melbourne, 1992

Hammond, Dorothy and Alta Jablow, *The Africa that Never Was: Four Centuries of British Writing about Africa*, Twayne, New York, 1977

Hancock, W. K., *Australia*, [1930], Australasian Publishing, Sydney, 1945

Harney, W. E. (Bill), *To Ayers Rock and Beyond*, Rigby, Adelaide, 1963

Hatfield, William, *Australia Through the Windscreen*, Angus & Robertson, Sydney, 1936

Hawdon, Joseph, *The Journal of a Journey from New South Wales to Adelaide (The Capital of South Australia) Performed in 1838*, Georgian House, Melbourne, 1952

Haynes, Roslynn D., *Seeking the Centre: The Australian Desert in Literature, Art and Film*, Cambridge University Press, Cambridge, 1998

Hayter, John, *The Landsman's Log-book, or, An Emigrant's Life at Sea: with some Account of South Australia*, Smith, Elder, London, 1842

Hennessey, John David, *The Bush Track: A Story Of The Australian Bush*, Hodder & Stoughton, 1913; originally published as *An Australian Bush Track*, Sampson Low, Marston, London, 1896

Hill, Barry, *The Rock: Travelling to Uluru*, Allen & Unwin, Sydney, 1994

Hill, Ernestine, *The Great Australian Loneliness* [1940], Robertson & Mullens, Melbourne, 1952

Hill, Hugh Robert, *The Record of the Royal Geographical Society*, RGS, London, 1930

Hippocrates, *On Airs, Waters and Places*, translated by Francis Adams, Sydenham Society, London, 1849

Hirst, John, *Convict Society and Its Enemies: A History of Early New South Wales*, George Allen & Unwin, Sydney, 1983

Holmes, J. Macdonald, *The Murray Valley: A Geographical Reconnaissance of the Murray Valley and a New Design for its Regional Organization*, Angus & Robertson, Sydney, 1948

Holt, Joseph, *Memoirs of Joseph Holt*, T. Crofton Croker (ed.), Henry Colburn, London, 1838

Hope, Jeannette, and Gary Vines, *Brewarrina Aboriginal Fisheries Conservation Plan*, A Report for the Brewarrina Aboriginal Cultural Museum, Brewarrina, 1994

Horton, David, *The Pure State of Nature: Sacred Cows, Destructive Myths and the Environment*, Allen & Unwin, Sydney, 2000

Howitt, W., *Land, Labour and Gold; or, Two Years in Victoria with Visits to Sydney and Van Diemen's Land* [1885], Lowden, Kilmore, Vic., 1972

Hunter, John, *An Historical Journal of Events at Sydney and at Sea, 1787–1792* [1793], Angus & Robertson, Sydney, 1968

Idriess, Ion, *The Great Boomerang*, Angus & Robertson, Sydney, 1941

Jeffcoat, Kevin, *More Precious than Gold: An Illustrated History of Water in New South Wales*, Department of Water Resources in association with Kangaroo Press, Sydney, 1988

Johnson, Michael and Stephen Rix, *Water in Australia: Managing Economic, Environmental and Community Reform*, Pluto, Sydney, 1993

Johnson, Richard, *The Search for the Inland Sea: John Oxley, explorer, 1783–1828*, Melbourne University Press, Melbourne, 2001

Jones, Philip, *Ochre and Rust: Artefacts and Encounters on Australian Frontiers*, Wakefield Press, Adelaide, 2007

Kahn, Douglas, *Noise, Water, Meat: A History of Sound in the Arts*, MIT Press, Cambridge, Mass., 1999

Kahrl, William L., *Water and Power: The Conflict over Los Angeles' Water Supply in the Owens Valley*, University of California Press, Berkeley, 1982

Kass, Terry and Carol Liston, John McClymont, *Parramatta: A Past Revealed*, Parramatta City Council, Sydney, 1996

Kelly, Robert, *Battling the Inland Sea: American Political Culture, Public Policy and the Sacramento Valley, 1850–1986*, University of California Press, Berkeley, 1989

Kelly, Max (ed.) *Nineteenth-Century Sydney: Essays in Urban History*, Sydney University Press, Sydney, 1978

King, Phillip Parker, *Narrative of a Survey of the Intertropical and Western Coasts of Australia performed between the years 1818 and 1822*, 2 vols, John Murray, London, 1827

Kingsley, Henry, *The Recollections of Geoffry Hamlyn* [1858], Hallcraft, Melbourne, 1952

Kirkpatrick, Jamie, and Bridle, Kerry, (eds), *People, Sheep and Nature Conservation: The Tasmanian Experience*, CSIRO Publishing, Melbourne, 2007

Kirmess, C., *The Australian Crisis*, Lothian, Melbourne, 1909

Kohen, James, *The Darug and their Neighbours: The Traditional Aboriginal Owners of the Sydney Region*, Darug Link with Blacktown and District Historical Society, Sydney, 1993

Kolodny, Annette, *The Land Before Her: Fantasy and Experience of the American Frontiers, 1630–1860*, University of North Carolina Press, Chapel Hill, 1984

Kolodny, Annette, *The Lay of the Land: Metaphor as Experience and History in American Life and Letters*, University of North Carolina Press, Chapel Hill, 1975

Kramer, Leonie (ed.), *My Country: Australian Poetry and Short Stories, Two Hundred Years*, 2 vols., Lansdowne, Sydney, 1985

La Nauze, John, *Alfred Deakin: A Biography*, 2 vols, Melbourne University Press, Melbourne, 1965

Lake, Marilyn and Reynolds, Henry, *Drawing the Global Colour Line*, Melbourne University Press, Melbourne, 2008

Lang, Rev. J. D., *A Sermon Preached on Sunday, June 15, 1823, to the Congregation of Scots Presbyterians, in Sydney, New South Wales*, Robert Howe, Sydney, 1823

Langley, Michael, *Sturt of the Murray*, Robert Hale, London, 1969

Laughton, A. M. and T. S. Hall (eds), *Handbook to Victoria, Prepared for Members of the British Association for the Advancement of Science*, Government Printer, Melbourne, 1914

Lawrence, A. E., *Taming the Wilderness: One Family's Contribution to Irrigation in Australia*, Melbourne, 1985

Lawrence, D. H. and Skinner, Mollie, *The Boy and the Bush* [1929], Cambridge University Press, Cambridge, 2002

Lawrence, D. H., *Kangaroo* [1923], Heinemann, Melbourne, 1963

Lawson, Henry, *While the Billy Boils*, Angus & Robertson, Sydney, 1896

Lawson, Henry, *When I was King*, Angus & Robertson, Sydney, 1905

Lee, Ida (ed.), *Early Explorers in Australia*, Methuen, London, 1825

Leichhardt, F. W. L., *Journal of an Overland Expedition in Australia from Moreton Bay to Port Essington, 1844–1845*, T. & W. Boone, London, 1847

Leonard, John (ed.), *Australian Verse: An Oxford Anthology*, Oxford University Press, Melbourne, 1998

Lighthall, William (ed.), *Songs of the Great Dominion: Voices from the Forests and Waters, the Settlements and Cities of Canada*, W. Scott, London, 1889

Lindsay, Joan, *Picnic at Hanging Rock* [1967], Penguin, Melbourne, 1970

Lines, William J., *An All Consuming Passion: Origins, Modernity and the Australian Life of Georgiana Molloy*, Allen & Unwin, Sydney, 1994

Lines, William J., *Taming the Great South Land: A History of the Conquest of Nature in Australia*, Allen & Unwin, Sydney, 1991

Lourandos, Harry, *Continent of Hunter-Gatherers: New Perspectives on Australian Prehistory*, Cambridge University Press, Cambridge, 1997

Lovelock, Bill (words and music), *Snowy River, Roll!*, Southern Music Publishing, Sydney, 1953

Luckin, Bill, *Pollution and Control: A Social History of the Thames in the Nineteenth Century*, Adam Hilger, Bristol, 1986

Luscombe, L. H. ('Veritas'), *Australia Replanned*, Ruskin Press, Melbourne, 1945

Macdonald, Alexander, *The Lost Explorers: A Story of the Trackless Desert*, Blackie & Sons, London & Glasgow, 1886

Macdougall, A. K., *The Big Treasury of Australian Folklore*, Currawong Press, Sydney, 1990

McEwan, Marcia, *Great Australian Explorers*, Bay Books, Sydney, 1979

McGrath, Ann, *'Born in the Cattle': Aborigines in Cattle Country*, Allen & Unwin, Sydney, 1987

Macintyre, Stuart, *A Colonial Liberalism: The Lost World of Three Victorian Visionaries*, Oxford, Melbourne, 1991

Macintyre, Stuart, *The Succeeding Age*, vol.4 of *The Oxford History of Australia*, Oxford University Press, Melbourne, 1986

McLaren, Glen, *Beyond Leichhardt: Bushcraft and Exploration of Australia*, Fremantle Arts Centre Press, Fremantle, 1996

McMinn, W. G., *Allan Cunningham: Botanist and Explorer*, Melbourne University Press, Melbourne, 1970

McPhee, John (ed.), *Joseph Lycett: Convict Artist*, Historic Houses Trust, Sydney, 2006

Macqueen, Andy, *Blue Mountains to Bridgetown: The Life and Journeys of Barrallier 1773–1853*, A. Macqueen, Springwood NSW, 1993

Madigan, C. T., *Central Australia*, Oxford University Press, London, 1936

Madigan, C. T., *Crossing the Dead Heart* [1946], Rigby, Adelaide, 1974

Marsh, George P., *Man and Nature; or, Physical Geography as Modified by Human Action*, Sampson Low, Son and Marston, London, 1864

Maslen, T. J. *The Friend of Australia: or A Plan for Exploring the Interior and Carrying on a Survey of the Whole Continent of Australia*, Hurst, Chance & Co., London, 1830, and 1836

Massola, A., *Bunjil's Cave: Myths, Legends and Superstitions of the Aborigines of South-East Australia*, Lansdowne Press, Melbourne, 1968

Matthews, Brian (ed.), *Readers, Writers and Publishers: Essays and Poems*, Australian Academy of the Humanities, Canberra, 2004

Maurice, Furnley, *Melbourne Odes*, Lothian, Melbourne, 1934

Meinig, D.W., *On The Margins Of The Good Earth: The South Australian Wheat Frontier, 1869–1884*, McNally, Chicago, 1962

Mill, Hugh Robert, *The Record of the Royal Geographical Society 1830–1930*, Royal Geographical Society, London, 1930

Millar, Ann, *'I See No End to Travelling': Journals of Australian Explorers 1813–76*, Bay Books, Sydney, 1986

Mitchell, T. L., *Journal of an Expedition into the Interior of Tropical Australia, in Search of a Route from Sydney to the Gulf of Carpentaria*, Longman, London, 1848

Mitchell, T. L., *Three Expeditions into the Interior of Eastern Australia, with Descriptions of the Recently Explored Region of Australia Felix*, 2 vols., Boone, London, 1839

Moorehead, Alan, *Cooper's Creek*, Hamish Hamilton, London, 1963

Morris, E. E., *Austral English* [1898], facsimile edition published as *Dictionary of Australian Words*, Currey O'Neil, Adelaide, 1982

Mountford, Charles P., *Ayers Rock, Its People, Their Beliefs and Their Art*, Angus & Robertson, Sydney, 1965

Mulvaney, D. J. and J. P. White (eds), *Australians to 1788*, Fairfax, Syme & Weldon, Sydney, 1987

Murdoch, Walter (ed.), *The Oxford Book of Australasian Verse*, Oxford University Press, Oxford, 1918

Murdoch, Walter, *Alfred Deakin: A Sketch*, Constable, London, 1923

Murgatroyd, Sarah, *The Dig Tree: The Story of Burke and Wills*, Text, Melbourne, 2002

Mussen, Sir Gerald, *Australia's Tomorrow*, Robertson & Mullens, Melbourne, 1944

Nash, Roderick, *Wilderness and the American Mind*, Yale University Press, New Haven, 1967.

Nevins, Allan and Henry Steele Commager, *America: The Story of a Free People* [1942], Oxford University Press, London, 3rd ed. 1966

Newland, Simpson, *Paving The Way: A Romance of the Australian Bush* [1893], Rigby, Adelaide, 1950

Nimmo, W. H. R., *The Bradfield Scheme*, Stanley River Works Board, Brisbane, 1947

Oxley, John, *Journals of Two Expeditions into the Interior of New South Wales, Undertaken by Order of the British Government in the Years 1817–18*, London, 1820

Palmer, Vance, *The Legend of the Nineties*, Melbourne University Press, Melbourne, 1954

Parker, Derek, *Outback: The Discovery of Australia's Interior*, Sutton, Phoenix Mill UK, 2007

Paterson, A. B., *Rio Grande and Other Verses*, Angus & Robertson, Sydney, 1917

Paterson, A. B., *The Man from Snowy River and other Verses*, Angus & Robertson, Sydney, 1895

Perry, T. M., *Australia's First Frontier: The Spread of Settlement in New South Wales 1788–1829*, Melbourne University Press, Melbourne, 1965

Petrie, C. C. (ed), *Tom Petrie's Reminiscences of Early Queensland*, Watson, Ferguson, Brisbane, 1904

Phillip, Arthur, *The Voyage of Governor Phillip to Botany Bay with an Account of the Establishment of the Colonies of Port Jackson and Norfolk Island*, John Stockdale, London, 1798

Pierce, Peter, *The Country of Lost Children: An Australian Anxiety*, Cambridge University Press, Melbourne, 1999

Plater, Diana, *Other Boundaries: Inner-city Aboriginal Stories*, University of Technology, Sydney, 1994

Powell, J. M., *An Historical Geography of Modern Australia: The Restive Fringe*, Cambridge University Press, Cambridge, 1988

Powell, J. M., *Griffith Taylor and 'Australia Unlimited'*, The John Murtagh Macrossan Memorial Lecture, 1992, University of Queensland Press, Brisbane, 1993

Powell, J. M., *Plains of Promise, Rivers of Destiny: Water Management and the Development of Queensland 1824–1990*, Booralong, Brisbane, 1991

Powell, J. M., *The Emergence of Bioregionalism in the Murray–Darling Basin*, Murray–Darling Basin Commission, Canberra, 1993

Powell, J. M., *Watering the Garden State: Water, Land and Community in Victoria, 1834–1988*, Allen & Unwin, Sydney, 1989

Praed, Mrs Campbell [Rosa], *My Australian Girlhood*, Unwin, London, 1902

Praed, Rosa, *Fugitive Anne: A Romance of the Unexplored Bush*, John Long, London, 1902

Pratt, Mary Louise, *Imperial Eyes: Travel Writing and Transculturation*, Routledge, London, 1992

Presland, Gary, *Aboriginal Melbourne: The Lost Land of the Kulin People*, McPhee Gribble/Penguin, Melbourne, 1994

Prichard, Katharine Susannah, *Straight Left: Articles and Addresses on Politics, Literature and Women's Affairs*, Ric Throssell (ed.), Wild and Woolley, Sydney, 1982

Priestley, Susan, *South Melbourne: A History*, Melbourne University Press, Melbourne, 1995

Quinn, Roderic, *Poems*, Angus & Robertson, Sydney, 1920

Raleigh, Sir Walter, *The Discovery of the Large, Rich, and Beautiful Empire of Guiana*, Hakluyt Society, London, 1848

Ransford, Oliver, *Livingstone's Lake: The Drama of Africa's Inland Sea*, Crowell, New York, 1966

Raxworthy, Richard, *The Unreasonable Man: The Life and Work of J. J. C. Bradfield*, Hale & Iremonger, Sydney, 1989

Reisner, Marc, *Cadillac Desert: The American West and its Disappearing Water*, Penguin, New York, 1993

Reynolds, Henry, *With the White People: The Crucial Role of Aborigines in the Exploration and Development of Australia*, Penguin, Melbourne, 1990

Reynolds, Wayne, *Australia's Bid for the Atomic Bomb*, Melbourne University Press, Melbourne, 2000

Richards, Jonathon, *The Secret War: A True History of Queensland's Native Police*, University of Queensland Press, Brisbane, 2008

Rickard, John, *Australia: A Cultural History*, Longman, Cheshire, Melbourne, 1988

Robertson, Craig, *Buckley's Hope: The Real Life Story of Australia's Robinson Crusoe*, Scribe, Melbourne, 1980

Roderick, Colin, *Leichhardt: The Dauntless Explorer*, Angus & Robertson, Sydney, 1988

Rolfe, Patricia (ed.), *The Blue Mountains*, Jacaranda, Sydney, 1964

Rose, Deborah Bird, *Nourishing Terrains: Australian Aboriginal Views of Landscape and Wilderness*, Australian Heritage Commission, Canberra, 1996

Ryan, Simon, *The Cartographic Eye: How Explorers Saw Australia*, Cambridge University Press, Cambridge, 1996

Sanderson, Marie, *Griffith Taylor: Antarctic Scientist and Pioneer Geographer*, Carleton University Press, Ottawa, 1988

Schaffer, Kay, *Women and the Bush: Forces of Desire in the Australian Cultural Tradition*, Cambridge University Press, Cambridge, 1988

Schama, Simon, *Landscape and Memory*, HarperCollins, London, 1995

Scott, Ernest (ed.), *Australian Discovery*, Dent, London, 1929

Scott, Ernest, *The Life of Captain Matthew Flinders, R.N.*, Angus & Robertson, Sydney, 1914

Scott, G. Firth, *The Last Lemurian: A Westralian Romance*, James Bowden, London, 1898

Seddon, George, *Landprints: Reflections on Place and Landscape*, Cambridge University Press, Cambridge, 1997

Seddon, George, *The Old Country: Australian Landscapes, Plants and People*, Cambridge University Press, Cambridge, 2005

Shaw, A. G. L., *The Economic Development of Australia*, Longman, Melbourne, 1944

Shillinglaw, John J. (ed.), *Historical Records of Port Phillip: The First Annals of the Colony of Victoria*, Melbourne, 1879

Smith, Bernard, *European Vision and the South Pacific*, Yale University Press, New Haven, 1985

Smith, John (chair), *Sydney Water Supply: Report of the Commission Appointed to Inquire into the Supply of Water to Sydney and Suburbs*, Government Printer, Sydney, 1869

Smith, Mark M., *Listening to Nineteenth-Century America*, University of North Carolina Press, Chapel Hill, 2001

Snowy Mountains Story, The, Snowy Mountains Authority, Cooma (c.1965)

Sprod, Dan, *Proud Intrepid Heart: Leichhardt's First Attempt to the Swan River, 1846–1847*, Blubber Head Press, Hobart, 1989

Stable, J. J. (ed.), *The High Road of Australian Verse: An Anthology for Australian Schools*, Oxford University Press, London, 1929

Stegner, Wallace, *The Sound of Mountain Water*, Doubleday, Garden City, N.Y., 1969

Stevens, Bertram (ed.), *An Anthology of Australian Verse*, Angus & Robertson, Sydney, 1906

Stokes, John Lort, *Discoveries in Australia, With an Account of the Coasts and Rivers Explored and Surveyed During the Voyage of H.M.S. Beagle, in the Years 1837–43*, 2 vols, T. & W. Boone, London, 1846

Stow, Randolph, *Selected Poems: A Counterfeit Silence*, Angus & Robertson, Sydney, 1969

Stuart, John McDouall, *Explorations Across the Continent of Australia 1861–62*, F. F. Bailliere, Melbourne, 1863

Sturt, Charles, *Journal of the Central Australian Expedition 1844–1845*, Jill Waterhouse (ed.), Caliban Books, London, 1984 (also referred to in the text as the 'Charlotte Diary')

Sturt, Charles, *Narrative of an Expedition into Central Australia 1844–6* [1849], Nicolas Rothwell (ed.), Corkwood Press, Adelaide, 2001

Sturt, Charles, *The Central Australian Expedition 1844–1846: The Journals of Charles Sturt*, Richard C. Davis (ed.), Hakluyt Society, London, 2002. This is the first publication of Sturt's field journals.

Sturt, Charles, *Two Expeditions into the Interior of Southern Australia, 1828–1831*, 2 vols, Smith, Elder & Co., London, 1833

Tauman, Merab, *The Chief: C. Y. O'Connor*, University of Western Australia Press, Perth, 1978

Taylor, Griffith, *Australia: A Study of Warm Environments and their Effect on British Settlement*, Methuen, London, 1947

Taylor, Griffith, *Environment, Race and Migration: Fundamentals of Human Distribution; With Special Sections on Racial Classification and Settlement in Canada and Australia*, Chicago University Press, Chicago, 1937

Taylor, Griffith, *Journeyman Taylor: The Education of a Scientist*, Robert Hale, London, 1958

Tench, Watkin, *1788*. Comprising *A Narrative of the Expedition to Botany Bay* [1789] and *A Complete Account of the Settlement at Port Jackson*[1793], Tim Flannery (ed.), Text Publishing, Melbourne, 1996

Tenison-Woods, Rev. Julian E., *A History of Discovery and Exploration in Australia*, Sampson Low, Son, and Marston, London, 1865

Thomas, Martin, *The Artificial Horizon: Imagining the Blue Mountains*, Melbourne University Press, Melbourne, 2003

Thoreau, Henry David, *The Maine Woods* [1864], Kessinger Publications, Whitefish, Montana, 2004

Thoreau, Henry David, *Walden* (1854) in Richard Lenat (ed.), *The Thoreau Reader*, http://thoreau.eserver.org

Timbury, F. R. V., *The Battle for the Inland: The Case for the Bradfield and Idriess Plans*, Angus & Robertson, Sydney, 1944

Tompson, Charles, *Wild Notes from the Lyre of a Native Minstrel* (1862), Australian Literature Electronic Gateway, Perth, 2002

Torney, Kim, *Babes in the Bush: The Making of an Australian Image*, Curtin University Books, Fremantle, 2005

Tucker, James, *Ralph Rashleigh*, Angus & Robertson, Sydney, 1952

Turner, Ethel, *Captain Cub*, Ward, Lock & Co., London, 1917

Tyrrell, Ian, *True Gardens of the Gods: Californian–Australian Environmental Reform 1860–1930*, University of California Press, Berkeley, 1999

Upton, Sydney, *Australia's Empty Spaces*, Allen & Unwin, London, 1938

Uren, Malcolm and Robert Stephens, *Waterless Horizons: The Extraordinary Life-story of Edward John Eyre*, Robertson & Mullens, Melbourne, 1941

Wadham, Samuel, *Land Utilization in Australia*, Melbourne University Press, Melbourne, 1939

Wahlquist, Asa, *Thirsty Country: Options for Australia*, Allen & Unwin, Sydney, 2007

Walker, David, *Anxious Nation: Australia and the Rise of Asia 1850–1939*, University of Queensland Press, Brisbane, 1999

Ward, Russel, *Concise History of Australia*, University of Queensland Press, Brisbane, 1992

Ward, Russel, *Finding Australia: The History of Australia to 1821*, Heinemann, Melbourne, 1987

Watling, Thomas, *Letters from an Exile at Botany Bay, to his Aunt in Dumfries* (1794), reprint with an introduction by George Mackaness, Ford, Sydney, 1945

Webster, E. M., *Whirlwinds in the Plain: Ludwig Leichhardt—Friends, Foes and History*, Melbourne University Press, Melbourne, 1980

Wellard, James, *Lost Worlds of Africa*, Hutchinson, London, 1967

Wells, William Henry, *A Geographical Dictionary or Gazetteer of the Australian Colonies*, W. & F. Ford, Sydney, 1848

Wentworth, William Charles, *Australasia: A Poem Written for the Chancellor's Medal at the Cambridge Commencement, July 1823*, G. and W. B. Whittaker, London, 1823

Wentworth, William Charles, *Statistical, Historical, and Political Description of the Colony of New South Wales, and its Dependent Settlements in Van Diemen's Land*, G. and W. B. Whittaker, London, 1819

White, Gilbert, *Thirty Years in Tropical Australia*, Society for Promoting Christian Knowledge, London, 1918

White, Graham and White, Shane, *The Sounds of Slavery: Discovering African American History Through Songs, Sermons, and Speech*, Beacon Press, Boston, 2005

White, John, *Journal of a Voyage to New South Wales*, Alec H. Chisholm (ed.), Angus & Robertson, Sydney, 1962

White, Patrick, *Voss: A Novel*, Eyre & Spottiswoode, London, 1957

Wigmore, Lionel, *Struggle for the Snowy: The Background of the Snowy Mountains Scheme*, Oxford University Press, London, 1968

Wilkinson, Mary E. (ed.), *Nature Poems: Gleanings from Australian Verse*, Whitcombe and Tombs, Melbourne, c.1919

Willshire, William, *The Land of the Dawning*, W. K. Thomas, Adelaide, 1896

Woltor, Robert, *A Short and Truthful History of the Taking of California and Oregon by the Chinese in the Year AD.1899*, A. A. Bancroft, San Francisco, 1882

Worgan, George, *Journal of a First Fleet Surgeon (1788)*, William Dixson Foundation, Sydney, 1978

Worster, Donald, *Rivers of Empire: Water, Aridity and the Growth of the American West*, Pantheon, New York, 1985

Wright, John, *Water Conservation etc.*, Paper read before the Engineering Association of New South Wales on March 23, 1882, John Sands, Sydney, 1882

INDEX

Abel, Robbie 9, 28–9
Aboriginal water 16–18
Aboriginal people
 conflict with convicts and soldiers
  20–1, 24–7, 31, 54
 conflict with explorers 117, 132,
  136
 conflict with settlers 71, 72, 73, 81,
  122, 191–7
 and fire-stick farming 78
 and fishing 17, 26, 73, 246–7
 health 112–13
 Luritdja people 228
 meeting with explorers 112–13,
  120–1, 132
 Myall Creek massacre 192
 and 'silence' 50–6, 58–9
 swamp drainage systems 246–7
 and *terra nullius* 54, 56, 62, 192,
  209–12, 244, 251
 and time 55–6
 and Uluru 241–5
Adelaide 125
America 23, 59–60, 62–3
America: The Story of a Free People 63
Anderson, James 32
Anderson, Marie-Louise 251
Angas, George French 60, 77
Argus 182
art 190, 243
artesian water 38, 115, 166–78, 179,
 183, 185, 188–9, 200–1, 208, 213

Asian invasion 210–11
Augustus Gregory and the Inland Sea
 85
Australasia 56
Australia Replanned 236
Australia Unlimited 220, 227
Australian Blue Book, The 242
Australian Bush Track, An 181, 182,
 183, 186
Australian Conservation Foundation
 249, 256
Australia's Empty Spaces 231
axe, symbolism of 14, 15, 56, 59,
 60–1, 159, 250
Ayers Rock 124, 241–5, 259
Ayres Rock and Beyond, To 243
*Ayres Rock, Its People, Their Beliefs and
 Their Art* 244

Bachelard, Gaston 15
Bali 246
Ball, Philip 83
Ballantine, James 104, 106
Bandler, Faith 244
Banks, Joseph 86–7, 88
Barkley, Henry 226
Barlow, Maude 256
Barnard, Marjorie 229
Barrett, Thomas 21
Barrier Ranges 138, 139
Barrington, George 15
Barwon River 72, 247

Batman, John 70–5, 77
Battle for the Inland, The 235
Bayldon, Arthur 164
Beagle 124, 125
Beale, Edgar 134
Being Australian 140
Bell, Edward 46
Blainey, Geoffrey 1, 51–4, 251
Blavatsky, Madame 180–1
Blaxland, Gregory 57, 58
Bligh, Captain William 33–4
Blood Tracks of the Bush 181, 187
Bloxham, H. K. 194
Blue Mountains 57, 159
Boake, Barcroft 162, 175–6
Boer, Roland 142
Bolton, Geoffrey 3
Bondi Ocean Outfall 46
Bonney, Charles 52
Bonyhady, Tim 3
Boote, H. E. 164
Botany Bay 10–11
Botany Swamps 46, 47
'The Boundary Rider' 152
Bourke, Governor Richard 42, 83
Bowen, Lieutenant John 77
Boyd, Alexander 153
Bradfield, John 234–5, 236, 237
Bradley, Lieutenant William 16, 22
Brady, Edwin 220–1, 223, 231, 233
Brantlinger, Patrick 50
Brock, Daniel 133–5, 137, 138, 142, 146
Brown, Bob 249
Brown, David 171
Browne, John Harris 132
Bruce, Stanley Melbourne 221, 226
Bulletin 181, 196
Burgess, Peter 43
Burke, Edmund 64
Burke, Robert O'Hara 155–7, 163, 213
Burke and Wills Expedition, The 157
Busby, John 37, 39–47
Busby's bore 39–47, 248
bushman 16, 132, 160–1, 194

Cadillac Desert 3
Cadigal stream 13, 20, 21, 28
Calder, James 51
Campbell, Charles 128, 129
Campbell, Judy 27
Canada 23, 60, 63, 251
Cannon, Michael 89
Carnegie, David 64
Carter, Paul 3, 4, 73, 80, 119
Cartographic Eye 4
Centennial Park 39–40
Chifley, Ben 239
Cilento, Raphael 237
civilisation, sound of 14, 15, 54, 59, 61, 62–3, 64–5, 148
Clark, Manning 156, 190
Clark, Lieutenant Ralph 20, 21
Clarke, George 'the Barber' 116–17
Clarke, Marcus 157–9, 162, 163, 185, 251
Clune, Frank 231, 242
Collins, David 11, 13, 14–15, 21, 32, 54, 69
Commager, Henry Steele 63
Commander, Philip 82
Cooper, Frederic 161–2
Cooper Creek 117, 118, 141, 155–7, 200
Cooper's Creek 83
Coorong wetlands 253
Cotton, John 65
Cowley, Joseph 144
Cox, Erle 181
Crosbie, Clarice G. 178
Cullen, Peter 253
Cummings, William 30
Cumpston, J. H. L. 84–5
Cunningham, Allan 90, 99, 106–9, 117
Curr, Edward 74

Dad Rudd MP 235–6
Dale, M. J. 43
Dampier, William 85
Daniel, Howard 231

Darling, Lt-Gen Ralph 41, 104–6, 108, 115, 116–17, 129, 131
Darling Downs 107, 117
Darling River 17, 95, 102, 109–16, 117, 129, 130, 135–6, 155, 169, 194, 200, 247, 252–3
Davidson, Bruce 202
Davis, Sam 24–5
Davison, Graeme 55
Dawe, Carlton 181
Dawson, Charles 186
de Lesseps, Ferdinand 177
Dead Heart of Australia 212
Deakin, Alfred 180, 202–4, 205, 208–9, 213, 214, 216, 221, 254
death 5, 58, 91, 114, 136, 137, 142, 143, 147, 154–6, 161, 162–3, 164, 171, 175–6, 187, 190, 212, 233
Depot Glen 87, 143–6
Despard, Lt-Col Harry 43
Diamantina River 200
Dixon, Robert 189
Dombrovskis, Peter 250
Drake-Brockman, Henrietta 239
drought 205, 209, 216

Elder, Catriona 140
Eldershaw, Flora 229
Eora people 12–13, 16, 19–21, 24–5, 27, 215
European Vision and the South Pacific 4
Evans, George Essex 90, 175
exploration and women 139–43
Exploration of Australia, The 89
explorers 6–7, 17, 48, 54, 60, 64, 79–81, 89, 92, 94, 96–7, 103, 104, 107, 113–14, 120, 124–6, 128, 134–6, 139–47, 150, 154–5, 163–4, 177, 190, 206, 220
  and the inland sea 82–98
Eyre, Edward 16, 79, 81, 125, 126–8, 129, 130, 132–3, 135, 142, 145
Eyre Peninsula 127

Falkiner, Suzanne 84, 139–40

farming 23, 25–6, 31–3, 77, 89–90, 150–1, 200–2, 204–5, 219–20, 252, 254–7
Farwell, George 56, 84, 115, 227
Favenc, Ernest 86, 160, 162, 181, 182, 201
Federation Drought 205, 209, 216
female metaphor of the land 141
Finlayson, Hedley 227–8, 231
fire-stick farming 78
Fitzpatrick, Kathleen 109
Flannery, Tim 3, 253
Fleming, James 68–9, 70
Fletcher, Brunsdon 223–4, 226
Flinders, Matthew 85–6, 99–100
Flinders Island 72
Flood, Robert 132, 138, 144, 145
Flynn, Frank 84
Flynn, Rev John 232
Franklin, Miles 164
Franklin River 249–50
Fraser, John Foster 216
Fraser, Malcolm 249
Fraser, Simon 172–3
Freeman, W.T. 50–1
Friend of Australia, The 101, 103
Fugitive Anne 181, 183, 186, 187, 188, 190–1, 196

Gardiner, Lyndsay 119
Gawler, Governor George 77, 125, 126, 128
Gay, William 177
Geelong 72
geography 48–53, 57–8
  and silence 14, 52–4, 58–65, 74–5, 126–7, 133, 136, 143–4, 148–50, 152–3, 157–61, 163, 164–5, 175–6, 218, 230, 250–1
Geography of Australia, A 223
Ghassemi, Fereidoun 240
Gibbs, Pearl 244
Gibson, Ross 88, 139–40
Giles, Ernest 64, 79–80, 97
Gipps, George 122
Goderich, Viscount 115

gold rush 151–2
Golden Lake, The 181, 182, 183, 184, 186, 195
Gordon, David J. 208, 210
Gove Land Rights Case 210
Goyder, George 150–1
Grand Victorian North West Canal Company 201
grasslands 57, 71, 72, 76–8, 81, 119, 121, 122, 136, 140, 160, 174, 194, 200
Great Artesian Basin 115, 166–78, 188, 213
Great Australian Explorers 84
Great Boomerang, The 232, 233, 234
Greenblat, Stephen 3
Gregory, Augustus 85, 147
Gregory, J. W. 212–13
Grey, George 128–9
Griffiths, Tom 3
Grimes, Charles 68, 69, 70
Grose, Major Francis 29–30
groundwater 17, 35, 42, 113, 166–74, 188–9, 205, 217, 252–3, 254
Gunn, Jeannie 162

Haeckel, Ernest 179
Haggard, H. Rider 176, 182, 189
Hall, Ken G. 235
Hardwicke, Dick 181, 182, 183, 186, 190, 195
Harney, Bill 243
Hatfield, William 230
Hawdon, Joseph 52–3
Hawke, Bob 250
Hawkesbury River 32–3, 47, 77
Haynes, Roslynn 2, 87, 228
Healy, John 183
Heney, Thomas 152
Hennessey, David 160
Hennessey, J. D. 141, 181
Herder, Johann Gottfried 1
Higgins, Henry Bournes 211
Hill, Ernestine 227
Hill, Samuel Prout 142
Hirst, John 42

History of Australia, A 190
History of Australian Exloration 86
History of Creation 179
History of New South Wales 15
History of the Discovery and Exploration of Australia 86
Hobart 32, 70–1, 77
Hogan, J. F. 181
Howard, Shane 250
Howard government 253
Hume, Hamilton 110, 112, 114
Hunter, Captain John 19–20, 30–1, 78
Huskisson, William 104
Hyde Park 41
hydro-electric schemes 231, 235–6, 238–9, 248–9
hydro-engineering 199–209, 235–7

Idriess, Ion 227, 232–4, 236, 237
Imperial Eyes 3, 4
inland sea 7, 81, 82–98, 104, 106, 108–9, 111, 113, 115, 123, 125–6, 130–1, 137, 138, 143, 145, 147, 176–7, 184–6, 188, 191, 213, 217, 236
Inland Sea and the Great River: The Story of Australin Exploration 84–5
irrigation 177, 185, 190, 199–205, 208–9, 213, 216–17, 220, 224, 231, 233, 236, 238, 239, 241, 246–7, 252, 254, 255, 257, 258

Jamison, Thomas 102
Johnson, Richard 89
Johnston, Major George 33–4
Jones, Rhys 77–8

Kahn, Douglas 4
Kelly, David 36–7
Kennedy, Edmund 118
King, Philip Gidley 31–2
King, Phillip Parker 99–101
King Solomon's Mines 176, 182, 189
Kolodny, Annette 139
Kulin nation 66, 69–70, 73

Lachlan River 90, 91–2, 95, 110
Lachlan Swamps 37, 39–43, 44, 45,
    46, 47, 110
Lake Eyre 119, 124, 127, 145, 151,
    155, 168, 169, 170, 171, 177, 200,
    212–13, 230, 241, 245
  flooding 232–8
Lake Pedder 248–9
Lake Salvator 119
Lake Torrens 127–8, 145, 155, 170
land and explorers 80–1
Land Half Won, A 52
landscape, Australian 3, 62, 72, 77,
    80–1, 103, 139–40, 148, 199,
    219–45, 250, 252
Landscape and Memory 3
Lang, John Dunmore 59, 71
Langley, Michael 131, 134
Langton, Marcia 18, 251
Last Lemurian, The 181, 188, 195
Lawrence, D. H. 5, 221
Lawson, Henry 5, 64, 174, 220
Lawson, William 57
Lay of the Land, The 139
Leeper, Geoffrey 238
Leichhardt, Ludwig 97, 118, 149,
    154–5, 163, 187–8
Lemuria 179–84, 185
Lindsay, Joan 163
Lines, William J. 3
Lingiari, Vincent 244
Living Heart, The 84
Liverpool Plains 116, 120
Lost Explorer, The 181, 187
Lost Explorers, The 181
Loughead, J. S. 173
Lourandos, Harry 55
Luscombe, L. H. 236
Lycett, Joseph 35

Mabo 210
Macarthur, Elizabeth 77
Macarthur, John 30, 31, 105
McCaughey, Samuel 171
McColl, Hugh 201–2
MacDonald, Alexander 181

McEwan, Marcia 84
McGrath, Ann 195
McIntyre, John 31
Mackellar, Dorothea 229
Macleay, George 130
Macquarie, Lachlan 34–8, 90
Macquarie River 90, 92–3, 95
Madigan, Cecil 230
Man and Nature 159
Marooned in Australia 181
Marsden, Rev. Samuel 33
Marsh, George Perkins 159
Martin, George 15
Marvelous Possessions 3
Maslen, Thomas John 101–4
Maurice, Furnley 164
Mead, Elwood 216
Melbourne 64–5, 66–75, 83
Menindee Lakes 102
Menzies, Robert 235, 239
Mermaid 99, 100
Mildura 204, 205, 224
Mill, Hugh 49
Milton, John 14
Mitchell, Major Thomas 1, 17, 54,
    55, 60, 78, 79, 80, 81, 96–7, 103,
    116–21, 123, 128, 140, 149, 164,
    175, 199, 200, 220, 246, 259
Moore, Charles 46
Moorehead, Alan 83, 156
Moorhouse, James 201
Mountford, C. P. 244
Mullett, H. A. 227
Murgatroyd, Sarah 157
Murray River 117, 135–6, 155,
    199–200, 204–5, 208–9, 239
Murray–Darling Basin 247, 252–3
Murrumbidgee River 216–17, 224,
    239
My Australia 229

Namatjira, Albert 243
Narrative of an Expedition into Central
    Australia 146
nationalism 7, 154, 162–3, 165, 201,
    213, 232

Nelson, Harry 225–6
Nepean River 28, 47
Never-Never 153, 161–2, 183, 187, 194, 211, 230
Nevins, Allan 63
New South Wales 15, 34–6, 45, 64, 68, 76, 91–2, 94–6, 101–6, 109, 116, 120, 122, 135–8, 151, 159, 168, 170, 173, 192, 208–9, 216, 224, 238, 250
Newland, Simpson 181, 187, 193
Niles, Hezekiah 59
Nimmo, William 237
Noise, Water, Meat: A History of Sound in the Arts 4
Nolan, Sidney 157, 190
Norfolk Island 29
Norman, Noel 213, 222
novels 142, 150, 154, 162–3, 180–97, 211
Nullarbor Plain 127, 128

O'Connor, Charles Yelverton 205
Okey, Bill 24–5
On the Fringe of the Never-Never 194
open country 76–8
Ord River 239
Outback: The Discovery of Australia's Interior 84
Out of the Silence 181
Oxley, John 64, 76, 89–98

Pacific Affairs 231
Palmer, Vance 164
Park, Mungo 87, 96
Parker, Derek 84
parks 76–8
Parramatta River 26
Paterson, 'Banjo' 5, 174, 177, 198, 199
Paterson, William 30
Paving the Way 193
Pemulwuy 31
Perkins, Charles 244
Phillip, Captain Arthur 9–10, 15, 25–6, 28–30

Picnic at Hanging Rock 163
Picturesque Atlas of Australia 164
place, individual's relationship to 55
Plains of Mulluba 120
Poole, James 87, 132, 137, 146
Port Essington 117, 119
Port Jackson 23, 27, 29, 36, 56, 71, 78, 100
Port Phillip 68, 69–70, 72, 73, 83, 88, 119, 122, 250
Powell, Joe 2
Praed, Rosa 181, 186, 196
Pratt, Mary Louise 3
'Pretty Dick' 162

Recollections of Geoffry Hamlyn, The 65
Red Centre: Man and Beast in the Heart of Australia, The 228
Red Heart, The 231
Reisner, Marc 3
reservoirs, Nepean and Hawkesbury rivers 47
Reynolds, Wayne 239–40
Richardson, Henry Handel 218
Riders to an Unknown Sea 84, 115
Rivers of Empire 3
Road to Botany Bay, The 3, 80
Roberts-Goodwin, Lynne 13
Rocks, the 38
Roe, Kohn Septimus 99
Roman civilisation 198–9
Rooney, Tom 255
Rose, Deborah Bird 251
Rose Hill 26, 29, 31
Ross, Major Robert 23, 29
Rudd government 253
Rum Corps 30, 31, 33, 34
Rum Rebellion 34
Rushcutters Bay 24
Russell, Henry Chamberlain 169
Ryan, Simon 4, 80, 140, 141

salinity 205, 208, 240, 252, 254
Schaffer, Kay 139–40
Schama, Simon 3, 14

Scott, George Firth 181
Search for the Inland Sea, The 89
Secret Doctrine, The 180
Secret of the Australian Desert, The
    181, 182, 184, 185, 187
Seddon, George 3
Seeking the Centre 2, 87
Shaw, A. G. L. 1
She 182, 189
Sibley, Gil 257
silence
  and Aboriginal people 50–6, 58–9
  and geography 14, 52–4, 58–65,
      74–5, 126–7, 133, 136, 143–4,
      148–50, 152–3, 157–61, 163,
      164–5, 175–6, 218, 230, 250–1
  howling wilderness 62–5
  see also sound; stillness of the bush
Silver Queen, The 181
Simpson Desert 145, 166, 228
smallpox 27
Smith, Bernard 4
Smith, Forgan 234
Smith, John 46
Smith, Mark M. 4, 5, 59–60
Snowy Mountains Scheme 238–41,
    248
Soldier Settlement Schemes 219–20
Sorrento 70
sound
  of the axe 14, 59, 60–1, 250
  of civilisation 14, 15, 54, 59, 61,
      62–3, 64–5, 148
  and silence 50–65
Sound in Between, The 4
Sounds of Slavery 4
South Australia 60, 61, 86, 150–1,
    168–70, 173, 193, 204, 208–9, 210,
    220, 234, 247
South of the West 139
Southwell, Daniel 23, 78–9, 80
squatters 104–6, 120, 121–3, 151,
    171, 172, 173, 193–4, 196, 199,
    201–2, 225
Squatting Investment Company 172
Stefansson, Vilhjalmur 224

Stegner, Wallace 64
Stephens, A. G. 161
Stevens, Bertram 215
stillness of the bush 14, 52–4, 58–65,
    74, 126–7, 133, 136, 143–4, 152–3,
    157–61, 163, 164–5, 175, 218, 230,
    250–1
Stirling, James 77
Stokes, John Lort 124–5
Stuart, John McDouall 79, 97, 132,
    137, 143, 144, 145, 149–50
Sturt, Charles 17, 36, 59, 79, 85, 86,
    103, 106, 109–16, 117, 119, 120,
    123, 125–6, 128–47, 148, 155, 171,
    184, 187, 204, 213, 220, 236
Sturt of the Murray 134
Sturt, the Chipped Idol 134
Sydney 12–13, 19, 21–4, 26–38,
    39–49, 79
Sydney Common 40
Sydney Corporation 44–5, 46
Sydney Cove 13, 15, 16, 19, 21, 23,
    29, 31, 36, 39, 54, 56, 59, 61, 78,
    88, 159
Sydney's water tunnel 39–47, 248

Tank Stream 12–13, 28–35, 36–7, 39,
    45, 47, 199, 248
Tasmania 249–51
Tasmanian Wilderness Society 249
Tate, Ralph 169–70
Taylor, Griffith 222–31
Taylor, Major James 35
Tench, Lieutenant Watkin 10–11,
    27–8, 54
Tenison-Woods, Julian 86, 88
terra nullius 54, 56, 62, 192, 209–12,
    244, 251
Thoreau, Henry 63
Timbury, Frederick 235
time
  and culture 55–6
  and the inland sea 184–6
Tompson, Charles 159
Torrens River 125, 168, 170
Tree of Man 190

Triumph of the Nomads, The 51
Tucker, Albert 190
Tucker, James 16
Tuckey, James 69–70
Tuitt, Len 243
Tully River 234
Turner, Ethel 217
Tyranny of Distance, The 1

Uluru (Ayers Rock) 124, 241–5, 259
Upton, Sydney 231

Victoria 202–5
Victoria River 124
'A Vision Out West' 175
von Mueller, Ferdinand 159
Voss 142, 150, 154, 162–3, 160

Wadham, S.M. 227
Walden 63
Walkabout 5, 227, 230, 242, 243
Walker, Willima Sylvester 181
Wallace, Alfred Russel 180
water
  artesian 38, 115, 166–78, 179, 183,
    185, 188–9, 200–1, 208, 213
  dreamers 165, 183, 208, 212–13,
    215, 232, 236, 238, 239, 248
  engineering 198–209
  Great Artesian Basin 115, 166–78,
    188, 213
  groundwater 17, 35, 42, 113,
    166–74, 188–9, 205, 217, 252–3,
    254
  irrigation 177, 185, 190, 199–205,
    208–9, 213, 216–17, 220, 224,
    231, 233, 236, 238, 239, 241,
    246–7, 252, 254, 255, 257, 258
  and salinity 205, 208, 240, 252,
    254
  schemes 199–205, 208, 209–12
  search for fresh 11, 12–13, 14, 15,
    16–18, 24, 32–3, 37, 39–49, 56–5,
    69, 72–3, 83, 88, 91, 93, 95, 108,
    116–18, 167–8, 224, 234, 244

  and song 164–5
  trading 254–6
Waterfind 255–6
Wathaurong people 72
We of the Never-Never 162
Wedge, John Hedler 73
Wentworth, W. C. 37–8, 56–8, 92,
  96
Wentworth Group 253
Werribee 73
Western Australia 64, 77, 100, 101,
  186, 205–7, 223, 237, 239, 252
Westgarth, William 74
wet-country people 8–12
wetlands 11, 17, 29, 39, 45, 46–7,
  66–7, 74, 91, 250, 252, 253
'Where the Dead Men Lie' 162, 176
White, Gilbert 212
White, Graham 4
White, Ian 240
White, John 19, 20
White, Patrick 142, 150, 154, 162,
  190
White, Shane 4
white Australia 11, 24, 48, 51, 54, 77,
  80, 82, 162, 189, 192, 210–11, 218,
  225, 226, 237, 240, 244, 258
White Australia Policy 211, 226
white optimism 189–91
Wigglesworth, Michael 62
wilderness 62–5, 74–5
William, John 122
Wills, William 155–7, 163, 190, 213
Wolcott, Roger 139
women and exploration 139–43
Women and the Bush 139
Wood, G. L. 5–6
Worster, Donald 3
Wright, John 172
Writers' Landscape: Wilderness 84
Writing the Colonial Adventure 189

Yarra Falls 66–9, 73–4
Yarra wetlands 74